FORGING THE MODERN AGE
——1900-14——

FORGING THE MODERN AGE

FOREWORD

To celebrate the turn of the century and the new millennium, **THE EVENTFUL CENTURY** series presents the vast panorama of the last hundred years – a century which has witnessed the transition from horse-drawn transport to space travel, and from the first telephones to the information superhighway.

THE EVENTFUL CENTURY chronicles epoch-making events like the outbreak of the two world wars, the Russian Revolution and the rise and fall of communism. But major events are only part of this glittering kaleidoscope. It also describes the everyday background – the way people lived, how they worked, what they ate and drank, how much they earned, the way they spent their leisure time, the books they read, and the crimes, scandals and unsolved mysteries that set them talking. Here are fads and crazes like the Hula Hoop and Rubik's Cube . . . fashions like the New Look and the miniskirt . . . breakthroughs in entertainment, such as the birth of the movies . . . medical milestones such as the discovery of penicillin . . . and marvels of modern architecture and engineering.

FORGING THE MODERN AGE describes the years of fizzing creative energy that marked the start of the century, from 1900 to the outbreak of the First World War in 1914. It was a time of daring inventiveness when the Wright brothers became the first to achieve powered flight, Marconi transmitted the first transatlantic radio message, Einstein propounded his theory of relativity and Marie Curie isolated radium. Artists, from Matisse to Picasso brought revolution to the arts, dazzling their contemporaries with outrageous use of colour, the strange new forms of Cubism and their first experiments in abstract art. Henry Ford brought motoring to the masses with his Model T while socialists championed workers' rights and suffragettes fought for a woman's right to vote. In this age of imperial pomp, a handful of mostly European powers controlled virtually the entire globe. Yet cracks were appearing in this imposing edifice. In 1905, Russia faced revolution at home and defeat abroad at the hands of Japan. In Europe, the Balkans were dogged by turbulence, while Germany was rich, powerful . . . and ambitious. The old balance of power was shifting and in the end would collapse altogether into the pit of war.

FORGING THE MODERN AGE
——1900-14——

Reader's
Digest

PUBLISHED BY
THE READER'S DIGEST ASSOCIATION LIMITED
LONDON NEW YORK SYDNEY MONTREAL

FORGING THE MODERN AGE
Edited and designed by Toucan Books Limited
Written by Antony Mason
Edited by Robert Sackville West and
Andrew Kerr-Jarrett
Designed by Bradbury and Williams
Picture research by Christine Vincent

FOR READER'S DIGEST
Series Editor Christine Noble
Editorial Assistant Caroline Boucher
Production Controllers Lorine Alexander,
Byron Johnson

READER'S DIGEST GENERAL BOOKS
Editorial Director Cortina Butler
Art Director Nick Clark

First English edition copyright © 1999
The Reader's Digest Association Limited,
11 Westferry Circus, Canary Wharf,
London E14 4HE

Reprinted 1999

Copyright © 1999
Reader's Digest Association Far East Limited
Philippines copyright © 1999
Reader's Digest Association Far East Limited
All rights reserved

Printing and binding: Printer Industria Gráfica S.A.,
Barcelona
Separations: Litho Origination, London
Paper: Perigord-Condat, France

ISBN 0 276 42363 1

FRONT COVER
Background picture: Crowds at the Henley Regatta,
1906, top; crowds listen to Kier Hardie at a
demonstration in Hyde Park, 1912, bottom.
From left to right: Albert Einstein; suffragette
medallion; Nijinsky; poster advertising the *Titanic*.

BACK COVER
Clockwise from top left: an early telephone-user;
an interior designed by Charles Rennie Mackintosh;
Leon Trotsky and his wife, Alexandra; medical
examination at Ellis Island, New York.

Page 3 (from left to right): French photographer;
German publication featuring naval manoeuvres;
Chinese patriot; *The Strand Magazine*.

Background pictures:
Page 15: Roentgen X-ray machine
Page 59: Textile workers' strike, USA, 1912
Page 125: Krupp arms factory, Germany, 1909

CONTENTS

SOWING THE SEEDS

THE EDWARDIAN ERA WAS A LIVELY AND OPTIMISTIC PERIOD DURING WHICH THE THEMES OF MODERN WORLD HISTORY BEGAN TO UNFOLD

The arrival of the 20th century was fêted like no other century before it. It was a new dawn in an exciting era of extraordinary technological breakthrough. The reigning monarch of Britain, Queen Victoria, had come to the throne in 1837 in an age of horse-drawn carriages, wooden sailing ships and paddle steamers. Now a web of railways spanned the continents; powerful steel-hulled liners plied the oceans; there were electric underground railways, and motor cars were poised to bring another revolution to land travel and transport. Messages could be sent instantaneously

FOR THE RECORD New technologies brought burgeoning markets for consumer delights, such as the gramophone (right) and photography (below).

NEW VICTOR RECORD CATALOGUE

NOVEMBER 1910

across the globe by telegraph, and people could talk between distant cities by telephone; electric lights would illuminate a room at the flick of a switch; there were skyscrapers and department stores, gramophones, typewriters, sewing machines, postage stamps, cameras and the very first movie films. Medical science had improved immeasurably with antiseptics, anaesthetics, immunisation and the first X-rays; and major advances in the understanding of mental disorder were being scored by doctors such as Sigmund Freud. Knowledge about the world was accumulating fast: most of the atlas had been painted in, leaving blanks only in the most inaccessible regions, such as the Amazon Basin, Tibet and around the poles. Important developments were unfolding in atomic and theoretical physics, evolutionary and behavioural biology, and the discipline that would soon be called genetics.

As the new century dawned, many people felt a buoyant confidence that the problems of the world could and would be solved through science, engineering, inventiveness and innovation. The industrial nations were booming, riding the crest of a wave of investment, production and international trade. The USA, Germany and Japan, in particular, were rising as the lions of the coming century.

Colonising the world

For many people in the West, industrialisation was synonymous with civilisation, and they assumed that the benefits of industrialisation should be spread throughout the world. This at least was one justification for

imperialism, particularly in the latter half of the 19th century. By 1900 the industrialised countries had stretched out their tentacles to reach virtually every part of the globe. While the initial incentive was usually trade – the search for cheap raw materials and new markets for manufactured goods – a trading presence was often followed by a military one, military intervention and then colonial rule. Despite the high costs and the catalogue of shameful abuses, advocates of imperialism pointed doggedly to the benefits it brought to subject nations – such as education, improved legal systems, access to industrialised goods, Western medicine and Christianity. Christianity played an integral role in this process; the conversion of heathens

THE RELIEF OF MAFEKING

For the British, the new century started with a war and a siege: the Boer War in South Africa, where the town of Mafeking had come under siege from the Boers in October 1899. Its garrison – led by Colonel Robert Baden-Powell, future founder of the Boy Scouts – held out for 215 days, until relieved by British and Canadian troops in May 1900. At news of this, the British public went wild with joy: it seemed to be a turning point in a war that had brought one humiliation after another. The writer Rebecca West, a girl of eight at the time, remembered the celebrations:

'One afternoon I was lying in bed because my chronic cough had become too outrageous . . . They had put me in an adult bedroom because there was more room on the bed for all the picture books; so at some time in the day or the afternoon or evening, I wakened in this strange room, listening to a strange sound. At first it seemed, improbably, as if a huge flock of sheep were being driven down the genteel suburban street, but human noises intervened. There was laughing and shouting and cheering . . .

'I should have expected our front door to be shut and bolted when such disorderly sounds were heard, but I was sure that our front door had opened, and that footsteps had run down the steps. Then I realised that not only my sisters were standing outside by the gate . . . but that my mother was in the porch, cheering too. I ran out on to the landing and leaned over the banisters, and, yes, indeed, my mother looked up at me from the open door, tears of joy running down her cheeks. As I ran down the staircase, I saw behind her, out in the road, a stream of shabby, happy men – one I remember wearing hessian overalls, with trousers tied round the knee with twine, carrying a garden broom over his shoulder like a rifle, and smiling like a buck-toothed angel. He wore on his chest a huge placard that hung between his shoulders and thighs to give all he passed the good news that the siege of Mafeking had been relieved after seven months.'

KING AND EMPEROR At his coronation in
August 1902, Edward VII was also crowned
Emperor of India. Eighteen months had
elapsed since the death of Queen Victoria,
allowing many representatives from Britain's
imperial possessions to attend.

and the fight against traditions deemed barbaric – such as slavery and the immolation of widows – often provided the moral justification for military intervention.

By 1900 the major imperial powers had neatly divided up the world into areas of influence, agreeing at the Conference of Berlin in 1884-5, for instance, how Africa should be carved among them in the so-called 'scramble for Africa'. A handful of nations – Britain, France, Russia, Germany, Austria-Hungary, the Netherlands, the USA, Spain, Portugal, Turkey and Japan – now accounted for most of the world. Those areas not ruled directly by them – such as China and South America – came under the umbrella of accepted international agreements or understandings.

A series of treaties forged in the late 19th century also served to maintain the balance of power among the imperial nations: France's treaty with Russia, for example, was designed to counterbalance Germany's treaty with Austria-Hungary and Italy. These did not resolve the intense historic rivalries among them, or the concern over the potential flashpoints where these rivalries converged, such as the Balkans, Tibet, Manchuria and Morocco. But at least they appeared to create a stable and reasonably flexible structure within which to operate. Indeed, with virtually the whole world now sewn up by international conventions, optimists foresaw a future of peace and prosperity gradually spreading to all.

THE DEATH OF QUEEN VICTORIA

When Queen Victoria's two surviving sons came to lift her body into her coffin, they were surprised how little she weighed. The tiny 81-year-old queen had virtually wasted away after months wracked by loss of sleep and an inability to eat. Dogged with ill-health and growing memory loss, her final years had been haunted by the war in South Africa, the price of which touched her personally as she was pushed in a wheelchair through hospital wards lined with the wounded. In 1900, it claimed the life of her own grandson, Prince Christian Victor. Also that year, her second son Alfred ('Affie') died, aged 56.

Having reigned since the age of 18 in 1837, she had seemed almost eternal to many of her subjects. The end came at Osborne House, the palace she and Albert had built on the Isle of Wight. As she began to fail on January 18, 1901, the immediate family was summoned, to be joined at his own insistence by her little-loved grandson, Kaiser Wilhelm II of Germany. On January 22 they gathered around her bed. In the afternoon the queen's physician, Sir James Reid, decided to raise her head to ease her breathing. Wilhelm offered his right arm to support her from the other side. Together they remained in this position for two and a half hours, until at 6.30 pm Victoria's face seemed to become more serene, and she passed away. When the news broke, the British Empire went into mourning. Everyone was affected. Children in school wore black armbands; even city street-sweepers – who kept crossings clear of horse manure – tied black crepe bows to their brooms.

No monarch had died for 64 years, so much of the protocol had to be improvised, but Victoria, meticulous to the end, had written out her wishes to the last detail. On February 1 her small coffin was taken on the royal yacht from Cowes to Portsmouth, passing down an avenue of warships to the chorus of naval guns. Then it was transported by train to Victoria Station in London. A huge military procession accompanied the coffin – placed on a gun carriage – across London to Paddington Station. Close to the gun carriage rode the new king, Edward VII; his brother Arthur, Duke of Connaught; the German Kaiser; and Lord Roberts, hero of the Boer War. They were followed by members of every European royal family, together representing the rulers of virtually the entire world. The coffin was taken by train to Windsor, where the gun carriage had to be pulled by sailors after the horse traces snapped. A funeral ceremony took place in St George's Chapel, then on February 4 the coffin was taken to the royal mausoleum at Frogmore. Here, Victoria was laid beside her beloved Albert, her tomb surmounted by an effigy of herself in younger days, which she had made for this purpose in 1862. Then the door was closed on the royal couple, and on an era.

Victoria was held in great esteem by her nation. She had brought stability to the monarchy; she symbolised the pride and responsibilities of British imperial rule. But the British also wanted to move with the times, and needed a figurehead for the era that beckoned with the new century. Edward VII, although broadly popular, came to his role aged 59 and with a reputation as a pleasure-seeker and womaniser. But he quickly made his mark. He handed Osborne House over to the Royal Navy, modernised Buckingham Palace and – with clear relish – set the course for a glittering nine-year reign, recalled as the 'Edwardian era'.

SILENT BUT FOR THE FALL OF HOOVES Solemn crowds cram London's pavements to watch Victoria's funeral cortege. Edward VII leads the mourners, accompanied by Kaiser Wilhelm on a white charger.

STREETS FOR PEOPLE Although the age of the motor car has begun, horse-drawn carts and bicycles still rule the road in Stuttgart in 1905 (right). A clam-seller (above) in 'Little Italy', New York, almost has the street to himself. By 1913, the vaudeville shows and electric signs in an American city (inset, right) are part of a more bustling scene.

But such optimism was based on a very selective view. Despite the veneer of high-minded intentions, and for all the pomp of imperial power, colonialism was driven less by ideals than by political and economic ambition backed by the force of superior arms and technology. As the new century began, the colonial powers continued to use force to maintain their borders, mop up unclaimed lands and protect their trading interests. Characteristically, two major international crises dominated the news in 1900, and horrified the public with their high death tolls: the Boxer Rebellion in China and the Boer War in South Africa – which made Britain an international pariah for several years. The century proceeded as it began.

Strife and nationalism

For most people in the world, colonialism meant not so much enlightenment as humiliating subjugation, and enforced conversion to export-oriented wage labour in mines and

THE BOXER REBELLION

For the readers of the newspapers in Europe and the USA, it was like having all their worst prejudices confirmed. The new century had turned, but the forces of barbarism were still at work. The Chinese were running amok, putting missionaries and Christian converts to the sword, and threatening businessmen, railway engineers and diplomats in the foreign legations. It was savage, it was incomprehensible – and the Chinese appeared to be attacking the very people who might help their backward and chaotic country.

The Chinese themselves had a different view. For most of the 19th century they had watched their country crumble, as the British, French, Germans, Russians, Portuguese and Japanese had all exploited its weakness to grab greater trading and territorial rights. Acts of violence against missionaries began in about 1896, and the rebels were soon identified as members of a secretive martial arts society called Yihe Quan, 'Fists of righteous harmony' – known in the West as the Boxers. Their goal was to rid China of foreigners; they believed that their rituals and talismans would protect them from the bullets of the 'foreign devils'. They won the backing of the imperial court, dominated by the elderly, ultra-conservative Empress Dowager Ci Xi.

In 1900 the Boxers stepped up their aggression. They attacked railways, telegraph lines, churches, trading posts – any symbols of Western presence. Some 140 000 Boxers – recognisable from their red sashes, ribbons and headbands – poured menacingly into Beijing (Peking), their numbers swelled by imperial Chinese troops who had adopted their cause. The Japanese legation chancellor was murdered, then Baron Klemens von Ketteler, the German ambassador. The foreign legation quarter was besieged – defended by a small troop of some 340 British, Russian, Italian, Japanese and US marines.

Although wrong-footed at first, the foreign powers assembled a multinational force under the command of the British vice-admiral Edward Seymour, and a column of 18 000 marched from Tianjin (Tientsin) to Beijing. The Boxers were well-armed with modern rifles; even so, they were massively outgunned. After a series of hard-fought skirmishes, the foreign troops reached Beijing on August 12. Two days later, the 56 day siege of the legation quarter was lifted. The Chinese paid a heavy price. Under a treaty signed in 1901, the imperial government had to agree to further trading concessions, pay an indemnity of $333 million and allow foreign troops to be stationed in Beijing. Russia took advantage of the situation to annexe Manchuria. The weakness of the 256-year-old Qing dynasty had been exposed; its days were numbered.

'THE BRITISH LION IS MUCH PERTURBED'
In 1900 Britain had to contend with three serious crises, involving the Boers in South Africa, the Boxers in China and the Ashanti in the Gold Coast colony of West Africa.

THE END Soldiers from the multinational force scale Beijing's walls in August 1900. Foreign troops stand by (right) as rebel leaders are executed.

plantations. Subject races were not easily convinced of the supposed benefits of colonial rule that were being thrust upon them. As a consequence, the early years of the century were spattered with countless demonstrations, protests, strikes and outright rebellions against the imperial powers, often accompanied by sudden outbursts of bloody violence and subsequently crushed by even more savagely punitive countermeasures. Many liberation movements were founded in this era, to develop further in the interwar years, and come to the fore in the troubled period of rapid decolonisation after the Second World War. Paradoxically, the spread of education and information by colonial powers helped to foster the notion of human rights and nationalist pride.

A fervour for national identity had developed in Europe during the 19th century, and by 1900 it had become a potent political force, particularly among dissatisfied minorities living in the shadow of the great European powers – such as the Slavs, the Poles and the Irish. Nationalism would come to dog the century: the grievances and political ambitions of the Slavic Serbs in the Balkans, for instance, triggered the First World War in 1914, and the bitter collapse of Yugoslavia in the 1990s; the German invasion of independent Poland set alight the Second World War, while the Poles' struggle for independence in the 1980s sparked the Soviet collapse; and the fallout from Irish nationalism is still claiming lives to this day.

The dark counterparts of nationalism – racism and xenophobia – manifested themselves in anti-Semitism, seen alike in the troubling 'Dreyfus case' that blighted French politics around the turn of the century, and the bloody pogroms in Russia that

FUELLING HATRED   Jews living in German Poland queue for petrol. All over central and eastern Europe Jewish communities were the target of anti-Semitic prejudices.

flared up in the wake of the 1905 revolution. This anti-Jewish prejudice was to evolve into one of the most disturbing stories of the entire 20th century.

Industrial squalor

But nationalism was not the only cause to which people pinned their grievances. While middle-class theorists and entrepreneurs boasted the merits of industrialisation, millions of workers were living the realities of industrial life. The huge scale of poverty and urban decay within the industrialised nations – and the attendant overcrowding, squalor, ill-health, crime and abuse – were only just beginning to be fully appreciated at the turn of the century. In Britain, Poor Laws forged in Tudor times were still in operation, and the sick, orphaned, aged and indigent often ended up together at workhouses, enduring conditions which Charles Dickens had excoriated in the 1830s.

Those who cared to open their eyes to these conditions were profoundly shocked, and many began to blame the very structure of a society that had produced the transparent inequalities of the industrialised world as well as its baby, colonialism. One analysis which seemed to offer a solution was socialism, or its more specific form, Marxism. This era saw the rapid rise of socialist political parties; it also witnessed the growing stridency of those who were

too impatient for traditional politics and promoted revolution as the most effective way to bump-start the transfer of power to the masses. In 1903 Lenin oversaw the division of Russian socialists into the revolutionary Bolsheviks and the more conciliatory Mensheviks. No one at the time foresaw quite where this would lead. Meanwhile, anarchists, with their own agenda to destroy the hierarchies of power, took matters into their own hands by assassinating a host of leading politicians and heads of state.

On another front, the trade unions were growing fast as they recruited millions of unskilled workers into their ranks, and increasingly well coordinated strike action gave clear indications of workers' potential power. On their extreme left flank, the syndicalists were pushing to use this power not just to win better wages and terms of employment for workers, but to bring down the entire capitalist system. By about 1911, it seemed as though they might succeed.

This pressure from below was proportional to the intransigence of the government – and the most hidebound and reactionary government of all, led by the Tsar of Russia, paid the ultimate penalty in the Revolution of 1917. Elsewhere, notably in Britain, Liberals and left-wingers in mainstream politics managed to defuse many of the social grievances by introducing embryonic welfare legislation. Old age pensions and sickness benefit, paid out of funds raised by national insurance schemes, went some way towards alleviating the deprivations to which so many workers

CHILD LABOUR   As long as school was regarded as a distraction from the task of earning a living, children – like these French miners – remained a key part of the work force. In 1900 the French government limited the working day for children to 11 hours.

AGE OF STRIFE   Striking textile workers (left) from Lawrence, Massachusetts, meet with armed confrontation in 1912. A 1908 illustration (below, right) shows the brutal suppression of a French strike. In the USA, a member of the radical group Industrial Workers of the World has a clear message for those in authority (below, left).

were condemned through no fault of their own. Meanwhile, essential services and utilities were placed increasingly in the hands of municipal authorities, ensuring fairer access to power, sewerage, mains water, street lighting and so on. The state also took greater responsibility for education and health.

In the USA, 'progressive' politicians followed a similar course; but in France and Germany, socialists found coalitions distasteful, and opted not to exert their potential to influence legislation, despite the fact that they represented a large percentage of the electorate. By the logic of opposites, this era also saw the development of the 'new right' – a breed of politician proclaiming a volatile mix of values such as deep conservatism, nationalism, monarchism, capitalism, Catholicism, anti-Semitism and militarism. The clash of interests across the industrial world would become ever more polarised as the early decades of the century progressed. In the years before the First World War, the result was disturbing levels of unrest, from which virtually all the industrialised nations suffered, regardless of the social reforms undertaken. Not only were millions of working days lost each year to strikes, but there was a distinct whiff of revolution in the air.

The new woman

By the first decade of the 20th century, roughly a quarter of the work force in industrialised countries was made up of women. There was not much new in this: women of the labouring classes had always worked, stopping only for a few weeks every year or so to give birth. This accounted to some extent for the continued high infant mortality rate, and a low average life expectancy of just 47 (compared to 75 today). What had changed was the growing number

In Britain the pressure for equal rights became focused on the vote; the 'suffragettes' led by Emmeline Pankhurst and her daughters, waged a high-profile campaign to win votes for women, using a strategy of well-publicised demonstrations and acts of disruption, which – mirroring the activities of the trade unions – became increasingly militant after 1912. This may have pushed them farther from their goal, which was eventually achieved only after the close of the First World War; but by their assertiveness and new-found sense of solidarity, they helped to lay the foundations for a general movement of this century, in which women have begun to liberate themselves from the limitations of a world largely defined by men.

A WOMAN'S PLACE Women are off to collect coal from waste heaps during the 1912 miners' strike in Britain. Emmeline Pankhurst's portrait adorns a suffragette medallion (right).

of middle-class and lower middle-class women in work, taking up jobs as teachers, shop assistants, secretaries, typists, clerks and telephonists. New opportunities for women also appeared in higher education, in the legal profession, in medicine and science.

By the 1880s, the term 'new woman' had been coined to describe members of a new generation that was more assertive, self-confident and independently minded – although not enough to alarm the male population. The early decades of the 20th century saw the rise to greater prominence of women such as the Nobel prize-winning scientist Marie Curie and the political activists Rosa Luxemburg, Emma Goldman and Beatrice Webb.

Women's rights soon became a burning issue: women – particularly middle-class women – pressed to be treated on equal terms as men on matters such as property, wages, divorce rights, access to education and careers. They no longer accepted that women's horizons should be restricted to marriage and the cycle of childbirth, the drudgery of housework and low-paid wage labour. They were becoming increasingly indignant that the current order of society left them undervalued, that their talents and potential were being wasted.

Mirror of the times

The Edwardian era is often painted as a kind of Indian Summer before the calamity of the First World War. Unquestionably, for the well-to-do and the expanding middle classes these were years of unprecedented comfort. They enjoyed better houses, transport and services, and could revel in busy rounds of dinner parties, dances, days at the races, outings to

OPENING UP NEW VISTAS A 1911 photograph shows a dissection class at the Women's College Hospital in Philadelphia, USA. A new world of work was unfolding for women.

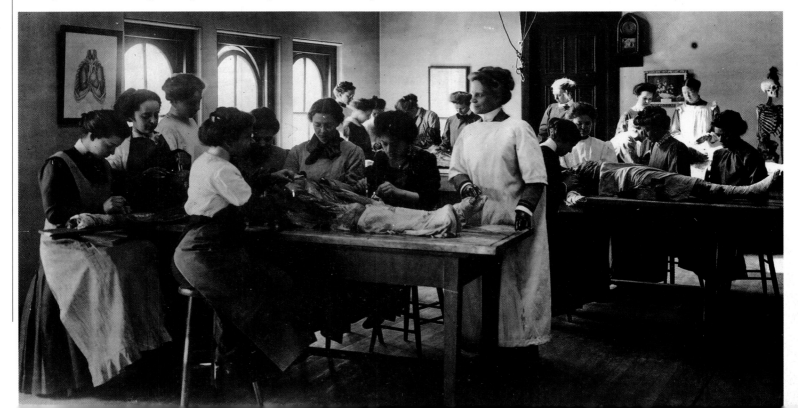

the theatre, cinema and music hall, and summer picnic expeditions in a motor car.

However, this was a period of rapid change, which delivered opportunities and frustrations in fairly equal measure. It was a complex and confusing time, characterised by a gathering pace of turmoil.

ART ON THE MOVE Futurist works, such as Giacomo Balla's *Velocity of Cars and Light* (1913 – right), brought a new sense of dynamism to art and poetry. The Ballets Russes' Tamara Karsavina (below) was a star of *Firebird* (1910), whose score by Stravinsky was the epitome of modernity.

All these trends were picked up in the arts. Ballet, for instance, went through its own revolution heralded by Isadora Duncan and brought to fruition by the Ballets Russes. Painters sought to reflect the mood of the modern era by throwing off the shackles of tradition: Fauvism, Cubism, Expressionism and Futurism followed one another in rapid succession. Their place in the history of art is now established, but in their day they were at the cutting edge, uncertain of success and guaranteed to provoke dismissive criticism and outrage. Soon, the very meaning, function and significance of art was being challenged. Vassily Kandinsky produced the first abstract paintings in 1909; and when Marcel Duchamp started to produce his 'ready-made' assemblages just before the First World War, he was putting forward ideas to which virtually all subsequent movements in 20th-century art can be traced.

The art world reflected multifarious strands of opinion. Many of the leading artists were committed socialists; the Futurists, by contrast, tended to be right-wing, antifeminist and militantly pro-war. Likewise, the rest of the world was fragmented into myriad opinions and viewpoints. In the frenetic era in the run-up to the First World War, dominated by an insatiable arms race, many people were convinced that war had become inevitable; and some held that it should be welcomed as a means of 'clearing the air' of all the industrial turmoil, political strife and militancy, international rivalry and xenophobia that had come increasingly to dominate events. On the other hand, there were those who sincerely postulated that the world had reached a level of sophistication which would make war – among the major powers at least – impossible. Many socialists, such as Jean Jaurès in France, fondly believed that the workers of the world could make war redundant by simply refusing to show up. In the end, war came about for old-fashioned reasons of national honour and historic rivalry, heated up by the jingoism disseminated by the popular press.

The socialists' pacifist dream evaporated. But those who thought that war would clear the air were also sadly deluded. Despite its devastating cost, the First World War did remarkably little to resolve the issues of the preceding era: it altered their appearance a little, then simply shunted them farther into the 20th century.

ANTI-WAR 'Down with War' reads a placard in a demonstration in the Hague in 1907. Hopes of an end to war were kept alive by socialists until the very eve of the First World War.

TIMES ON THE TURN

PARIS GREETED THE NEW CENTURY WITH A UNIVERSAL EXPOSITION, WHOSE STAR WAS ELECTRICITY, A POWER SOURCE NOW COMING INTO ITS OWN. SCIENTISTS WERE UNRAVELLING THE SECRETS OF THE ATOM AND RADIOACTIVITY, WHILE MOVEMENTS SUCH AS CUBISM WOULD TRANSFORM THE ARTS FOR EVER. THE CINEMA HAD ALREADY ARRIVED. AN APT SYMBOL OF THE AGE WAS A YOUTHFUL NATION: THE UNITED STATES, FLEXING ITS MUSCLES AS AN ECONOMIC SUPERPOWER.

PARIS 1900

PARIS WAS EUROPE'S MOST EXHILARATING CITY – SO WHERE BETTER TO CELEBRATE THE NEW CENTURY WITH AN INTERNATIONAL EXPOSITION?

The correspondent from *The Times* was ablaze with enthusiasm. 'In a hundred varied kiosks,' he exclaimed on April 11, 1900, eve of the opening of the Paris Universal Exposition, 'in the numberless galleries surrounding the Champ de Mars, in the vast spaces where the products of the whole world are displayed . . . all [that] the human brain and hand can conceive and execute will be displayed by competing nations.'

There had been a rash of international exhibitions in various major cities of the Western world ever since the hugely successful Great Exhibition of 1851 in London's Crystal Palace. They offered industrialists, inventors and designers an ideal platform on which to display state-of-the-art technology and fashion – and gave countries an opportunity to broadcast nationalistic pride. Paris had held exhibitions in 1855 and 1867, and then at intervals of 11 years. The 1900 one was the biggest and best yet. Spread over a site of 547 acres (221 ha) on both sides of the River Seine, and encompassing both the Champ de Mars and the Esplanade des Invalides – vast open spaces at the heart of the city – it contained the pavilions of some 50 nations, and 80 000 stands and exhibits. It made more money than any of the previous international fairs, and over the six months and three weeks it remained open, it attracted 48 million visitors.

Child of its times

The exposition was a public reassertion of French self-confidence. The nation was still haunted by memories of defeat in the Franco-Prussian War and the subsequent horrors of the Paris Commune (1870-1) when a revolutionary government established itself in the capital and was brutally suppressed by the army. France had remained troubled by the restless growth of Germany, and in 1892 had hastened to lay claim to the turn-of-the-century fair for fear that the Germans might put in a rival bid. As the opening day drew closer, patriotic French agitators threatened to disrupt proceedings because of the presence of large numbers of Germans – who, gallingly, boasted the biggest and most impressive exhibit of industrial products. Russia, on the other hand, had been accorded special status early on in the proceedings, having become a formal ally of France against the might of Germany in 1894. Russia had four pavilions, and the new bridge over the Seine, Pont Alexandre III, had been named in honour of the father of the current tsar, Nicholas II.

Anti-German sentiment, combined with anti-Semitism, had been responsible for the Dreyfus case, which still cast a dark shadow over French politics – and was the reason why, at the inauguration of the Pont Alexandre III, Emile Loubet, President of France (1899-1906), suffered the indignity of having his carriage pelted with vegetables. In 1894 the French had discovered that military secrets had been passed to the German embassy in Paris. A trumped-up case was made against a blameless Jewish army officer from Alsace

Turkey

United States

Austria

RIVER-FRONT PROFUSION From tiny Monaco to the mighty USA, each nation had its pavilion, creating a glorious jumble of styles along the banks of the River Seine.

THE POWER AND THE GLORY Visitors make their way to the Palace of Electricity. An aerial view (right) shows the swathes of central Paris encompassed by the Exposition.

called Alfred Dreyfus, who was then tried in a secret court-martial and condemned to life imprisonment on Devil's Island, the infamous penal colony off the coast of French Guiana. The disgraceful behaviour of many high-ranking officers and politicians involved in the case gradually came to light,

1 Porte Monumentale.
2 Petit Palais.
3 Grand Palais.
4 Pont Alexandre III.
5 Pavillon de la ville de Paris.
6 Pavillon de l'Horticulture.
7 Pont des Invalides.
8 Palais du Congrès.
9 Vieux Paris.
10 Trocadéro et Colonies.
11 Pont d'Iéna.
12 Palais de la Navigation.
13 Tour Eiffel.
14 Palais des Eaux et Forêts.
15 Tour du Monde.
16 Palais du Champ de Mars.
17 Château d'Eau et Electricité.
18 Agriculture salle des fêtes.
19 Village suisse.
20 Grande Roue.
21 Hôtel des Invalides.
22 Exposition de l'Esplanade.
23 Gare des Invalides.
24 Rue des Nations (sections étrangères.)

EXPOSITION
universelle
1900.

Bosnia Herzegovina

Hungary

Britain Belgium Norway

Germany

Spain Monaco

Greece Serbia

SPARKLING SPLENDOUR Inside, the Palace of Electricity presented a dazzling spectacle of domes and arches sprinkled like a magic cavern with thousands of electric bulbs.

however, causing an international outcry and great public indignation. In 1899 Dreyfus was brought back to France and retried, found guilty again, but condemned to a lesser sentence; he was then pardoned by a government unsettled by street violence and the threat of an international boycott of the forthcoming Universal Exposition. This series of events did little to dignify public office in France; even then, Dreyfus was not fully exonerated until 1906.

The Universal Exposition proved, however, that hatchets could be buried, at least temporarily. Even the British – arriving in droves on package tours arranged by Thomas Cook & Son – were tolerated: it had been feared that vigorous anti-British sympathies engendered by the Boer War might spill over into violence. At the opening ceremony on Saturday, April 14, held in a holiday atmosphere in bright spring weather,

JAUNTY TOURER The motor car was a 15-year-old novelty. Manufacturers such as the French company De Dion Bouton, makers of this 'Phaeton', used the Exposition as a showcase.

President Loubet expressed the hope that the Exposition would herald a new century of world peace and technical progress to benefit all.

All the fun of the fair

The public was not inclined to let anything spoil its enjoyment of the Exposition. The avenues were lined with fanciful pavilions in national styles: there was a Chinese pagoda, Swiss chalets, a Russian palace, a replica of medieval Paris. In restaurants, cafés and brasseries visitors could sample Russian caviar, Indian curry, Scandinavian smorgasbord, Tunisian couscous – served by staff dressed in their national costumes.

If the Universal Exposition had a star, it was electricity. The centrepiece was the Palace of Electricity, embracing a tiered, illuminated fountain. The Eiffel Tower, star of an earlier exposition in 1889, was decked with electric bulbs from head to toe, and the whole fairground glittered with lights in a

way that had never been seen before. Music specially composed by Camille Saint-Saëns, and played by an orchestra of 2000, took up the theme with a hymn to electricity entitled 'Heavenly Fire'.

There was nothing new about electricity. Electric street lighting had been installed in the city of Lyons as early as 1855. What was new was the emphasis: it was clear now that electricity was the power source of the future. One of the highlights of the Exposition was the electrically powered *trottoir roulant*, the 'moving pavement'. This was an ingenious belt-like wooden platform on which visitors could travel around the centre of the exhibition area, choosing one of the three tiers moving at different speeds.

Manufacturers of motor cars were showing off their latest models. Some models were fragile toys inspired by the traditions of horse-drawn carriages. Others, such as the more robust Italian Fiats, presaged the future of the motor car, which was about to revolutionise road transport and sweep the horse-drawn carriage aside. But for the time being, horses still ruled the roads: there were some 200 000 working horses in Paris.

One answer to the growing problem of city traffic congestion was underground railways. In 1890 the London Underground became the first to provide a regular service using electrified trains. The first Paris Métro line was built to serve the 1900 Exposition.

The visitors to the fair would have been able to record their impressions of it with snapshots. In 1888 the American George Eastman, inventor of Celluloid film, had produced the first box camera – ideally suited to amateur photographers. This proved such a success that in 1900 he launched the 'Brownie' – a camera simple enough for children to use. Moving pictures, projected onto a screen, were just five years old. The Lumière brothers, Louis and Auguste, had given their first public performance of a *Cinématographe* movie in Paris in 1895. The idea had caught on quickly, and was already a major attraction. Raoul Grimoin-Samson had hoped to show cinema-in-the-round at the Exposition, featuring

POINT AND CLICK
The 'Brownie' camera, first sold by George Eastman in 1900, would remain in production in various forms for 60 years.

panoramic film of Paris taken as he rose from the fairground in a balloon to the height of 2000 ft (600 m). Sadly, the projectors at his *Cinéorama* overheated and the exhibit had to be abandoned.

Other new inventions on display included X-ray photography, first used in clinical trials in 1895, and wireless telegraphy, first demonstrated by Guglielmo Marconi in 1896. The 1889 Exposition had the Eiffel Tower: the 1900 Exposition had a giant Ferris wheel, rising 350 ft (107 m) above the crowds and with seating capacity for 1600 people. The first such wheel, designed by G.W.G. Ferris, had been constructed for the Chicago Exposition of 1893. To some critics, the Paris Ferris wheel represented a rather blunt symbol of

MOVING PAVEMENT Tenants of adjacent apartments complained that visitors using the *trottoir roulant* (below) could see through their windows. The Métro (left) – dubbed the *Nécropolitain* by those opposed to the scheme – was built in time for the Exposition and caused temporary chaos, but in the long term helped to relieve traffic congestion.

PAST AND FUTURE

The travel writer Eric Whelpton was a child living in the semi-rural outskirts of Paris at the turn of the century. In *Paris Cavalcade* (1959), he described the wondrous impressions that the Universal Exposition made on his young mind, and his later reflections on this pivotal moment of history:

'In a sense 1900 was as much the last year of the old century as the first year of the new one. Many of the peasants who flocked to Paris from the provinces still wore their traditional costumes, and the lives they led were not far removed from those of their great-grandfathers before the Revolution.

'Occasionally, a noisy, clumsy contraption would rattle down the street making reports like those of a machine-gun. I can well remember seeing such a one for the first time, and being told that it was a horseless carriage. Although there were a few thousand optimists who believed that this same contraption had a future, most people thought that the craze would soon die out. After all, if you used one of the noisy, smelly things you could never be sure of getting to your destination, whereas with a train or even a good horse . . .

'Electricity was a different matter altogether – it was clean, it was brilliant, and it was cheap. The large illuminated fountain was one of the greatest successes of the Exhibition, and also there were the electric lamps that decorated the Eiffel Tower at night. Only the most reactionary old fogies proclaimed that oil lighting was better for the eyes and far pleasanter for reading.'

ART NOUVEAU

THE FOUNDERS OF THE 'NEW ART' WERE DETERMINED TO CREATE A STYLE
THAT WAS TRULY NEW – FREE OF THE BAGGAGE OF THE PAST

By the 1890s a new set of wealthy middle-class patrons was looking for a fresh style to reflect changing times – one that was elegant, luxurious and entirely modern. Responding to this demand, architects and designers came up with a sensuous style of flowing, organic lines and poetic motifs drawn from nature – poppies, lilies, sheaves of wheat, peacocks, billowing women's hair, stars. It was unlike anything seen before.

The first house built like this was the Hôtel Tassel in Brussels, designed by the Belgian architect Victor Horta and completed in 1893. Soon furniture, fittings such as door handles and lamp brackets, stained-glass windows, jewellery, book covers – all aspects of design were being rethought and reworked. At this point it was known as the *style anglais*, in recognition of the influence of the designs of William Morris and the Arts and Crafts movement. But there were other important influences, such as Japanese design and Celtic interlacing patterns. The Belgian designer Henri van de Velde chose to call the style Art Nouveau – a title picked up in 1895 when Samuel Bing, an American dealer, opened La Maison de l'Art Nouveau in Paris. It became truly international, known as *Jugendstil* in Germany and the Netherlands (after a design journal called *Jugend*), *stile Liberty* in Italy (after Liberty's of London, a store which promoted Art Nouveau goods) and *modernista* in Barcelona.

It was at the Paris Universal Exposition of 1900 that Art Nouveau first really came to public attention. Samuel Bing organised La

Pavilion d'Art Nouveau, and some of the great names of Art Nouveau were awarded Grands Prix, such as the Frenchman Emile Gallé for his glassware and the American Louis Comfort Tiffany for his vases and lamps. Visitors with large budgets could order jewellery by René Lalique. Nobody could help noticing the ironwork entrances to the new Métro stations designed by Hector Guimard.

The Art Nouveau of Victor Horta was restrained and functional. The Scottish designer Charles Rennie Mackintosh went farther down this path, discovering freshness and novelty in pared-down, angular forms. But in other hands Art Nouveau became frenzied, seething, sometimes suffocatingly voluptuous, even sickly. Art Nouveau motifs were widely used and abused until the First World War; thereafter, the style was rejected for its associations with the decadent world that had created the war, and was largely reviled until its re-evaluation in the 1960s.

THE NEW ART Female revellers, *bacchantes*, adorn a Lalique vase (below). Below left: This pectoral – a jewelled ornament worn on the breast – was created for the actress Sarah Bernhardt. One of the style's most idiosyncratic geniuses was Barcelona's Antoni Gaudí, architect of the Casa Milà (left).

the cultural and industrial challenge posed by the USA. The telephone, electric lighting, box cameras, the Ferris wheel – the USA seemed to be stealing the limelight. It was a sign of things to come: the impact of the USA on European history and culture would be a recurrent theme for the rest of the century.

A backward glance at the arts

The technological theme of electricity was diluted by 'grand art'. The principal art galleries were in the Grand Palais, a building of cast-iron, glass and stone, designed in the ornate 'eclectic style' specially for the Exposition. It faced the slightly less imposing Petit Palais.

In the Grand Palais – dubbed 'A monument consecrated by the Republic to the glory of French art' – technically brilliant but old-fashioned academic paintings and sculpture were on show; these included work by such revered and popular painters as William Bouguereau and Jean Léon Gérôme. A separate room was given over to various Impressionist and post-Impressionist painters, such as Renoir, Monet, Sisley, Pissarro and Degas. This might have been interpreted as a sign that they were now accepted as major contributors to French art. However, as Gérôme was showing

---

THE FIRST TALKIES

The Jazz Singer (1927), starring Al Jolson, has gone down in cinema history as the first 'talkie'. However, experiments with synchronised sound, using a separate soundtrack played on an amplified record player, date back to the early days of the 'silent' cinema. A selection of such films, made by the French Gaumont company, were presented at the 1900 Paris Universal Exposition. One of these showed Sarah Bernhardt, the greatest French actress of her day, performing the duel scene from Shakespeare's *Hamlet*.

President Loubet around the Grand Palais, he planted himself bodily in the entrance of the Impressionist exhibit and declared: 'Go no further, *Monsieur le Président*; here France is dishonoured!'

The sculptor Auguste Rodin had a retrospective exhibition with a pavilion entirely to itself. It was one of the triumphs of the Exposition. The collection included *The Kiss*, a work of stunning sexual frankness and naturalism that caused a sensation.

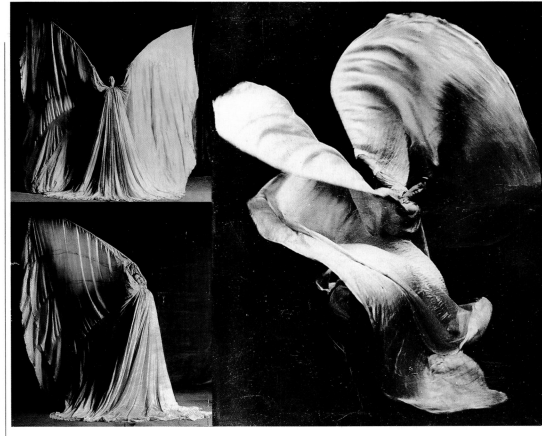

The Paris Exposition had a significant impact on modern dance. The American dancer Loïe Fuller was given her own pavilion to perform her novel 'free-form' dance. Another American, Isadora Duncan, then aged 22, was among the many who came to see her.

Olympic Games were also held to coincide with the Exposition. The original Greek games had lapsed at the end of the 4th century AD. The Frenchman Pierre de Coubertin revived the concept, and the first of the modern series was held in Athens in 1896, to huge acclaim. The Paris Olympics of 1900 attracted teams from 23 countries and 1335 competitors. They were, however, poorly organised and, overshadowed by the Exposition, attracted only sparse crowds. The contests were strung out over several months, from May 20 to October 28. Some competitors were unaware that these Amateur World Championships had been designated the Olympics.

Paris for pleasure

Paris at the turn of the century was famed as the European capital of art, fashion, gastronomy and pleasure. Food and wine were good, plentiful and cheap, and the lively mood and entertainments – with more than a hint of naughtiness – drew visitors from all over the world.

DANCE AS NEVER SEEN BEFORE The American Loïe Fuller took audiences by storm with her 'serpentine' dances. Enhanced by lights and flowing costumes, they created an image that coincided with the current Art Nouveau style.

It had 2.7 million inhabitants – about half as many as London. Some 500 000 of these went to the theatre, or a comparable entertainment, at least once a week. In addition to thriving theatre and opera, there were 300 or so music halls and *cafés-dansants*, where crowds could dance, drink and eat, and watch shows laid on by acrobats, magicians, singers, cabaret artistes – and the famed can-can dancers showing their undergarments.

The young Pablo Picasso, attracted to Paris from his native Spain at the young age of 19, painted his impression of the famous dance hall, the Moulin de la Galette, in 1900. But the artist par excellence of the music hall was still Henri de Toulouse Lautrec, who had won celebrity status for his lithograph posters before his death in 1901 at the age of 36.

For many of the most influential players in both the arts and society – from Picasso to the Prince of Wales, the future Edward VII – Paris, with its fun-loving, liberal atmosphere, had an essential place on the map.

THE FRONTIERS OF SCIENCE

SCIENCE TOOK BREATHTAKING LEAPS FORWARD IN THE FIRST YEARS OF THE CENTURY, OVERTURNING MANY EARLIER ASSUMPTIONS

Alfred Nobel, the Swedish chemist and industrialist, was deeply concerned about the potentially lethal seeds he had sown with his invention of dynamite. He died in 1896 and left in his will an endowment to fund five prizes for the sciences, literature and peace, to be awarded 'to those who, during the preceding year, shall have conferred the greatest benefit to mankind'. Fittingly, the first of these prizes were awarded in the first year of a century that was to produce a feast of major scientific advances – as well as two of the most deadly wars in human history. The Nobel prize was born in the midst of a period of intense scientific achievement, and much of this was of direct and tangible benefit to mankind. For example, the first Nobel prize for physics, awarded in 1901, went to the German Wilhelm Conrad Roentgen for his discovery of X-rays. Although the Austrian Karl Landsteiner had to

FIRST PRIZE-WINNER A certificate from the Royal Swedish Academy of Sciences confirms Wilhelm Conrad Roentgen as the winner of the 1901 Nobel prize for physics. X-rays, which he discovered in 1895, were already being put to clinical use (bottom left).

wait until 1930 before he won the Nobel prize for medicine, his main breakthrough was accomplished, also in 1901, when he discovered a way of identifying the various blood groups, named by him A, B and O (AB followed in 1902). The chief impact of this was in blood transfusions, which previously had been haphazard: patients given blood from a non-matching group risked fatal clotting or kidney failure. Bloodtyping based on Landsteiner's work was introduced to blood transfusion in 1907, though the donor still had to be present. Modern blood transfusion

GIVING BLOOD An early transfusion kit has a glass jar for storing blood along with needles and tubes for bleeding the donor and introducing the blood into the patient.

began in 1914 after the discovery of the citrate method of blood preservation.

Medicine was also the beneficiary of important studies in radioactivity. Early on in her research, Marie Curie noted that skin burns caused by contact with pitchblende (uranium ore) healed comparatively quickly. She concluded that radiation could be used in the treatment of diseased cells: by bombarding them with radiation, malignant cells could be killed off, while the healthy cells would recover. Within three years of her isolation of radium in 1902, this powerful radioactive element was being widely used as the only effective treatment for cancer. Characteristically, Marie Curie refused to patent radium: even though she stood to earn a fortune from its manufacture, she found distasteful the idea of profiting from the treatment of disease.

Reviewing the atom

The practical and industrial spin-offs from science had been increasingly appreciated in the latter part of the 19th century, resulting in the rapid growth of technical colleges. In

1900 Freud's *The Interpretation of Dreams*

1901 First Nobel prizes awarded

1902 Marie Curie isolates radium

1905 Einstein first describes relativity

MOSQUITO MAN Ronald Ross, winner of the 1902 Nobel prize for medicine, was born in British-ruled India and returned there after completing his training. It was in India that he identified the *Anopheles* mosquito as the transmitter of human malaria.

Germany the number of science students increased eightfold between 1880 and 1910, providing German industry with considerable advantage in fields such as metallurgy, chemical manufacture, mechanics and electrical engineering.

National rivalries and imperialism played their part in driving forward scientific goals – in medicine as well as industry. For instance, advances in bacteriology and immunology were inspired in part by the need for the imperial powers to combat the lethal diseases they encountered in their tropical colonies. The 1902 Nobel prize for medicine was awarded to the British bacteriologist Ronald Ross for identifying the mosquito that transmits malaria.

But the really revolutionary scientific advances of the age belonged to the rarefied world of scientific theory. Initially they had little impact on the world at large. It was hard for the public even to conceptualise, for example, the advances in atomic physics when the focus of research was invisible.

The idea that the material world is composed of minute particles was first proposed by the ancient Greek Democritus, who coined the term atom, from *atomos* meaning 'indivisible': matter could get no smaller than these indivisible building bricks. This concept was revived during the 17th century, when the atom was conceived as a kind of

THE FIRST WOMAN TO WIN A NOBEL PRIZE

The 1903 Nobel prize for physics was shared by three scientists researching radioactivity: Marie Curie, her husband Pierre and Henri Becquerel. Marie Curie was the first woman to win a Nobel prize, and in 1911 she became the first person to win it a second time.

The young Marie Sklodowska had overcome enormous hardships to go from her native Poland to study at the Sorbonne in Paris in 1891. Life was tough: on occasions she fainted for lack of food. After graduating, she worked under Pierre Curie. They married in 1895. Following Becquerel's discovery of the unique properties of uranium, Marie opted to study the phenomenon for her doctorate. The raw material of her researches was pitchblende (uranium ore), mined for the glass industry. She knew that pitchblende contained uranium, but pitchblende was more radioactive than pure uranium, indicating the presence of other elements with higher radioactivity. Unassisted, Marie had to stir large quantities of heated pitchblende, filtering and refiltering the residue in an attempt to track down this further element. 'We had no money, no proper laboratory and no help in the conduct of our important and difficult task,' she later recalled. 'In the evening I was broken with fatigue.' One evening in 1902, Marie and Pierre returned to their laboratory – a shed with an earth floor – to find crystallised radium salts glowing bluish-purple in their glass-covered bowls. It was a moment of joy: the element had at last been distilled out of the pitchblende.

In 1906, Pierre was killed in a road accident. In 1910 Marie at last succeeded in producing a sample of pure radium. She became director of the Curie Laboratory in Paris and continued her researches before succumbing in 1934 to leukaemia brought on by her long exposure to radioactivity.

PARTNERS IN LIFE AND LEARNING Marie Curie stands with her husband Pierre in their Paris laboratory.

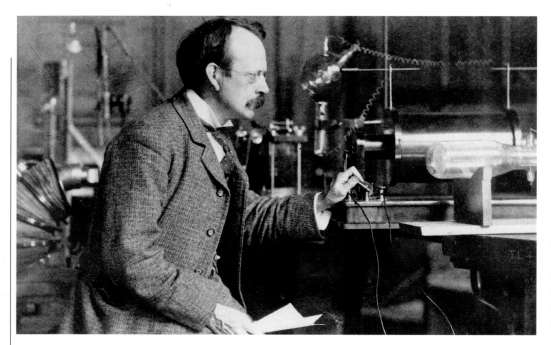

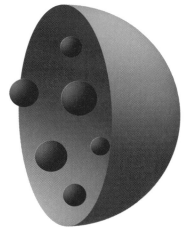

IDENTIFYING THE ELECTRON J.J. Thomson (left), working at the Cavendish Laboratory in Cambridge, devised an image of the atom (above) as a cluster, like a plum pudding, with negatively charged electrons embedded in it like currants.

billiard ball; by the early 19th century, it had been established that each element possessed its own unique type of atom. Then, in 1897, the British physicist Joseph John Thomson, working at the Cavendish Laboratory in Cambridge, identified the electron, a negatively charged particle within the atom. For this discovery Thomson won the 1906 Nobel prize for physics.

A key inspiration behind a number of such ground-breaking discoveries was radioactivity. This had first been identified in uranium ore in 1896 by the French physicist Henri Becquerel, who shared the 1903 Nobel prize with the Curies. Another pioneer was Ernest Rutherford. He was already an expert in electromagnetism when he came to Britain from New Zealand in 1895; he worked alongside J.J. Thomson at the Cavendish Laboratory and helped in the discovery of the electron. He transferred to Canada in 1898 where, in collaboration with Frederick Soddy, he demonstrated that radioactive elements are transformed into other elements through radiation. Rutherford won the 1908 Nobel prize for chemistry for this work.

He returned to Britain in 1907 to become professor of physics at Manchester University. Here he began a series of experiments using alpha particles of radiation – positively charged particles emitted by some radioactive substances – fired at a screen of metal foil. He was assisted by a young English physicist Ernest Marsden and a German, Hans Geiger, who designed an electrical device to measure radioactive emissions – later developed into the Geiger Counter.

Their work led to what Rutherford described as 'the most incredible event' of his life: the discovery of the nucleus in 1911. A series of experiments suggested that atoms must have powerful positive and negative charges. Rutherford concluded that they

THE GREAT AND THE BRILLIANT The Belgian Ernest Solvay (seated, third from left) organised conferences bringing together the best scientific minds of the day. Participants here include Marie Curie (seated, second from right), Ernest Rutherford (behind her) and Albert Einstein (standing, second from right).

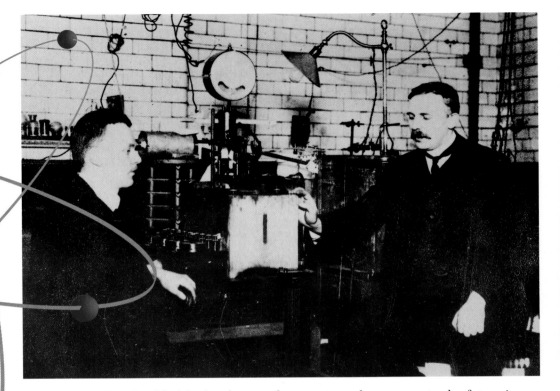

HOW THE ATOM WORKS
For Rutherford, the atom consisted
of electrons in orbit around a nucleus. Just two
years after this photograph (above right) was taken,
Rutherford (right) and Hans Geiger (left) would be
separated by the First World War, in which Geiger
served in the German artillery.

were not a solid mass, but a composite
structure consisting mainly of space, with
negatively charged electrons orbiting around
a positively charged nucleus. The quantity of
space was surprisingly large: if the nucleus
were a pea, the space defined by the electrons' orbit would be the size of a football
stadium. It was a strange and bold concept
to suggest that solid matter consisted mainly
of space. The identification of the nucleus
conferred upon Rutherford the title 'father
of nuclear physics'.

The quantum theory

Back in 1900 the German physicist Max
Planck had come up with an astonishing new
theory. He had been intrigued by the problem posed by 'black bodies' – substances
such as lampblack (a sooty, almost pure form
of carbon often used as a pigment and in
matches) which absorb almost all the energy
that falls upon them. According to traditional
theories of physics, the energy should be

converted into heat, but black bodies do not
give off heat. Clearly the laws of physics
were at fault.

Planck came up with a new explanation:
energy was not transmitted as a continuous
wave as had previously been thought, but as
a flow of little, indivisible packets, similar to
atoms. Planck called these packets 'quanta'.
Waves simply described the approximate
pattern of these quanta. Planck's 'quantum
theory' was greeted with little enthusiasm at
first, but in 1905 it received the significant
backing of the young German-born theoretical physicist Albert Einstein.

In 1912, Ernest Rutherford was joined in
Manchester by a young Danish physicist
Niels Bohr, who was concerned about the
older man's model of the atom with planet-
like electrons orbiting a sun-like nucleus.
According to existing scientific law, the atom
would run out of energy at some point and
collapse. Why did this not happen? Bohr
felt that the answer might lie in quantum
mechanics. By applying Planck's theories to
Rutherford's concept, he devised a model of
the atom in which the electrons travel round
the nucleus in orbits determined by specific
packets of energy or quanta. This model,
with modifications, is still used today.

Relativity: breaking the old laws

In 1931 Planck said: 'We have no right to
assume that physical laws exist, or if they have
existed up to now, that they will continue to

do so in a similar manner in the future.'
Planck's own quantum theory and Einstein's
theory of relativity represented the two most
radical breaks with prior physical laws, and
formed the bases for much of the physics of
the 20th century.

GENIUS AT WORK

Ernest Rutherford commanded immense
respect from his colleagues, who were in little doubt of
his stature. He was acknowledged both for his own
achievements and for his abilities to galvanise the team
around him into producing first-class work. Niels Bohr, a
colleague at Manchester University, put it like this:

'This effect [the wide scattering of alpha particles],
though to all appearances insignificant, was disturbing to
Rutherford, as he felt it difficult to reconcile it with the
general idea of atomic structure then favoured by
physicists. Indeed it was not the first, nor has it been the
last, time that Rutherford's critical judgement and
intuitive power have called forth a revolution in science
by inducing him to throw himself with his unique energy
into the study of a phenomenon, the importance of
which would probably escape other investigators on
account of the smallness and apparently spurious
character of the effect. This confidence in his judgement
and our admiration for his powerful personality was the
basis for the inspiration felt by all in his laboratory, and
made us all try our best to deserve the kind and untiring
interest he took in the work of everyone. However modest
the result might be, an approving word from
him was the greatest encouragement for which
any of us could wish.'

For a man who became the greatest scientific theorist of the century – whose very name was used as a synonym for genius by the time he had reached 40 – Albert Einstein had an extraordinary background. Born into a Jewish manufacturing family, he was slow to speak as a child, and his parents worried that he might be mentally impaired. He had poor results at school, and after doing low-paid teaching jobs, he took up a mundane post at the patent office in Bern, Switzerland. Then, in 1905 at the age of 26, he published four papers which demonstrated the brilliance of his mind. The first was a formula for the movement of particles suspended in a liquid or gas (known as Brownian motion), which helped to support current atomic theory. The second explained photoelectric effects in terms of the quantum theory (for which he was awarded the 1921 Nobel prize for physics). The third was the most significant. Called 'On the Electrodynamics of Moving Bodies', it was his first attempt

PATENT GENIUS In 1902 Einstein was employed by a Swiss patent office. The undemanding work allowed him to devote a great deal of his time to thinking. One fruit of this was his theory of relativity.

NEW THEORY FOR A NEW CENTURY Max Planck announced his revolutionary findings about radiation, the basis of quantum theory, at a meeting of the German Physical Society in Berlin on December 14, 1900.

to describe relativity. The fourth was an extension of this, a short paper entitled 'Does the Inertia of a Body Depend on its Energy Content?' This contained his formula $E=mc^2$ (energy is mass multiplied by the speed of light squared), which suggested that mass has a direct correspondence with energy. It anticipated the vast energy released by splitting atoms in bombs and in nuclear power.

Relativity completely undermined traditional approaches to physics. Until then people believed that they lived in a world in which everything could be explained by measurable and constant phenomena, such as distance and time. Einstein showed that all such perceptions were relative to the standpoint of the observer: the only constant is the speed of light.

Einstein's theories were quickly recognised as revolutionary by the academic world, and he took up a series of academic posts before becoming director of the Kaiser Wilhelm Institute of Physics in Berlin. In 1916 he published 'The Foundations of the General Theory of Relativity', in which he demonstrated the broader application of relativity, and showed how space, time and mass are all interdependent. He also suggested that space and time form a curve, and that light can be bent by gravity. This was proved by observations of the 1919 solar eclipse, which did much to enhance Einstein's fame.

FREUD UNLOCKS THE UNCONSCIOUS

THE BIRTH OF PSYCHOANALYSIS BROUGHT UNPRECEDENTED SCRUTINY TO THE INNER WORKINGS OF THE MIND AND GAVE A HUGELY ENLARGED ROLE TO THE UNCONSCIOUS

In 1900 Sigmund Freud (1856-1939), an Austrian doctor of psychiatry, published *The Interpretation of Dreams*. Although it sold slowly at the time, it is widely seen as his masterpiece – and was later described as 'epoch shattering' by the Swiss doctor Carl Jung (1875-1961), who that same year had begun work at a mental hospital in Zurich.

Since 1882 Freud had been working at the department for nervous diseases at the General Hospital of Vienna, where he had developed a partnership with Joseph Breuer. Breuer had evolved a set of techniques to treat patients suffering from psychosomatic illness: by allowing them to talk about their feelings and symptoms, sometimes under hypnosis, he hoped to understand the causes of the illness, and so find a cure. Freud valued this technique as a means of revealing feelings suppressed by the conscious mind, but during the 1890s, he found he could dispense with hypnosis. Instead he used 'free association' in which the patient recounted a train of thoughts as they came into his or her head. The recollection of dreams was also important.

Through practise of this technique, and self-analysis, Freud concluded that many of the symptoms of neuroses had their origin in childhood experiences – particularly in suppressed infantile sexual feelings towards the parent of the opposite sex (the 'Oedipus complex').

Freud's theories were highly contentious, causing both heated debate and a certain amount of outrage. Yet Freud also commanded great respect among many at the cutting edge of the psychiatric profession. From 1902 to 1938, he held the chair of neurology at the University of Vienna, while continuing private consultations. In 1902 he also began regular meetings at his home, which later evolved into the International Psycho-Analytical Society. Among those who attended were Jung and the Austrian psychiatrist Alfred Adler (1870-1937). Each eventually found Freud's dogmatic insistence on the primacy of infantile sexuality too restrictive, and went his separate way.

Adler was noted in particular for his theories, developed around 1907, about the way that people compensate for a feeling of inadequacy – the 'inferiority complex'. He concluded that this was a stronger driving force than sexuality, and by 1911

had broken with Freud. Jung had a very close relationship with Freud for several years after they first met in 1906, but this turned sour in 1912 when Jung published *The Psychology of the Unconscious*, which demonstrated the degree to which his ideas were at variance with Freud's. Jung's 'analytical psychology' essentially embodied a more positive and generous attitude toward the workings of the mind. Later, Jung developed a keen interest in personality types, coining the terms extrovert and introvert. He also studied myths and fairy tales in search of shared ideas or 'archetypes' belonging to the 'collective unconscious', inherited in a similar manner to physical attributes derived from a common ancestry.

PROBING THE DEPTHS By 1900 Freud had established his consulting room, in which the patient reclined on a rug-covered sofa. Freud, out of sight and smoking a cigar, gently directed proceedings from a chair at the head of the sofa.

PAVLOV AND HIS DOGS

While other scientists were opening up new ground in genetics, the Russian physiologist Ivan Pavlov was making significant advances in the study of animal behaviour. His starting point for this was research into digestion. He demonstrated that dogs will salivate at the mere sight of food; by using surgery to isolate the stomach from the salivary glands, he proved that this reaction was prompted by mental association alone. He also carried out a series of experiments during which dogs were fed to the sound of a beating metronome: later, when the metronome was set in motion without the presence of food, the dogs still salivated. Pavlov called this response 'conditioned reflex', a concept that has had an important impact not only in studies of behaviour and psychology, but also in practical fields such as advertising. Pavlov won the 1904 Nobel prize for medicine.

SECRETS OF DIGESTION Pavlov (right) was a deft surgeon as well as researcher, able to perform operations on dogs' digestive systems (above) without anaesthetics and without causing the animals undue pain.

Much later, in 1949, Einstein himself gave a wry layman's explanation of his famous theory: 'When you are courting a nice girl an hour seems like a second. When you sit on a red-hot cinder a second seems like an hour. That's relativity.'

Genetics and the workings of heredity

Einstein was one of very few scientists who have radically altered our perceptions about the world. Another was the pioneer of evolutionary theory, Charles Darwin. Darwin's theories, however, were more easily absorbed than Einstein's; published between 1858 and 1871, they had been broadly accepted by as early as the 1880s – a remarkably short time

given that they completely redefined humankind's place in nature.

Inevitably, Darwin's concept of the 'survival of the fittest' was also applied to the contemporary human world, and bent to the purposes of those who wanted to give a scientific spin to theories about the inferiority of other races or classes of people. For some, 'social Darwinism' took on a political hue, which smacked of authoritarianism and racism: superior classes and races should see to it that they breed with care for the betterment of humankind. Some saw imperialism as an expression of Darwinian evolution. In

1883 the term 'eugenics' was coined for the concept of applying some form of selective breeding controls to maintain, or improve, inherited features in humans; by the turn of the century it was a burning issue.

Eugenics was closely tied to scientific studies of heredity, and many of the scientists involved came to the subject out of a concern for the future of the human race. Work in the field had received a considerable boost from the rediscovery of the work of Gregor Johann Mendel, an Austrian monk who in the 1850s and 60s had made a close study of inheritance factors observed in the hybridisation of peas in the garden of his monastery. One of several zoologists working independently on Mendel's theories was the Englishman William Bateson, who devised the term genetics in 1905 and then became the first professor of genetics at Cambridge in 1908.

Meanwhile, the Dutch botanist Hugo de Vries proposed a theory that heredity was carried by chromosomes, which form at the moment of cell division in reproduction. Kansas-born Walter Sutton reached the same conclusion by studying grasshoppers; and the German scientist Theodor Boveri, working quite independently with roundworm eggs, concurred. The theory was proven in 1908 when the American Thomas Hunt Morgan showed that genes were carried by the chromosomes – the result of his studies of inherited mutant characteristics in fruit flies.

The politics of science

Later in the century, many of the scientists who had made such a mark at its start would face rougher times. The Nazis, in particular, persecuted a large number of them, especially if they had Jewish connections. Sigmund Freud had Jewish parentage: the Nazis outlawed psychoanalysis, and forced him, now 82 years old and sick with cancer, to flee to London. Einstein left Berlin for the USA in 1933.

This was a tragic time for a fading generation of some of the greatest figures in the history of science. They could look back wistfully upon the years that preceded the First World War as a golden age of exceptional achievement, and of remarkably fruitful international cooperation.

THE AGE OF THE MASSES

A NEW BREED OF ENTREPRENEURS TAPPED THE SPENDING POWER OF WORKING PEOPLE TO TRANSFORM THE MEDIA AND COMMUNICATIONS

The launching of the *Daily Mail* in Britain in 1896 was a landmark for the modern press. The man behind it was the dynamic journalist Alfred Harmsworth, already the founder and owner of a variety of popular publications with names like *Home Chat* and *Comic Cuts*.

Before this time, all the leading British newspapers had been densely printed, erudite and stodgy. Hidebound by traditions that dated back several hundred years, they appealed to a narrow, literate and conservative readership. Harmsworth recognised that these newspapers failed to capture a vast potential readership of men and women who were eager for daily news, but wanted it served up in a more digestible form. News

stories needed to be shorter, punchier, more entertaining, more sensational if necessary, presented with the pazzazz of bold banner headlines and plenty of photographs. Sports pages, human-interest stories, forthright comment, gossip, fashions, big-prize competitions, cartoons, crossword puzzles and illustrated advertisements could all be added to spice up the brew.

The *Daily Mail* was an overnight success. Selling for just half a penny, it was the first newspaper in the world to reach a circulation of more than a million people. The formula clearly won approval, even if, by the standards of modern tabloid journalism, it was actually rather sedate, respectful and cultural: a review of Sir Edward Elgar's First Symphony, for example, appeared on the front page in 1908.

As advertising revenue poured in, Harmsworth became a wealthy and powerful man. In 1903 he founded *The Daily Mirror*, which the next year became the first paper to be illustrated entirely with photographs. Initially conceived as a women's paper, it failed in this guise, but worked when it was later relaunched as a more general paper. In 1908 Harmsworth took over a controlling interest in the venerable but ailing *Times* and rescued it from oblivion. His influence over public opinion was now significant – enough to earn the respect of politicians. He was rewarded with honours: elevated to the peerage, he took the title Lord Northcliffe, while his brother Harold, the financial wizard behind his empire, became Lord Rothermere.

New journalism

Alfred Harmsworth was in fact applying in Britain, and extending, a pattern that had already been successfully tried and tested across the Atlantic. The pioneer of popular journalism was a Hungarian-born immigrant to the USA, Joseph Pulitzer – later the founder of the Pulitzer prizes for journalism and literature.

Pulitzer made his name as owner, from 1878, of the St Louis *Post-Dispatch*. Being a

TABLOID APPROACH The use of photography and an emphasis on 'shock horror' – the death of a policeman in the course of his duties – distinguishes the British *Daily Graphic* from two continental counterparts.

LINOTYPE REVOLUTION Machines like these enabled operators to punch out type three times as fast as in the old, laborious days of hand composition.

was a large untapped market for geographical articles, but also that ordinary people wanted to feel they were contributing to exploration and research.

National Geographic had a circulation of no more than 1000 when Bell took over; by 1912, now under the editorship of Bell's son-in-law Gilbert H. Grosvenor, it had risen to 107 000. Sustained by this level of public interest, the Society was able to give active support to a number of high-profile expeditions, such as Admiral Robert Peary's quest for the North Pole in 1909, and Hiram Bingham's second expedition to Machu Picchu in 1912.

By the 1900s, newspapers and magazines were also benefiting from major advances in the printing industry following the invention of Linotype and Monotype machines, both

first-generation arrival in America with an imperfect command of English, he understood the kind of journalism required by a population of limited literacy: short and uncomplicated. Pulitzer's success at the *Post-Dispatch* led to his purchase of the New York *World* in 1883. His main rival after 1900 was William Randolph Hearst who had built up a press empire as a young man, starting with his father's San Francisco *Examiner*.

Newspapers were just one contender among a vast range of printed products on the newsvendors' stands. This was a great age for magazines and periodicals, catering for all manner of tastes and special interests – fashion, gardening, hobbies, railways, motor cars, electrical inventions and so on. For instance, *Strand Magazine*, founded in 1891 by Sir George Newnes, another British newspaper mogul, was a popular monthly, providing a mixed bag of articles including new Sherlock Holmes stories by Sir Arthur Conan Doyle. Newnes also launched *Country Life* in 1897.

The *National Geographic Magazine*, journal of the US National Geographic Society,

provided a typical example of the huge potential for successful publications. In 1898 Alexander Graham Bell, the inventor of the telephone, took over as the journal's second president and set about broadening its appeal, confident in his instinct not only that there

"What a time we'll have."

VOICE TO VOICE Making a date was so much easier with the telephone – a postcard celebrates the new freedom. This candlestick phone (right) was a gift to Britain's future King George V.

1901 Marconi's first transatlantic wireless transmission

1902 Venice campanile collapses

1904 Caruso records 'La Donna è Mobile'

1905 Candlestick telephone introduced

developed in the USA. Previously, compositors had assembled type by hand, at a rate of about 2000 characters an hour. The new machines had keyboards onto which operators typed the letters, which were converted into code on punched tape, then cast and composed at a rate of 6000 characters per hour. This represented the most significant technological advance in printing since the invention of movable type in the 15th century and would remain so until computerisation arrived in the 1970s.

Communications technology

The telephone, meanwhile, was continuing its own communications revolution, with a million subscribers in the USA by 1900. Users, by and large, had to go through two operators. The act of lifting the handset of the 1905 'candlestick' telephone sent a signal to the local operator, who responded by asking 'Number, please'. This operator then had to get through to the operator at the exchange of the person being called. Long-distance connections could take several hours to arrange. The introduction of automatic exchanges (and hence telephones with built-in dialling facilities) was slow as long as the labour costs of the operators, mainly women, remained competitive. The first automatic exchange in Britain was opened in Epsom in 1912.

Intercontinental communications had been possible since the laying of trans-oceanic cables in the latter part of the 19th century. These carried telegraph messages in Morse code. By 1907 newspapers could even receive photographs by cable, by means of the first kind of facsimile machine which had been invented several years earlier by the German Professor Arthur Korn.

The telegraph system depended upon a network of wires. In 1894 the young Italian

THE COLLAPSE OF THE VENICE CAMPANILE

For nearly 1000 years, the elegant red-brick campanile had stood opposite the cathedral in St Mark's Square in the centre of Venice. First built in AD 888-912 and completed in 1173, it served as a lighthouse and also contained five famous bells that rang out the hours of the working day throughout the centuries of Venice's glory – and more ominously announced executions. Topped by the Golden Archangel of the Annunciation on the pyramidal summit 324 ft (99 m) above the square, the campanile was a major landmark. During the 18th century the campanile was struck by lightning, then a crack appeared, causing concern about the safety of the structure, but otherwise there was little warning of the moment, on July 14, 1902, when it suddenly collapsed and disintegrated in a pile of rubble. Incredibly, the only casualty was the keeper's cat. That same day, the city fathers vowed to rebuild the campanile *'dov'era e com'era'* ('where it was and as it was') and, assisted by generous international donations, an exact but lighter replica was completed in 1912.

TUMBLED IN A MOMENT In less than a minute, St Mark's campanile had become a pile of rubble.

Guglielmo Marconi had hit upon a new form of 'wireless' communication. By experimenting with equipment developed by the German Heinrich Hertz to demonstrate atmospheric electromagnetic waves ('Hertzian waves'), Marconi – working in the attic of his home – found that he could use an electrically induced

ACROSS THE OCEAN The first transatlantic wireless transmission, from Cornwall (below right) to a waiting Marconi in Newfoundland (below left), succeeded because the radio waves bounced off the ionosphere.

spark to pass signals to an unconnected bell on the other side of the room. Gradually, he increased the range of his experiment to 2 miles (3.2 km). When the Italian military showed no interest in his discovery, Marconi took his equipment to Britain (his mother was from a wealthy Irish distilling family). In 1899 he transmitted a signal across the English Channel.

But Marconi had greater ambitions. He wanted to prove that he could send wireless messages around the world. But would the waves bend to the Earth's curvature, or travel

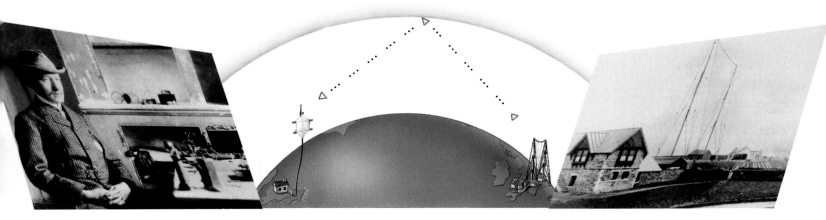

1908 Pathé brothers introduce weekly newsreels

1911 D.W. Griffith's *Enoch Arden*

A BRAND NEW ENTERTAINMENT

**THE MOVIE INDUSTRY, JUST FIVE YEARS OLD AT THE TURN OF THE CENTURY, WAS
ALREADY MAKING ITS MARK WITH STEADILY GROWING AUDIENCES**

The early pioneers of the cinema made no bones about it: perceiving film as a form of mass entertainment, they went unashamedly for laughs and sensation, and rode the crest of a wave funded by the thousands who paid for cheap tickets – and came back repeatedly for more. Film was tailor-made for the age of the masses.

Although the cinema was developed in the first instance in France, launched by the Lumière brothers in 1895, the USA soon proved to be the driving force behind its escalation as a business.

Silent films were a perfect form of entertainment for a nation with a large immigrant population of mixed backgrounds and languages. At first, films were shown as fairground entertainment, and audiences were satisfied by the thrill of seeing moving photographic images projected onto a screen. In 1900 most films lasted no more than 90 seconds; over the next few years they grew to about 10 minutes or so – long enough to develop a story line. Westerns were among the first of these dramatic films, including in 1903 *The Great Train Robbery* and *Kit Carson* – which stretched to an almost unprecedented 21 minutes. The first film cartoons date from 1906.

By 1905 films were being shown in specially adapted premises, although a converted shop kitted out with wooden benches and a bedsheet for a screen was still a far cry from the picture palaces to come in later years. At one of these, at McKeesport, Pennsylvania, the cost of entry was a nickel (five cents), so the cinema was proudly named the Nickelodeon. The name caught on, and within three years there were 10 000 nickelodeons across the USA, serving an audience of 26 million cinema-goers.

The film world attracted a wide variety of entrepreneurs, many of whom made such a success of it that their empires remain a force in cinema to this day. Russian-born Louis B. Mayer was a scrap

BIRTH OF A GENRE The booty is heaved out to accomplices in *The Great Train Robbery* of 1903 (left). Films were often shown in travelling 'cinemas' (below), which tried to assure customers of their respectability.

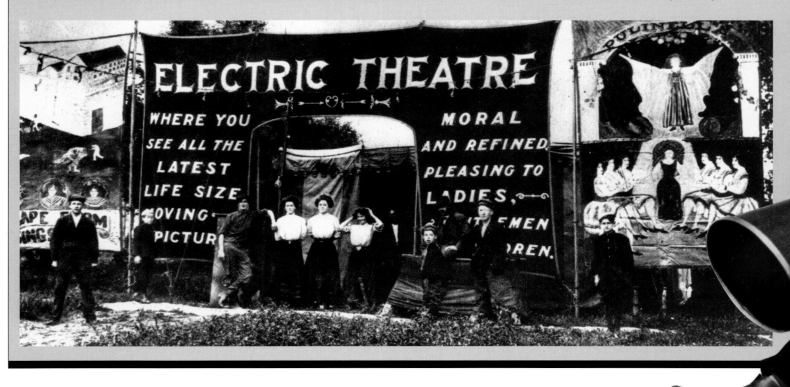

director in search of authentic sagebrush country for Westerns set up a primitive studio in a remote settlement near Los Angeles called Hollywood. Within just two years, it became the main production centre of American film. At about this time, directors began to recognise the audience-pulling power of certain favourite actors, such as Mary Pickford, and began to give special emphasis to their 'stars' – who soon responded by demanding higher fees. The 'star system' was born.

Films were screened initially with piano accompaniment, but in 1911 the first powerful Wurlitzer organ was produced in New York State. Based on the traditional church organ, it was enhanced for the movies with features such as extra percussive devices. Primitive colour was introduced to some films at this time, but, like integrated soundtracks, commercially successful colour did not arrive until the interwar years.

The silent cinema had one advantage over sound: it could cross international boundaries with ease – and films were made all around the world for international distribution. In Europe the film-going public was considered more up-market than the American equivalent, and French directors were noted for their more serious output, such as film versions of literary classics. For similar reasons, cinemas in Europe tended to be more luxurious. The world's first purpose-built cinema, the Cinema Omnia Pathé, opened in Paris in 1906.

The French Pathé brothers, Emile and Charles, dominated world production and distribution of film stock and equipment in the years 1900 to 1914, and were also responsible for the development of weekly newsreel bulletins from 1908, bringing moving pictures of world events to cinema audiences for the first time.

TRAITOR'S KISS Judas betrays Jesus in a French re-creation of the life of Christ from 1902. The Pathé brothers set out to conquer the world – as seen by a contemporary cartoonist, Barrère.

dealer in Canada before he began taking over picture houses in New England in 1907 and became a distributor. Warner Brothers, Fox Films (founded by William Fox), Universal Films (founded by Carl Laemmle) all began in these early years of the century. D.W. Griffith, formerly a stage actor and aspiring playwright, entered cinema in 1907 and directed some 150 one-reel films before making his first two-reeler *Enoch Arden* in 1911. By experimenting with now-familiar techniques, such as flashbacks, crosscutting and close-up, he demonstrated the freedoms offered by film compared with theatre.

To begin with, the American film industry was located on the east coast, but in 1911 a

DIRECTOR AT WORK All is concentration as D.W. Griffith, loudhailer in hand, directs one of the silent classics that earned him the title, 'the father of the cinema'.

SPEAK INTO THE HORN In a programme sponsored by the US government, native Americans in 1913 record some of their traditional songs and folklore.

in a straight line into space? Nobody knew, until Marconi made a dramatic experiment on December 12, 1901. From a large aerial set up at Poldhu Cove in western Cornwall, his assistants sent out a simple repeated signal: the letter S (three dots) in Morse. In St John's, Newfoundland, with his receiving equipment attached to an aerial suspended from a kite, Marconi listened in on headphones. Yes – there it was! A weak signal could be heard. Radio waves had bounced over the Atlantic in the ionosphere, a phenomenon only fully understood later, in the 1920s.

Initially, it was in communications with ships at sea that wireless showed its clearest practical benefits. By 1905 some 80 ships of the British Royal Navy were able to communicate with the Admiralty in London, via

shore stations, from as far away as Gibraltar. In 1910, wireless messages between a liner in the mid-Atlantic and Scotland Yard in London led to the arrest of the murderer H.H. ('Peter') Crippen who was attempting to flee Europe for America.

Radio and speech

Marconi improved his wireless equipment over succeeding years, but it suffered from the great handicap that the signals were weak. A huge advance was made when the American Lee de Forest invented the triode thermionic valve, patented in 1907, which improved on the diode valve invented by the British electrical engineer John Ambrose Fleming in 1904. Designed initially to strengthen transmission signals by amplifying the current without distortion, the triode valve could also be used to amplify signals received. This not only improved wireless telegraph communications, it also paved the way for the transmission of speech by wireless

methods, and to the development of radio, radar and television in the interwar years. De Forest became known as the 'father of radio'.

The first public transmission of speech and music by radio was made from a wireless station in Massachusetts in 1906 by the Canadian-born Reginald Aubrey Fessenden. The signal was weak but it was picked up by ships off the coast, demonstrating the possibilities both of radio telephony and of radio broadcasting.

Phonographs and gramophone

Radio remained a remote concept to most people in these years: recorded sound played on the phonograph or gramophone, however, was familiar – even if only heard as a fairground entertainment.

The phonograph was just one invention to spring from the fertile mind of the American Thomas Alva Edison, a man who held over 1000 patents covering such things as the modern electric light bulb. His first phonograph, involving a cylinder turned by a hand-operated crank, dates to 1877. In 1887 the German-born American Emile Berliner came up with a rival machine called the 'gramophone', in which a flat disc revolved on a turntable. In 1892 Berliner also invented the 'master disc', enabling the record producer to manufacture multiple copies from a single recording. By the turn of the century, the gramophone had come of age.

OPERA ON DISC

At the turn of the century, most recorded music was limited to music-hall and parlour hits. The stars of serious music were wary of leaving such imperfect legacies of their art. All this changed in 1902 when the Italian tenor Enrico Caruso made a recording of 'Vesti la Giubba' ('On with the Motley') by Ruggiero Leoncavallo. It sold over a million copies. Two years later, Caruso had equal success with 'La Donna è Mobile' ('Women are Fickle') from Verdi's *Rigoletto*.

At first, the public was fascinated by the sheer wonder of experiencing sound captured and reproduced at will. Soon they could listen to their favourite singers and musicians at leisure, and were able to entertain guests to sounds that had previously been available only in public places or at vast cost. By 1902 recordings were selling in their millions and another new industry was born.

BRAVE NEW WORLD

BY 1900 THE USA WAS THE WORLD'S LEADING INDUSTRIAL NATION. TO MILLIONS AROUND THE WORLD, THIS WAS THE LAND OF OPPORTUNITY

It was a glorious sight. Rising up from its island in the approaches to the New York docks was that icon of American dreams, the Statue of Liberty. The immigrants, dressed in their best clothes, crowded the ship's rails to salute this outsized monument, then barely two decades old. It heralded a new life in the most exciting country on earth – a country offering opportunities to work and make a fortune, the chance to own land, to educate the children, to glory in democracy, individualism and political freedom.

But there was one agonising hurdle yet to come. As the ship came to a halt, barges arrived to take its passengers to Ellis Island, the notoriously strict immigrant processing centre, whose tight-lipped officials and doctors were charged with rooting out 'undesirables'. Under pressure from an American public alarmed by the tidal wave of immigration, the US government had introduced increasingly stringent rules for new arrivals. In the long and soulless alleys of the Ellis Island 'Receiving Station', all were carefully screened, both officially and surreptitiously, for signs of the listed disqualifying faults: serious disease or mental illness, which could make the immigrant a burden on the state, or any record of a criminal past, of prostitution, bigamy or anarchism. Any one of these could lead to immediate detention and subsequent deportation back to the homeland that the immigrant had struggled so hard to leave. Ellis Island was also known as 'Heartbreak Island'.

By the early 1900s, however, immigration had become less of an ordeal than in the preceding decades. It was now a well-oiled process, organised in Europe by specialist agents who advertised and recruited, and arranged the paperwork and ticketing. The shipping lines, operating out of Naples, Liverpool, Hamburg and Bremen, had been saddled with the responsibility of ensuring that immigrants would pass the health criteria. As the cost of the repatriation of failures had to be met by the shippers, they took trouble to screen their passengers before the

BOUND FOR AMERICA For the immigrants on the Hamburg-America Line's *Patricia* (below) the first port of call was Ellis Island in New York harbour (left). The Hungarian authorities (right) grant permission for two children to emigrate to join their parents in America.

journey, thereby reducing the burden on US immigration officials.

The days of 'steerage' were all but over. In the 19th century, the poorer immigrants had suffered appalling conditions in the bowels of the ship – airless, uncomfortable, insanitary, often crime-ridden. By the turn of the century, operators such as Cunard had introduced 'third class' or 'tourist class' on its new ships, with spartan but acceptable accommodation in small cabins of six berths only, adequate access to bathrooms and toilets, medical staff in attendance, full meals served in a dining room, and promenade decks for all.

In their millions

During the 1890s, 3.5 million new immigrants came to the USA. By the turn of the century, about a million were arriving every year. The year 1907 was the

high-water mark, with 1 285 000 arrivals. Ellis Island was capable of processing 8000 immigrants a day.

The ethnic background of immigrants had changed over the years. In the middle decades of the 19th century, they had come largely from Britain, Ireland, Germany and Scandinavia, but after the American Civil War (1861-5), they had come from eastern and southern Europe. They included Poles, Hungarians, Italians, Russians, Turks, Greeks, Croats, Serbs, Syrians and Lebanese. By the early 1900s, the majority were either Roman Catholic or Jewish. The ethnic and linguistic make-up of the USA, founded by north European Protestants, was changing rapidly.

Immigrants were needed to underpin a massive industrial boom that had been gathering momentum since the end of the Civil War. The USA had the technology, the raw materials, the agricultural base and, through immigration, plentiful cheap labour to fuel rapid and sensational growth.

OPEN WIDE Immigrant children peer at the camera as a New York City health officer examines them for signs of typhus. Immigration statistics for 1900-14 (below) show Austria-Hungary as the largest source of new arrivals.

MENTAL TESTING Immigrants had 20 seconds to find the four sad faces – or they might be judged 'mentally defective'. Immigrants marked with a chalk X (below) are suspected of being 'defective'.

Netherlands 76 462
France 109 000
Portugal 112 822
Norway 230 046
Greece 273 843
Sweden 315 004
Asia (inc China, Japan, India) 352 075
Germany 471 410
Rest of the Americas 813 516
Great Britain (inc Ireland) 1 212 099
Russia 2 465 122
Italy (inc Sicily, Sardinia) 2 935 173
Austria-Hungary 3 016 182

Make AMERICA
Your COUNTRY
As Well As
YOUR HOME

HOW TO
TAKE OUT YOUR
FIRST PAPERS

AN EASY BOOK IN PLAIN ENGLISH
FOR THE COMING CITIZEN

PREPARED FOR POLICYHOLDERS
Metropolitan Life Insurance Co.

BECOMING AMERICAN American patriotism is already being drummed into children sitting in an 'Uncle Sam wagon' on Ellis Island's rooftop playground. An insurance company offered would-be immigrants this booklet (left) with helpful hints on becoming an American citizen.

Uncle Sam Co

LAND OF OPPORTUNITY The bustle of New York, a city rapidly expanding through immigration, is captured in this 1908 photo of a street market. Immigrants might find employment in rural settings, however, like these apple pickers in West Virginia (inset).

During the period 1900-14, US industrial output expanded at an average rate of 5.4 per cent per annum.

The prospect of new opportunities appealed to a range of Europeans, dissatisfied with the economic conditions of their own countries, trapped by poverty or facing political or religious oppression. The USA was promoted as a land where merit and hard work were rewarded by money and status – a huge and largely unexploited country, where vast tracts of land had recently been opened up all the way to the Pacific. The USA was where an immigrant family could come and make something of themselves, in factories, in the mines, in the high street, in the forests, or in the farmlands of the West.

Politics begins at home

For many immigrants, however, the first experience of the land of their dreams was in overcrowded urban tenements, rife with disease and the haunt of con men and racketeers who exploited the newcomers' lack of English and experience. A series of government administrations had helped to provide the conditions for the USA's industrial expansion, and in the early 20th century they sought to curtail the abuses that had arisen from it.

Despite the USA's new-found prominence on the world economic stage, its governments concentrated on domestic issues. American foreign policy maintained an air of reluctance: even the robust and charismatic Theodore Roosevelt (president from 1901 to 1909), who prided himself on his international vision, was more concerned with domestic issues, such as the conservation of America's natural heritage. This lack of foreign distraction gave the USA an enviable record of political stability.

With a combination of immigration and native growth, the population of the USA almost doubled from 50 million to 92 million between 1890 and 1914. The rapid expansion in the domestic consumer market was one of the driving forces behind the economic boom. Cities such as New York, Boston, Philadelphia, Pittsburgh and Chicago

1901 Theodore Roosevelt becomes president

1903 Wright brothers achieve powered flight

1906 San Francisco earthquake

1907 A record 1.3 million immigrants arrive in USA

had likewise grown rapidly. New York, with a population of 1 515 000 in 1900, was now the nation's largest city.

The spiralling cost of land in the city centres gave rise to the new symbol of US dynamism: the skyscraper. By building upwards, large numbers of people could be accommodated on a comparatively small plot of land. Skyscrapers had become practicable only after the creation of the first passenger lift, or elevator, in New York in 1857, and they began to appear in New York and Chicago in the 1870s. (Europe had to wait half a century for its first skyscraper, built in Antwerp in 1928.)

One of the leading designers was Louis Sullivan of Chicago, who pioneered the concept of creating skyscrapers around a metal skeleton. He also foreshadowed modernism in his desire to create an aesthetic that was free from any reference to past historical styles of architecture.

By 1913 the tallest building in New York – and the world – was 60 storeys high. Significantly, this was the new Woolworth Building, and it symbolised the triumph of a revolution in retailing forged by Frank Winfield Woolworth.

From a modest background as a store clerk in the 1870s, Woolworth had built up a chain of stores that stretched across the USA

WORK AT THE MILL The industrial heartlands, dominated by mammoth enterprises such as this Pennsylvania steelworks, swallowed up millions of immigrant labourers.

1908 Ford introduces Model T

1910 Carnegie Endowment for International Peace founded

1913 Woolworth Building completed

and to Britain. He brought two major changes to retailing. First, he saw how customers liked to be able to browse and to inspect goods before they bought them: he put open displays and shelving in his shops, replacing the tradition whereby only clerks behind the counter had access to the goods. Second, Woolworth understood how retailers could eke out competitive advantages by selling cheaply but in large volume.

The same kind of approach was adopted by the 'all-under-one-roof' department stores of the big cities. In 1909 the American Gordon Selfridge exported this idea to London. When Selfridges opened in Oxford Street, its bright window displays, its sales staff of 1800, its free gifts and high-profile advertising became the talk of the town.

For Americans who could not easily reach a major town or city, there was always mail order. Sears, Roebuck & Company, founded in 1893 by Richard Sears and Alvah Roebuck, sought to bring a huge range of goods at competitive prices to customers anywhere in the USA. Its free catalogue – featuring anything

HARRY HOUDINI: MASTER OF ILLUSION

Erik Weiz, otherwise known as Harry Houdini, knew how to bring his audiences to the brink of hysteria. Many minutes after he had been locked into an airless safe and shrouded by a curtain, the public would be screaming for his assistants to rescue him. Then, just when they thought that he must be dead, 'The Great Houdini' would reappear, bursting breathlessly through the curtains to tumultuous clamour. Little did his admirers know that Houdini had, in fact, been sitting on a chair behind the curtain for the last half hour reading a book, having escaped the safe in a couple of minutes using secret hidden catches.

Houdini was a master illusionist. Born in 1874 of Hungarian immigrant parents, he trained in fairgrounds and vaudeville shows from the age of 16, where he quickly exploited a talent for escaping from handcuffs, chains and shackles. Gradually his feats became more spectacular, including a highly publicised escape from the condemned cell in Washington jail.

One of Houdini's specialities was to be dropped into a river bound in shackles and chains. He knew how to wriggle out of chains, and used a key concealed in his mouth to release shackles and handcuffs. But, notwithstanding the use of deception, his breathtaking effects depended on daring brinkmanship. In November 1906, he was dropped, fully bound, into a hole in the ice in the Detroit River. The current swept him downstream, and he survived only by locating some air bubbles trapped beneath the ice.

His most popular trick was the Chinese Water-torture Cell. He was suspended upside-down from locked leg shackles in a tank full of water. Behind the closed curtains he would simply curl upwards and press a catch to release his legs – even so the trick required great agility and fitness.

Houdini took immense pride in his physique, and this proved his undoing. In Montreal, Canada, in 1926 he challenged a student to punch him in the stomach, but received the blow before he had tensed his muscles. He died of aggravated appendicitis two days later.

ON THE BRINK Wrapped in chains, Houdini prepares to jump into the Charles River in Boston in 1906.

from ladies' shoes, crockery and fob watches to agricultural implements – was being dispatched to tens of thousands of customers by the early 1900s. At the company's headquarters near Chicago, orders were processed and dispatched with model rapidity and the assistance of state-of-the-art machinery.

Tycoons and philanthropists

Thrusting business methods and a booming economy resulted in huge new corporations, headed by figures such as John Davison Rockefeller of the Standard Oil Company and the financier John Pierpont Morgan.

Many of these magnates were admired in America for their business success, but many, too, were labelled 'robber barons' for their unscrupulous dealings with both rivals and employees. Monopolising 'trusts' – groups of companies in the same business or industry that organised themselves

DEMOCRACY IN ACTION
Theodore Roosevelt, Republican president from 1901 to 1909, campaigning in 1912 for the short-lived Progressive Party.

TOWERING ACHIEVEMENT When finished in 1913, the Woolworth Building was the world's highest skyscraper. It had 19 lifts and could accommodate 14 000 office workers.

so as to reduce competition and control prices – were another well-publicised abuse. 'Trust-busting' became a key plank in the administrations of both President Theodore Roosevelt and his successor, William Howard Taft (1909-13).

It was the tycoons' vision of market potential that projected so many of them from comparatively modest backgrounds into the stratosphere of vast wealth. Andrew Carnegie was a good example. The son of an immigrant Scottish linen worker, he had arrived in the USA at the age of 13, and soon began work in a cotton factory. He then found a job as a telegraph messenger and joined the Pennsylvania Railroad, where, at the age of 18, he was promoted to a managerial position. He also made a series of astute personal investments, notably in oil, then in steel. With the growth of the engineering industry, steel became an increasingly vital element of manufacturing. Carnegie bought and developed plants around Pittsburgh, applying the Bessemer method of decarbonising iron ore. He also bought controlling interests in the supplies of raw materials.

In 1901 Carnegie sold out to J.P. Morgan, earning a personal fortune of $300 million in the transaction. Although he had a reputation for the ruthless treatment of trade unions, Carnegie believed that his wealth should benefit all and devoted much of the latter part of his life, and a great deal of money, to philanthropic works, endowing libraries in the USA, Canada and Britain.

THE SAN FRANCISCO EARTHQUAKE, 1906

At 5 am on April 18, 1906, most of San Francisco slept. After half a century of rapid growth, this was a large and prosperous city of 400 000 people, with a cluster of skyscrapers in the downtown commercial district, a 'cable-car' tram network, and gentle hills cloaked with thousands of timber-framed homes.

Suddenly the earth roared and rumbled in a mighty jolt lasting 40 seconds; there was a brief pause, then another 25 second jolt. An eyewitness described what he saw: 'Big buildings were crumbling as one might crush a biscuit in one's hand. Great gray clouds of dust shot up with flying timbers, and storms of masonry rained into the street . . . Ahead of me a great cornice crushed a man as if he were a maggot . . . Everywhere men were on all fours in the street, like crawling bugs.'

Thousands were killed and injured as their homes collapsed; the floors of multistorey hotels concertinaed, crushing their occupants. The able-bodied came running out into the streets, bleary-eyed and bewildered, then began the hunt among the wreckage for survivors. But worse was yet to come.

As cooking stoves and heaters were overturned, and gas pipes ruptured, dozens of fires spread through the city, demolishing wrecked houses and setting light to undamaged ones. The city's main fire station had been damaged in the earthquake, trapping many of its horse-drawn vehicles, while the Fire Chief lay fatally injured. Those appliances that did manage to get out into the street found their way blocked by wreckage, and their water supplies depleted by broken pipes.

As the fires raged, sending palls of thick smoke high into the sky, troops from the local garrison attempted to dynamite streets of houses in order to create firebreaks, but in doing so, they not only destroyed undamaged houses, but started new fires. Some householders, knowing that their house insurance explicitly precluded earthquake damage, deliberately torched their wrecked homes so as to claim fire insurance.

Looters began to strip shops, businesses and homes. The troops were authorised to shoot looters on sight, and other armed citizens followed their example. They also carried out mercy killings, dispatching badly injured people trapped in wreckage, if they begged to be put out of their misery.

For three days the fires burnt, until a damp drizzle arrived that helped to put them out. By this time four-fifths of the city – nearly 30 000 buildings – had been destroyed; many of the 300 000 people made homeless were now camping in the city parks and suburbs. About 2500 people had died from the earthquake, in fires, through jumping from burning buildings, and in stampedes of terrified citizens and animals. Yet within a decade San Francisco had recovered and had been completely rebuilt – on the same earthquake-prone site.

DEATH AND DESTRUCTION Smoke billows from fires raging across San Francisco after the earthquake.

Among other donations, he gave $50 000 to the scientist Marie Curie in Paris for her research into radium. He also financed the creation of the Peace Palace in the Hague, which was built in 1907-13.

Morgan, meanwhile, was an investment banker who made his fortune by amalgamation and consolidation. He, too, started with the railways. By the late 19th century, many of the thousand or so existing railway companies had run into serious financial problems through fierce competition. J.P. Morgan saw ways of pooling resources by buying clusters of railways, and then rationalising them. By the early years of the new century, he had controlling interests not only in railways, but also in steel, creating the United States Steel Corporation in 1901.

J.D. Rockefeller, the other great tycoon of the times, had cornered the market in domestic oil production with his Standard Oil Company before the dawn of the motoring industry. Like Andrew Carnegie, he also had a desire to help those who were less fortunate than himself, and endowed the Rockefeller

THE TYCOONS The thin-lipped Rockefeller (right) contrasts with the bearded Carnegie (below). Morgan (below right) is the image of the swashbuckling financier.

Institute for Medical Research (1901), and the Rockefeller Foundation (1913), as well as the University of Chicago.

A genius for manufacture

There was a fever of inventiveness in the United States in the decades around the turn of the century. A large number of now-familiar brand names also became current during this era. Coca-Cola, first invented in 1886, was now sold across the USA, King Camp Gillette put the safety razor into production in 1903, and William Kellogg produced his first cereal as a health food in 1906.

Manufacturers profited from American inventiveness, and had the knack of wringing the commercial potential from foreign inventions. The vacuum cleaner was first developed in England by Hubert Cecil Booth in 1901, but it was a US leather manufacturer, William Hoover, who marketed a model light enough for domestic use and turned it into a popular success. An even more dramatic example of the American flair for adaptation was the motor car. This may have been pioneered by Karl Benz and Gottlieb Daimler in Germany, but it was the genius of American industry that pushed it through the vital transition into a machine of mass transport.

AIRBORNE Watching a buzzard in flight was a key inspiration for the Wright brothers. They realised that a flying machine, like a bird, would have to be able to move on three axes: up and down, to left and right, and by banking from one side to the other.

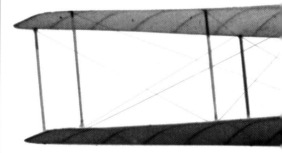

FIRST FLIGHT

One of the handful of people to witness the Wright brothers' historic flight on a cold December day in 1903 was John T. Daniels, an employee of a service that later became the US Coast Guard. In 1927 he recalled the experience:

'Wilbur and Orville walked off from us and stood close together on the beach, talking low to each other for some time. After a while they shook hands, and we couldn't help notice how they held on to each other's hand, sort o' like they hated to let go; like two folks parting who weren't sure they'd ever see each other again.

'Wilbur came over to us and told us not to look sad, but to laugh and hollo and clap our hands and try to cheer Orville up when he started.

'We tried to shout and hollo, but it was mighty weak shouting, with no heart in it. . .

'Orville climbed into the machine, the engine was started up, and we helped steady it down the monorail until it got underway. The thing went off with a rush and left the rail as pretty as you please, going straight out into the air maybe 120 feet [36 m], when one of its wings tilted and caught in the sand, and the thing stopped. I like to think about that first airplane the way it tailed off in the air at Kill Devil Hills [the dunes near Kitty Hawk] that morning, as pretty as any bird you ever laid your eyes on. I don't think I ever saw a prettier sight in my life.'

Alexander Winton of Cleveland, Ohio, was an important early manufacturer. Born in Scotland, he emigrated to the USA at the age of 20, and set up a workshop making patented bicycle parts. He built his first 'horseless carriage' in 1896, and demonstrated the reliability of a second vehicle the following year by travelling the 800 miles (1300 km) from Cleveland to New York in an actual running time of 73 hours 40 minutes.

heavier-than-air machine in December 1903, but the feat received little press at the time. Greater interest was shown in balloons and the dirigible airship built by the German Count Ferdinand von Zeppelin in 1900, which was making commercial passenger flights by 1910.

The delayed appreciation for powered heavier-than-air flight can in part be ascribed to Wilbur Wright's desire for secrecy, as he hoped to exploit its commercial prospects himself. It was only after 1905 that the Wright brothers' achievement became widely publicised. They demonstrated their plane to early aviation enthusiasts at Le Mans in France in 1908, and it was France that proved to be the crucible of aviation's subsequent development.

By 1898 he was producing 21 cars a year. By 1900 the single-cylinder 3.8 litre Winton was taking part in international motoring rallies.

Manufacturers needed to show that automobiles could perform long-distance journeys to compete with railways. One inhibiting factor, however, was the state of the roads. These were little more than muddy tracks in rural areas. Winton attempted to cross the entire continent in one of his cars in 1901. Having started in San Francisco, his attempt came to grief in the sands of the Nevada Desert. But two years later, H. Nelson Jackson and the mechanic Sewell J. Crocker succeeded where Winton had failed – by taking a new Winton from San Francisco to New York, covering the 5600 miles (9000 km) in 63 days.

It was the first crossing of America by car, and a remarkable feat. Jackson and Crocker had to traverse two mountain ranges on deeply rutted wagon trails, crossing some rivers over the sleepers of railway bridges. In rural towns they were mobbed by crowds of bemused onlookers who had never seen a car before. The automobile, though still expensive, was proving its worth as an adaptable means of transport; the commercial genius of Henry Ford would bring it within the reach of ordinary people.

The flying machine

Strangely, perhaps the single most important American invention of the early 20th century, the aeroplane, initially evaded the acquisitive gaze of American manufacturers. The brothers Wilbur and Orville Wright achieved their first manned and powered flight in a

BRINGING MOTORING TO THE PEOPLE

Motor cars were too expensive. This was the problem addressed by Henry Ford (1863-1947) when he declared: 'I am going to democratize the automobile, and when I am through, everybody will be able to afford one and about everybody will have one.' He produced his Model T in 1908. In 1913 he introduced the moving assembly line, which enabled him to apply economies of mass production to create his 'people's car'. Simple but reliable, the Model T sold at a much more accessible price than that offered by any of the other leading manufacturers of the day, such as Winton, Packard and Oldsmobile.

Initially the moving assembly was operated by ropes pulling the chassis along the line. It enabled Ford to increase production from about seven cars an hour to 146 an hour. When production of the Model T eventually ceased in 1927, 15 million of these 'Tin Lizzies' had been manufactured. Ford ploughed his profits back into manufacture, and by increasing production he benefited customers by lowering the price yet further. In 1908 a Model T cost $850; by 1923, this was down to $290.

Ford had been brought up on a farm near Detroit, Michigan, but as a youth he had shown more interest in mechanics than farming. He built his first car in 1896. Perhaps influenced by his background, he had in his mind's eye the very people who had gawped at H. Nelson Jackson's Winton in 1903: people from rural and small-town America, where 50 per cent of the US population still lived. The sheer force of numbers introduced to motoring by Ford brought about changes to favour the motorist: better road networks, more garages, and improved technology such as the self-starter, first introduced by Cadillac in 1912 as a welcome alternative to the hand crank.

CENTRE OF ATTENTION Picnickers admire a Model T at Poughkeepsie on the banks of the Hudson River.

THE AMERICAN WEST: MYTH OR REALITY?

**IN FACT, MYTH AND REALITY OVERLAPPED. MANY OF THE MEN WHO WROTE AND ACTED
IN THE FIRST WESTERNS HAD BEEN COWBOYS AND OUTLAWS IN THE REAL WILD WEST**

By 1900 the American West had been 'opened up', and the bittersweet age of the early pioneers was over. The railways had long since superseded the wagon trains; the Indian Wars had reached their conclusion at Wounded Knee in 1890, and the decimated Native Americans had been corralled into reservations; the vast herds of bison had been brought to the verge of extinction; and after the 1880s, cattle were fenced into ranches by barbed wire, bringing to a close the romance of the cowboy and the long-distance cattle trails. The Frontier had disappeared and the Wild West had been tamed.

But even before the great age of the West was over, its myth was being created, promulgated by those who had been actively involved. William 'Buffalo Bill' Cody had been a scout and buffalo hunter before he set up his hugely successful Wild West Show in 1883. Complete with cowboy gunslingers, costumed Native Americans and trick horseriders, the Wild West Show toured the USA and Europe for 25 years, offering a flavour of the West to audiences whose imaginations had been fired by Western dime novels and the paintings of 'cowboy' artists such as Frederic Remington.

Given this public interest, it was not surprising that many of the earliest American movies were Westerns. Some of the actors were former cowboys, soldiers and Native Americans who had actually taken part in the Indian Wars. Brutal reality dovetailed with movie mythmaking. Caught in a stake-out at a bank raid at Coffeyville, Kansas, in 1892, all but one of the Dalton brothers, a notorious band of outlaws, were killed. The survivor, Emmett Dalton, served his stint in prison, and on his release in 1907 began writing Western movie scripts, which provided him with a new career until his death in 1937.

Movies developed side-by-side with a vogue for still photographs of Native Americans. A number of photographers travelled widely, recording 'vanishing America' – the traditional Native American way of life. Such pictures were often sentimental, employing deliberately archaic props, and portraying the Native American as a proud and noble people. Nonetheless, these photographers have left a stunning record of Native Americans, seen particularly in the work of the greatest of them all, Edward Sheriff Curtis.

Largely sponsored by the tycoon J.P. Morgan and his son, Curtis visited just about every Native American tribe over the first three decades of the century, creating a collection of 40 000 photographs that still provide a powerful stimulus to the world's enduring fascination with the American West.

STRANGE CONTRASTS Edward S. Curtis took this photo of the Cañon de Chelly, Arizona, in 1904. In his youth, the Apache chief Geronimo had waged war on whites; in old age (right), he sits in a steam car.

NEW NATIONS

FOUR LARGE COUNTRIES, LONG SETTLED BY EUROPEANS, ENTERED THE NEW CENTURY WITH A FRESH SENSE OF NATIONHOOD

For Australians, January 1, 1901, was the first day of a new era. Despite a downpour the night before which had left banners and flags sodden and bedraggled, a magnificent procession of bands, troops from various parts of the British Empire and visiting dignitaries – watched by a cheering crowd of half a million people – paraded through Sydney to mark the inauguration of the Commonwealth of Australia. Four months later, even grander celebrations, including an international exhibition, took place in Melbourne to mark the opening of the national parliament.

Australia's emergence as a Western-style nation had taken just 113 years from the time its earliest European settlement was established as a penal colony in 1788. The first Australian Federal Convention had been called in 1891, bringing together representatives of the different colonies – New South Wales, Victoria, Queensland, South Australia, Western Australia and Tasmania – which until then had retained stronger links with Britain than with each other. A constitution was hammered out and then approved after two referendums in 1898 and 1899. This was ratified by Britain, which maintained a controlling interest in the appointment of a governor-general to represent the monarch as head of state. 'A nation for a continent, a continent for a nation', was the slogan of the New South Wales lawyer and statesman Edmund Barton, who after tireless work to bring about the federation became its first prime minister in 1901.

The next question was where to locate the new national capital. Sydney and Melbourne were arch rivals; one of the stipulations of federation was that neither would become the capital and that a new one would be created somewhere between the two. In 1911 a site in New South Wales was selected: Canberra, until then a modest farming community, its name derived from the Aborigine word for 'meeting place'. An international competition to design the new city was won by Walter Burley Griffin, an American architect from

CELEBRATING FEDERATION A large family marks the day on which Australia became one nation with a picnic among the gum trees at White Cliffs, New South Wales.

SLICING THROUGH THE ISTHMUS: THE PANAMA CANAL

In 1869 the Suez Canal had opened: a triumph of engineering that reduced the voyage from Europe to India and the Far East by as much as 7000 miles (11 000 km). The next challenge was to create a way to sail from the Atlantic to the Pacific without having to face the long and treacherous journey around Cape Horn. In 1881 the mastermind behind the Suez Canal, the Frenchman Ferdinand de Lesseps, began driving a canal through the Isthmus of Panama, the narrowest neck of land between North and South America, and at that time a possession of Colombia. But de Lesseps had chosen a lowland region of marsh and swamp-land, plagued by disease. He was forced to give up in 1889 in a financial and political storm, following the bankruptcy of his company and the loss of 20 000 labourers killed by malaria and yellow fever.

The USA took a keen interest in this canal, which promised a convenient shipping lane to link its east and west coasts. One American group was actively surveying a route through Nicaragua, while another sought an alternative route through Panama. After the eruption of Mont Pelée in Martinique in 1902, the fate of the project in earthquake-prone Nicaragua was sealed. The US government, led by President Theodore Roosevelt, put aside a fund of $40 million to buy the concession for a canal in Panama, and sup-ported a rebellion to give Panama its independence. Under the Canal Treaty of 1903, the USA acquired sovereign rights over a strip of land 10 miles (16 km) wide and 51 miles (82 km) long across the isthmus, and began a campaign of fumigation and drainage to minimise health risks to construction workers.

Building work began in 1907, led by the formidable US army engineer George Washington Goethals. Six huge locks were constructed to take the canal up to Lake Gatún, 85 ft (26 m) above sea level, and back down the other side. The most difficult challenge was the Culebra Cut – a passage blasted through 8 miles (13 km) of solid rock. On October 10, 1913, the new US president, Woodrow Wilson, blew away the last obstacle by pressing a remote-control button in the White House, and five weeks later the steamer *Louise* became the first ship to pass through the canal. Officially opened in August 1914, the Panama Canal was the first major engineering triumph of the 20th century. It had cost $352 million, and the lives of a further 5600 labourers killed by accidents and disease.

A CUT ABOVE THE REST The Culebra Cut (below) proved the greatest test for the engineers. Left: A cartoon portrait of George Washington Goethals, the driving force behind the canal.

GRAND PLAN Walter Burley Griffin's plan for Australia's new capital, Canberra, was based on a set of concentric circles centred on the Capitol and government buildings.

Chicago who was strongly influenced by the work of Frank Lloyd Wright. He arrived in Australia in 1913; just 14 years later, in 1927, Canberra hosted its first parliament.

'White settler' colonies

By the turn of the century, the larger cities of Australia were as sophisticated as any in Europe. They had produced, for instance, the internationally acclaimed diva soprano, Dame Nellie Melba – after whom the Savoy Hotel of London named its toast, and who inspired a pudding of peaches served with raspberry sauce. She was born in Melbourne in 1861 and trained there; it was in Sydney in 1885 that she made her non-operatic debut.

In the years following federation, the new nation set up new universities and a distinc-tively Australian cultural life continued to emerge. The University of Queensland was established in 1909, the University of West-ern Australia in 1911. The Sydney paper, the *Bulletin*, provided the focus for a small group of proudly nationalist writers and artists. They included the goldminer-turned-novelist Joseph Furphy whose epic masterpiece *Such Is Life* was published in 1903.

Despite its thriving cities, however, Australia remained essentially agricultural, its economy based on the exports of wool, meat and mined raw materials. It had little incentive to industrialise, as it could import manufactured goods from Britain. The situa-tion was similar in New Zealand, which had developed rapidly during the 19th century, primarily through sheep farming. By 1905 it had more than 10 million sheep, as against a

1901 Inauguration of the Commonwealth of Australia

1902 End of the Boer War

1905 Alberta and Saskatchewan are newly created provinces of Canada

1907 Work begins on the Panama Canal

THE END OF SPANISH COLONIAL RULE

THE SPANISH WERE GONE, BUT THE PEOPLE OF CUBA AND THE PHILIPPINES FOUND THEMSELVES AT THE MERCY OF A NEW POWER: THE UNITED STATES

Speak softly and carry a big stick; you will go far: this 'homely adage', quoted by President Theodore Roosevelt in 1901, came to summarise his country's foreign policy in the early years of the century. Since the 1820s, the USA had operated behind the protective screen of the Monroe Doctrine. This had generally succeeded in keeping foreign powers out of its backyard, while the old Spanish Empire collapsed before the pressures of independence. By the late 19th century, Spain had just two major overseas possessions, Cuba and the Philippines.

The USA kept a close eye on Cuba, lying just 200 miles (320 km) off its mainland. When Cubans rioted in Havana in January 1898, it sent a battleship, the USS *Maine*, to protect American lives and property. On February 15, 1898, the *Maine* was blown up in Havana harbour, probably by mines. The US public was outraged and in April Congress authorised President McKinley to declare war on Spain.

The Spanish-American War lasted just 16 weeks. A US expeditionary force had overrun Cuba by the end of July. Another force took Spanish-ruled Puerto Rico. On May 1 the US Asiatic Squadron annihilated a Spanish fleet off Manila in the Philippines. As it happened, the Philippines were already in a state of revolutionary turmoil; insurgents had scored considerable success and were cheered to find that the Americans had brought the exiled revolutionary Emilio Aguinaldo. The Spanish quickly sued for peace. Under the Treaty of Paris, signed in December 1898, they ceded Cuba, Puerto Rico, the Pacific island of Guam and the Philippines to the USA.

At this point, the interests of the USA and the Filipino rebels diverged. The USA installed a military government, against which Aguinaldo waged a bitter two-year guerrilla campaign. The Americans poured money into the infrastructure, building new roads, harbours, schools and medical clinics. However, by nurturing the support of the powerful land-owning elite, they tended to

DISAPPOINTED REBELS These Filipinos were captured near Manila after opposing US forces at the start of the Spanish-American War.

replicate the iniquities of the old Spanish regime. Things went more smoothly in Guam and Puerto Rico. Guam was administered by the US Navy until 1950; Puerto Rico became an 'incorporated territory', whose inhabitants were considered US nationals after 1901.

Cuba posed problems similar to the Philippines. Here, too, the rebels had expected to win independence. In 1901 the US military government was replaced by a civil one, with Tomás Estrada Palma as president; the last US troops left Havana in 1904. However, under the Platt Amendment passed by the US Congress, the USA had reserved extensive rights to intervene in Cuba. By 1906 Palma's corrupt and feckless government had caused such resentment that the Cuban Liberals rebelled. In September Palma resigned. Roosevelt, now US president, sent in the army, which remained in occupation until 1909.

The USA supervised new elections in 1908; but troops were once again dispatched to protect American interests in May 1912.

CUBA LIBRE President Tomás Estrada Palma (centre ninth from left) reviews a parade held in Havana in 1902 to mark Cuban independence.

1910 Britain grants South Africa dominion status

1911 Canberra is chosen as the site for the new capital of Australia

1914 The Panama Canal is officially opened

COMMANDOS AND CONCENTRATION CAMPS: THE BOER WAR

The First Boer War was fought in 1880-1 and ensured the independence of the Boer republic of Transvaal from Britain. It brought only a short-term respite, however. In October 1899, a steady rise in political and military pressure from the British incited Paul Kruger, the elderly President of the Transvaal, to issue an ultimatum demanding a guarantee of Transvaal's independence and an end to the British military build-up in the Cape Colony and Natal. This was taken by Britain as an unacceptable infringement of imperial rights, and the Second Boer War began.

Much to the shock of the British, the well-armed Boer 'commandos' quickly gained the initiative and laid siege to Ladysmith, Kimberley and Mafeking. British troops then suffered a serious defeat at Spion Kop in January 1900. The tide began to turn only after the arrival of massive British reinforcements under Lord Roberts later in 1900. The Boers were defeated at Paardeberg and Diamond Hill; one by one the sieges were lifted; Pretoria, the Boer capital, fell in June 1900, and the Boer states were annexed. In this the British were assisted by troops volunteered from other 'white settler' nations, including 16 500 Australians, many of them in 'bushmen' cavalry brigades accustomed to the conditions found in South Africa.

The war, however, was not yet over. The Boers, led by men such as Louis Botha and Jan Smuts, began to adopt successful hit-and-run guerrilla tactics. Lord Kitchener, now in command, responded with a brutal scorched-earth policy – destroying Boer farmsteads, sectioning off or 'blockading' vast areas of the veldt with barbed wire controlled by 8000 military blockhouses and imprisoning Boer families in concentration camps. By 1902, concentration camps contained 117 000 people, mainly women and children, living in filthy conditions that caused disease and a mortality rate of one in six. The policy caused widespread revulsion, especially in the foreign press, but it brought the Boers to their knees. When Kruger failed to elicit German support in early 1902, the Boers sued for peace. Under the Treaty of Vereeniging, signed in May 1902, they accepted British rule.

A BITTER GAME A Dutch board game invites players to move around the main scenes of confrontation between the Boers and British. The British were initially outclassed by the Boers, led by men such as General Jan Smuts (left).

human population of only 770 000. By 1910 it had the highest export value per capita of any nation in the world. New Zealand was also remarkable for a string of mould-breaking social measures, introduced by the Liberal government of the Lancashire-born former goldfield trader, R.J. Seddon, prime minister from 1893 until his death in 1906. These included giving women the vote, setting up an arbitration court to settle labour disputes and the world's first non-contributory old-age pension scheme.

Across the Pacific in Canada, meanwhile, politics were dominated by Sir Wilfred Laurier, prime minister from 1896 to 1911. A French Canadian of outstanding ability and charm, he presided over a period of booming growth. Canada had opened up its western prairies in the late 19th century, following completion of the transcontinental railway in 1885. In 1905 two new provinces, Alberta and Saskatchewan, were carved out of this increasingly wealthy and densely populated region. By 1913 wheat production in the prairies had quadrupled since 1890. Forestry and mining also provided valuable export commodities, as well as inviting some wild speculations. In the decade after 1897 the gold rush to the Klondike, in the far west close to the frontier with Alaska, was the most spectacular of these.

In parallel with Australia, both New Zealand and Canada pressed to turn self-government into independence. So long as they stayed within the overall fold of empire, Britain had no reason to object. Compared with other British possessions, such as India, where the divisions between rulers and ruled remained firmly drawn, the 'white settler' colonies were allowed considerable leeway. New Zealand, a self-governing colony since 1852, became a 'dominion' – a separate state with its own international representation, though still a part of the British Empire – in 1907. Most of Canada had formed a confederation and been given dominion status in 1867. British Colombia joined the confederation in 1871, Prince Edward Island in 1873; Newfoundland would contribute the final piece in the jigsaw in 1949.

Within these new countries, however, were minorities that did not form part of the political agenda. In Australia the Aborigines – the indigenous people, with a history

MAKESHIFT HOME The British promoted this kind of image of the concentration camps into which Boer families were herded. Their true horror was disclosed after the social reformer Emily Hobhouse visited the camps in 1901.

stretching back more than 40 000 years – were ignored and oppressed. The first Australian parliament of 1901 also passed the Immigration Restrictions Act, forming the basis of a 'whites only' immigration policy, which was not fully repealed until 1973. This was originally designed to restrict the Chinese, who had flooded into Australia in tens of thousands in the wake of a series of gold rushes from the 1850s onwards. People not only feared competition from the cheap labour of the Chinese but also felt threatened by their alien culture.

In New Zealand the Maoris were the first settlers, having arrived on the islands 1000 years before the British. By 1900, however, they represented only 7 per cent of the population, and remained in possession of just one-fifth of the land. In Canada the Native Americans barely appeared in the political equation, and were generally marginalised or driven northwards.

Canada also had its large French population. The French in Quebec commanded the St Lawrence River, the main waterway into the eastern heartlands. Their geographical, numerical and political significance had to be accommodated in negotiations with Britain. In fact, the French Canadians had a major stake in national government and did not prove an obstacle at home. Their begrudging loyalty to the British Crown did not, however, extend to supplying French-speaking troops to support the British cause in South Africa.

Complexities in South Africa

A far more complex racial and political map existed in South Africa, which had to come to terms with the tensions that had boiled over in the Boer War (1899-1902). The Cape Colony had originally been established in 1652 by the Dutch East India Company to provide a staging post for its ships en route to Indonesia. It was taken by the British in 1795. After 1834, when Britain banned slavery throughout its empire, serious friction began to develop between the Dutch settlers (called Boers or 'farmers') and the British. This culminated in the Great Trek, starting in 1835, when the Boers headed north across the Drakensberg mountains, taking their black slaves with them.

The situation might have been tenable, had it not been for the discovery of gold in 1886 in the Rand region of the Transvaal. Gold brought wealth to the Boer republics but also upset their way of life, attracting thousands of African labourers, immigrants from the Indian subcontinent as well as immigrant miners from Europe and elsewhere, who became known as the *Uitlanders*. Moreover, it turned the Boer lands into a strategic and commercial prize that British imperialism found hard to ignore.

The Boer War resolved the issue at the expense of the Boers, who came under British rule, but with the promise of self-government. The Boer states later combined with the British ones to form the Union of South Africa, which was granted dominion status by Britain in 1910, thus joining the club of the other independent 'white settler' nations with special historic ties to Britain.

SOUTH AFRICAN WAR The prizes of the war were the gold-rich Witwatersrand near Johannesburg and strategic links with Bechuanaland and Rhodesia to the north.

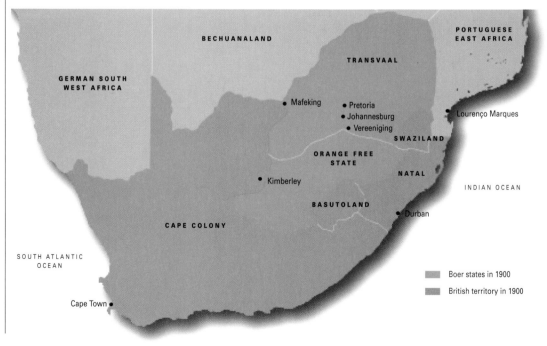

THE SHOCK OF THE NEW

A SPIRIT OF INNOVATION INSPIRED DYNAMIC MOVEMENTS IN THE ARTS – PROVOKING ADMIRATION AND OUTRAGE IN EQUAL MEASURE

In 1905, in a leafy southern suburb of Brussels, beside a broad avenue plied by horse-drawn wagons, trams and early automobiles, a shockingly modern private mansion was taking shape. The building was the Palais Stoclet, one of several buildings designed by the Austrian architect Josef Hoffmann. A

PALAIS STOCLET The interior of this Brussels mansion was as uncompromising as its exterior. Its architect, Josef Hoffmann, combined the luxury of polished marble with an almost brutal rejection of ornament.

configuration of strident horizontals and clean, rectilinear shapes, the only immediate key to the building's age was the figurative whimsy of four muscular statues on the central tower. The mansion showed virtually no links with the past, only to the future, foreshadowing the functional modernism of Bauhaus in the 1920s and the International Style thereafter.

The Palais Stoclet was the product of an era of radical change in design and art. Josef Hoffmann belonged to the movement known as the Vienna Secession, one of several such movements that sprang up in the 1890s when a number of artists and designers publicly seceded from the academic mainstream in order to form their own radical groups. Hoffmann was joined by two other influential architects in Vienna, Joseph

Olbrich and Kolomon Moser. Despite their mould-breaking approach, they were not working in complete isolation from the past: one of their key influences was the Scottish designer Charles Rennie Mackintosh, more usually associated with Art Nouveau, and they also owed a debt to the British Arts and Crafts movement which they followed in seeking to unify architecture, design and painting into a single discipline.

In fact, the Vienna Secession is perhaps best known for its painting. One of the leading figures of the group was Gustav Klimt, a creator of richly decorative, mosaic-like paintings and murals. These often had strongly erotic undertones that link Klimt's

NEW LINES The clean lines and restraint of traditional Japanese interiors influenced the designs (above) of the Glaswegian Charles Rennie Mackintosh. His serenity contrasts with the sensuousness of the Viennese painter Gustav Klimt in works such as *Death and Life* (below). Klimt's works often reveal a strong streak of the morbid.

work to the *fin-de-siècle* Romanticism of the late 19th century. His young acolyte Egon Schiele, by contrast, injected his emaciated nudes with a raw aggression and anguish which ties him more to the work of another emerging group, the German Expressionists.

Like all significant artistic movements, the Vienna Secession was a vital stepping stone between the past and the future. At the time, however, it challenged the standards of the present – and with a burning and deeply committed urgency.

Wild beasts

At the turn of the century, Paris remained the main focus of European art. To the Parisians, art was a passion, a topic of common discussion. Hence, when a critic reported that there were 'wild beasts' (*fauves*) exhibiting at the 1905 Salon d'Automne everyone had to have an opinion about it all. The Fauves, as they were happy to call themselves, shot to fame – or notoriety.

One of their leading spirits was the 36-year-old Henri Matisse, who had spent the previous summer in the south of France with two younger, like-minded artists, André Derain and Maurice de Vlaminck. They were searching for a new direction in which to take painting. After the great Impressionist era of the 1870s, painting had undergone numerous transformations in the hands of Vincent van Gogh, Paul Cézanne and Paul Gauguin. Such developments had failed to produce an '-ism' to match the success of Impressionism, while photography had usurped the skills of the artist to portray representational reality.

Matisse and his colleagues focused on the expression of feelings, and they embarked on a series of brash experiments with colour. They used unmixed primary colours, seen for example in Derain's *The Pool of London* (1906) – all vivid reds and blues in place of the muted greys and greens of London's industrial docklands.

The Salon d'Automne placed Matisse at the forefront of the Parisian avant-garde. But the Fauves – who also included the painters Raoul Dufy and Georges Rouault – soon began to go their separate ways. Matisse became increasingly interested in two-dimensionality, simplified forms and harmony, and began painting large works saturated with colour. By 1908 Fauvism had effectively come to a close.

One of the most ambitious young painters in Paris was the Spaniard Pablo Picasso. By 1906, he had already scored some success among art collectors with the innovative figurative paintings of his 'Blue' and 'Rose' periods. Not to be outdone by Matisse, he launched himself into a radical reappraisal of the very foundations, the concepts of perspective and naturalism, upon which Western art was built.

In this, he – like the Fauves and many other artists of the day – was in part inspired by sculpture from Africa and Oceania, which demonstrated that immense artistic power existed beyond the confines of Western traditions of art. In 1907 Picasso painted *Les Demoiselles d'Avignon*, a large and deliberately shocking work which featured angular and simplified nudes, representing prostitutes from the red-light district of Barcelona. Until 1916 the painting was never displayed in public; Picasso showed it only to his artist

EXPERIMENTING WITH COLOUR Matisse's portrait of his wife, *Madame Matisse – The Green Line* (1905), provoked derision for the line down the middle of her face, not to mention the blue hair.

1908 Term 'Cubism' coined

1911 *Der Blaue Reiter* founded in Munich

1913 Stravinsky's *The Rite of Spring* first performed by Ballets Russes

THE PAINTING THAT SHOCKED **Even artists among Picasso's friends were dismayed by *Les Demoiselles d'Avignon* (1907). It played havoc with traditional notions of perspective and the two nudes on the right, with African-like masks instead of faces, scandalised many viewers.**

friends. For all that, the picture represents a major watershed in modern art, for from this moment Picasso drove forwards with his experimentation that culminated in Cubism.

In making the imaginative leap into Cubism, Picasso was attempting to make painting do what had never been asked of it before. Subject and background were broken down into geometrical forms, seen from a variety of angles simultaneously, then reassembled like a jigsaw. Picasso found a soul mate for his endeavour in the French

CUBIST REVOLUTION In *Still Life with Chair Caning* (1912), Picasso took the revolutionary step of attaching real rope to a painted canvas. Right: Picasso's Cubist colleague Georges Braque in his Paris studio in 1912.

painter Georges Braque, formerly associated with the Fauves. They exhibited together at the Salon d'Automne of 1908, at which the term 'Cubism' was coined.

The Cubist work of this early 'analytical' era tended to be sombre in tone, and almost mechanical and metallic in finish. Picasso and Braque were pushing their experiment to see just how broadly it could be applied – to still life, to figure painting and even portraiture. 'Roped together as mountaineers', as Braque put it, they worked on excitedly, gradually lightening the palette and the mood of their work, then adding printed

THE BIRTH OF ABSTRACT PAINTING

Some of the Cubist and Futurist paintings may look abstract, but they were not: they were evocations of things in the real world, and thus, ultimately, representational. Picasso always rejected the idea that his work was in any way abstract: 'There is no such thing as abstract art. You must always start with something.'

The first steps towards pure abstraction can be traced to work by the Expressionist Vassily Kandinsky, a founder-member of *Der Blaue Reiter* in Germany. He recalled how the idea of entirely nonrepresentational painting occurred to him. At dusk one day in 1909 he walked into his studio:

'Suddenly my eyes fell upon an indescribably beautiful picture that was saturated with an inner glow. I was startled momentarily and quickly went up to this enigmatic painting in which I could see nothing but shapes and colours, the content of which was incomprehensible to me. The answer to the riddle came immediately: it was one of my own paintings leaning on its side against a wall.'

words and bits of collage, such as sandpaper, wallpaper and newspaper cuttings. By 1912 Picasso was producing painted three-dimensional constructions made of 'found' objects such as upholstery trimmings, tin cans and teaspoons. Painting and sculpture were being taken down totally uncharted paths in this new period of 'synthetic Cubism', liberated not just from traditions of Western art appreciation, but also from the straitjacket of technical art skills.

In 1911-12 the French artist Marcel Duchamp painted his pair of Cubist-inspired works entitled *Nude Descending a Staircase*; the second of these caused outrage in 1913 when exhibited at the highly controversial Armory Show of modern art in New York, a city that was fast becoming a new centre for the avant-garde. That same year Duchamp produced the first of his 'ready-mades', *Bicycle Wheel* – a bicycle wheel mounted on a kitchen stool.

This apparently nonsensical construction seemed like an affront to traditional art. It was art simply because Duchamp said it was. His ready-mades foreshadowed the Dada movement of 1916 onwards – and laid the foundations for just about every subsequent art movement of the 20th century.

Expression through Expressionism

'I paint objects as I think of them, not as I see them', declared Picasso during his Cubist phase. Cubism was essentially an intellectual exercise – the result of careful analysis of the visual world and of the possibilities of extending the techniques of representation.

READY-MADE With works such as *Bicycle Wheel* Marcel Duchamp posed fundamental questions about what constitutes a work of art.

Other artists were concerned more with the way that painting could express emotion; they likewise found inspiration in the sculpture of Africa and Oceania, but also in Fauvism and in the work of precursors such as Van Gogh, Gauguin and the Norwegian painter Edvard Munch, who had created his extraordinary emblematic work *The Scream* in 1893.

In Dresden, Germany, a group of artists formed their own guild-like group called *Die Brücke* (The Bridge) in 1905. Among its

OMENS OF THE FUTURE

Of all the art movements of the 1900-14 period, Futurism could claim the most popular appeal at the time. It began as a self-conscious movement, promoted by the Italian poet Filippo Tommaso Marinetti, who announced the *Futurist Manifesto* in Paris in 1909. Iconoclastic, frenetic and apocalyptic, Futurism championed the machine age, speed and energy, as witnessed in Marinetti's famous statement: 'A screaming automobile that seems to run like a machine-gun is more beautiful than the Victory of Samothrace [an ancient Greek sculpture in the Louvre].' Futurist poetry has largely been forgotten but its artists, mainly Italian, produced some significant work. In the sculpture *Unique Forms of Continuity in Space* (1913), Umberto Boccioni gives a physical presence to the abstract sensation of muscular movement in a striding figure. Some of the paintings of Giacomo Balla, such as *Abstract Speed: the Car has Passed* (1913), border on abstraction. Futurism alienated many through its posturing machismo and its concepts of racial superiority and right-wing reforms that later made it a natural bedfellow of Fascism. In the tense years leading up to the First World War, many Futurists claimed that they welcomed war as an apocalyptic clash that would shake out the past and lead to a brilliant, machine-age future. The Futurists had no idea that the war would spell the end of their own movement, as of Cubism, *Die Brücke* and *Der Blaue Reiter* – although the reverberations of all of them would be felt for the rest of the century.

MOTION PICTURE Experiments with multi-exposure photography led Giacomo Balla to paint *Dynamism of a Dog on a Leash,* a wryly humorous picture of a dachshund being walked by its fashionable mistress.

SELF PORTRAIT WITH A MODEL Ernst Ludwig Kirchner was one of four architecture students who founded *Die Brücke* (The Bridge). The group lived and worked together, consciously aiming for a collective style.

founders were Ernst Ludwig Kirchner and Karl Schmidt-Rotluff, whose work superficially resembled Fauvism, but was more strident, distorted and emotionally charged. Karl Schmidt-Rotluff, in particular, painted with an angry vehemence expressed in lashings of thick, vivid paint, his images strongly influenced by African sculpture. But this German 'Expressionism', as it became known after 1911, also had a gentler, more mystical voice, seen for instance in the work of Emil Nolde, who was influenced by naive folk art. A recurring theme of *Die Brücke* artists was the tawdry unpleasantness of urban life, lambasted in particular in Kirchner's work, and contrasted to the mystical purity of nature.

In 1911 another Expressionist group was founded in Munich, led by Franz Marc, Auguste Macke and the Russian-born artist Vassily Kandinsky. They called themselves *Der Blaue Reiter* (The Blue Rider), simply because of Kandinsky's love of blue and Marc's predilection for painting horses. Their Expressionism took a variety of forms, generally softer and more lyrical than that of *Die*

Brücke: Kandinsky had begun to toy with abstraction in 1909, while the Swiss painter Paul Klee developed a charmed world of inner landscapes, reflecting the workings of the unconscious exposed by Freud and Jung. But their agenda was nonetheless radical. As Marc put it: 'We must be bold and turn our backs upon almost everything that until now good Europeans like ourselves thought precious and indispensable.'

A balletic revolution

Radical and provocative developments were not confined to painting; changes in ballet caused a sensation that few, among the more educated classes at least, could fail to notice.

IMPROVISING TOWARDS ABSTRACTION   In works such as *Improvisation 28 (Second Version)*, painted in 1912, Vassily Kandinsky was well on the way to abstract art.

At the heart of the maelstrom was the Russian company called the Ballets Russes, formed by the aristocratic impresario Sergei Diaghilev. Inspired by the free and expressive dancing of the Americans Loïe Fuller and Isadora Duncan, Diaghilev created his new company with the dancer and choreographer Mikhail Fokine and launched it in Paris in 1909. It was an instant success.

The Ballets Russes created an alluring spectacle of lavish, spellbinding sets and costumes, most of them designed by the artist Leon Bakst, who had first made his name as a painter at the Imperial court in St Petersburg. The music was radically modern – challenging, yet for the most part approachable – by avant-garde composers such as the Russian Igor Stravinsky and the Frenchmen Claude Debussy and Maurice Ravel. Diaghilev also managed to recruit the greatest dancers of the century, including the

Russians Vaslav Nijinsky, Tamara Karsavina and Anna Pavlova.

The Ballets Russes went from strength to strength, particularly with *L'Oiseau du feu* (*Firebird*; 1910) and *Petrushka* (1911), which gave the young Stravinsky his reputation as the most exciting composer of the day. While women's fashions were soon being influenced by Bakst's exotic designs, the Ballets Russes never lost its controversial image: Debussy's *L'Après-midi d'un faune* (*The Afternoon of a Faun*; 1912) was held to be scandalously erotic, while Stravinsky's *Le Sacre du printemps* (*The Rite of Spring*; 1913), choreographed by Nijinsky, caused a riot on its opening night. Faced with music of ferocious dissonance, one part of the audience laughed, heckled, catcalled and jeered, while the other – led by Ravel shouting 'Genius! Genius!' – vigorously voiced its defence of the performance and exchanged insults.

Various leading artists were invited to design sets and costumes for the Ballets Russes, such as Matisse, Derain and Picasso, who in 1917 created extraordinary Cubist costumes for *Parade*, a ballet with music by Erik Satie. The Ballets Russes eventually dispersed after the death of Diaghilev in 1929.

Le Sacre du printemps provoked the most prominent musical controversy of its day, but it was part of a growing radical tendency that was to lead classical music farther and farther from popular taste. Among the cognoscenti, the real *enfant terrible* of modern music was the Austrian Arnold Schoenberg.

At the turn of the century, the music of the German composer Richard Wagner was still the most influential in classical music, reverberating even in the works of figures such as Sir Edward Elgar, a great favourite among the English. Various composers had analysed the power and novelty of Wagner's music; they

HUMAN TIGER Nijinsky (1890-1950) dances the 'negro slave' in the ballet *Scheherezade* in 1910. One contemporary, the Englishman Cyril Beaumont, remembered his first entrance, shooting out 'like an arrow from a bow in a mighty parabola which enabled him to cross in one bound a good two-thirds of the width of the stage'. It was 'the kind of leap a tiger might make'.

identified his use of chromatic notes as the key to his modernity. Traditionally, harmony in classical music had been bound by a tonality based on a chosen key (such as B flat major) consisting of a scale of eight notes. Chromatic notes were notes introduced from outside this scale to create the frisson of dissonance. Schoenberg decided to do away with tonality altogether, and to give equal weight to a full scale of 12 notes (the octave plus all the flats and sharps). In 1909, in Vienna, he produced the first of what he

AN ILL-FATED INSPIRATION

Movement 'springing from the soul' was how Isadora Duncan described her form of dancing. Born in San Francisco in 1878, her early performances in the USA met with a stony response, so in 1898 she travelled to England where she established a reputation as a free spirit. In 1905 she went to Russia and deeply impressed Diaghilev and Fokine, who was inspired by her to develop the freer dance style that later became the hallmark of the Ballets Russes. Mercurial and headstrong, Duncan had two children, a daughter by the theatre director Gordon Craig, and a son by Paris Singer, the millionaire heir to the sewing-machine business. In 1913 both were drowned in France when the car they were travelling in stalled and slid into the River Seine. In 1921 Duncan married a Russian peasant poet called Sergei Yesenin, 17 years her junior. In 1925 he committed suicide. Her own death came two years later: in 1927 in Nice, southern France, she was setting off for a drive in a Bugatti when her trailing shawl caught in the spokes of a rear wheel and broke her neck.

BAREFOOT DANCER Isadora Duncan danced to highly charged music by Schubert, Beethoven, Brahms and Wagner, wearing flowing costumes inspired by Greek sculpture in the British Museum.

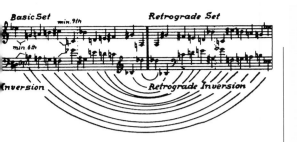

named 'pantonal' music, later called 'atonal'. It was an uncompromisingly new sound, and, although potentially anarchic, it was capable of stirring, dreamlike beauty.

Writers and readers

Of all the creative arts, literature probably had the most broad-based popular appeal. Successful novels, available in high-street shops, at railway station retailers, through book clubs and the many private libraries, sold in large quantities. Then, as now, they made a fortune for the handful of best-selling authors at the top of the profession.

The British writer Rudyard Kipling had acquired a reputation as the 'poet of empire' by evoking the imperial experience with a mixture of wonderment, reverence and patriotism. His *Kim* (1901) is a tale of the 'Great Game' of spying and intrigue played out between the British and Russians in the borderlands of northern India.

A similarly broad canvas was adopted by the Polish-born Joseph Conrad, who drew on his experiences during 20 years of seafaring. He published *Lord Jim* in 1900, *Nostromo* in 1904 and *The Secret Agent* in 1907. Although now acclaimed as one of the century's greatest writers in the English language – all the more remarkable in that it was not his native tongue – Conrad never enjoyed more than moderate success in his day. His popularity was easily outstripped by the American Jack London, whose *Call of the Wild* (1903) and *White Fang* (1906) were based on his experiences in the American far north.

At the turn of the century, one of the leading authors was H.G. Wells, an international celebrity who had written his futuristic *The Time Machine* and *The War of the Worlds* in the 1890s. Even greater success lay ahead

MUSIC HALL AND RAGTIME

By far the most popular form of entertainment during the era was the music hall, known as 'variety' in Britain and 'vaudeville' in the USA. Every town had at least one variety theatre, providing an enthusiastic, even boisterous public with a medley of nightly acts: singers, dancers, comedians, acrobats, magicians and illusionists. Richly costumed and painted, the best singers would bring an audience to tears with songs of unashamed sentimentality and nostalgia for the past, then leave the stage to knock-about clowns, sword-swallowers and contortionists.

Although essentially born of the provinces, the apogee of the music hall world was in the city, where large theatres dedicated to the art were given grand and exotic names, such as the Tivoli, Hippodrome, Alhambra, Empire and Palace. These provided the setting for the great stars, such as the English comedienne Marie Lloyd, who earned stuff-of-dream salaries. But the days of the music hall were numbered as audiences were drawn increasingly to the entertainment that would usurp it: films. Music hall performers were beginning to translate their skills to the screen. Charlie Chaplin had joined the music hall acts of Fred Karno as a 17-year-old, but went over to film in 1913; one of his understudies in the music hall was Stan Laurel. Similarly, the Marx Brothers were leading vaudeville acts until they became Broadway stars in the 1920s and then turned to film.

In 1912 a different sort of show reached the London Hippodrome. It was called *Hullo Rag-Time!*, and featured the American star, Ethel Levey, and an all-girl chorus line. British audiences loved it, particularly the brash and driving rhythm of the syncopated ragtime music. The great progenitor of ragtime was the gifted black pianist Scott Joplin.

Joplin had made a fortune from the sheet-music sales of tunes such as 'Maple Leaf Rag' (1900) but this had all but disappeared in attempts to get a black ragtime opera off the ground. He was now living in modest circumstances in Harlem, New York. Meanwhile, ragtime had been projected onto an international stage by a new generation of performers and writers, notably Russian-born American Irving Berlin, whose 'Alexander's Ragtime Band' (1911) was an international success.

FOLLIES OF 1912 The vaudeville comedians Leon Errol and Bert Williams share the stage with Nicodemus, a 'race horse' (below). Across the Atlantic, *Hullo Rag-Time!* introduced syncopated rhythms to enthusiastic London audiences.

REMEMBERING THINGS PAST Marcel Proust opened up a new vein in literature with his exploration of memory and perception.

with *The First Men in the Moon* (1901), *Kipps* (1905) and *The History of Mr Polly* (1910). His work in these years also shows a sociological bent, notably in *Tono-Bungay* (1909) which vilifies the new class of English rich, and *Ann Veronica* (also 1909), a sympathetic portrait of the modern woman, a suffragist battling for social and sexual equality.

The most significant European novel was *Buddenbrooks* (1901) by the young German Thomas Mann. The rising star of French literature was Marcel Proust, who started his monumental *A la recherche du temps perdu* (*Remembrance of Things Past*) in 1909, though its impact would not be widely felt until after the First World War.

Sir Arthur Conan Doyle's creation Sherlock Holmes had achieved such popularity that he was forced by public demand to resurrect his sleuth – despite having killed him off. In 1901-2, Conan Doyle produced *The Hound of the Baskervilles* and he continued to reel off Holmes stories until his death in 1930.

Some of the era's most remarkable achievements, however, lay in children's literature. In 1900 the American journalist Lyman Frank Baum wrote *The Wonderful Wizard of Oz*, which was transformed into a musical the following year with resounding success. *Peter Pan* by J.M. Barrie, first performed on stage in 1904, met with similarly rapturous acclaim. A string of other classics emerged, including Kipling's *Just So Stories* (1902), *Peter Rabbit* (1902) by Beatrix Potter, *The Railway Children* (1906) by Edith Nesbit, *The Wind in the Willows* (1908) by Kenneth Graham, and *The Secret Garden* (1911) by Frances Hodgson Burnett.

The theatre was still reverberating to the ideas of the Norwegian Henrik Ibsen, who had broken new ground with tragedies written in prose rather than verse and featuring ordinary people as its heroes and heroines. No less radical was the influence of his contemporaries the Swede August Strindberg and the Russian Anton Chekhov, whose *The Cherry Orchard* was produced in 1904, the last year of his life. In England, the Irish-born George Bernard Shaw was using theatre to explore progressive ideas, seen for example in *Three Plays for Puritans* (1900).

In Ireland itself, where a cultural revival was in full swing, led by figures such as the poet W.B. Yeats and his patron Lady Gregory, Dublin's Abbey Theatre opened in 1904. In 1907 it staged *The Playboy of the Western World* by J.M. Synge. Synge was trying to reflect the 'rich and living' language of the Irish people, but the frankness of it was too much for some, who felt that it cast a slur on the nation. The audience rioted at the play's first performance in Dublin, and there were similar scenes when it opened in New York in 1911 and later in Boston and Philadelphia.

TALE-TELLING Kipling (left) gives a shipboard rendering of his *Just So Stories*. Other favourites were Conan Doyle's Sherlock Holmes stories (top), Wells's *The First Men in the Moon* (middle) and *The Wonderful Wizard of Oz*.

FORCES FOR CHANGE

THE ALTERED HORIZONS OF INDUSTRY AND TECHNOLOGY ENCOURAGED THE DESIRE TO RESHAPE POLITICS AND SOCIETY. AS NATIONS JOCKEYED FOR POSITION ON A WORLD STAGE, THE OPPRESSED SOUGHT TO REDRESS HISTORIC INEQUALITIES. THIS WAS A TIME OF GROWING POLITICAL TURBULENCE, AS THE OLD ORDER STRUGGLED TO COME TO TERMS WITH NEW HOPES AND IDEOLOGIES – SUCH AS NATIONALISM, SOCIALISM, CIVIL RIGHTS AND VOTES FOR WOMEN.

THE RISING SUN

WITHIN HALF A CENTURY, JAPAN SHOT FROM BEING AN INWARD-LOOKING DICTATORSHIP TO A WESTERNISED, INDUSTRIALISED NATION

It was the irresistible drive of Western commerce that prised Japan out of its isolation. In 1853 Commodore Matthew Perry of the US navy had steered a squadron of four ships into Tokyo Bay and demanded that Japan open its door to international trade. For 250 years the Tokugawa shogunate had enforced a policy of strict isolationism: foreign trade was restricted to a trickle arriving through Nagasaki and controlled by Dutch and Chinese merchants. Any Japanese citizen who left the fatherland, and dared to return, faced execution.

The opening up of trade caused a political crisis in Japan, and in 1867 this ushered in a new regime with the authority of the monarchy restored under the youthful Emperor Meiji. The new rulers encouraged trade and industrialisation and the growth of a merchant class. Foreign experts were invited to develop commerce, railways and telecommunication systems, and to teach Western medicine. Students were sent abroad to study Western sciences and industrial techniques. During the 1880s, Japan established a Prussian-style bicameral parliament or Diet, a constitutional monarchy and a legal framework based on French and German models. The old *daimyo* feudal estates were broken up, and a Western-style tax regime was imposed on a newly enriched peasantry. This helped to provide vital capital for industrialisation.

GATEWAY FROM THE PAST Japan held firm to its traditions, such as the geishas (right), and its religious heritage, symbolised by the old *torii* (ceremonial) gate of the island shrine of Miyajima, near Hiroshima (below).

While drawing on foreign expertise, however, Japan was careful to avoid overreliance on it or foreign capital. Self-sufficient in agriculture, and with a healthy domestic market, the country was able to fund almost

1902 Japan forms an alliance with Great Britain

1904 Japan attacks the Russian Pacific Fleet at Port Arthur on February 8

1905 Russians surrender at Port Arthur on January 2. The Treaty of Portsmouth, signed on September 5, ends the Russo-Japanese War

THE ROAD AHEAD Compared with Japan, Korea remained mired in the past. Telegraph poles line a street in the capital, Seoul, still serving transport from the 19th century.

all its industrial development from its own sources. Industries that helped to reduce imports received government sponsorship: silk-production was transformed into a major industry; cotton textiles followed in the 1880s, then heavy industry in the 1890s.

The Japanese population grew rapidly, from 35 million in 1873 to 55 million in 1918. By 1918 half of the people lived in the cities, where they adopted many Western ways – such as the wearing of suits for men. Nonetheless, modern development was underpinned by Japan's confidence in its own culture. The traditions of the samurai, the geisha girls, the No and Kabuki theatre, the tea ceremony, Shintoism, Zen Buddhism and calligraphy may have been sidelined, but they did not die.

The fashion for imperialism

The proud martial tradition of Japan was also part of its modern development. '*Fukoku kyohei*' ('Rich country, strong army') was the slogan of the modernisers, who introduced military conscription and invested heavily in a modern navy. Closely observing the Western powers, they noticed the emphasis these placed on the acquisition of imperial possessions abroad. Acquiring an overseas empire of its own became a Japanese priority. First it stamped its authority on neighbouring islands formerly claimed by China, then it cast a covetous eye towards the mainland.

The main fields of conflict were Korea and Manchuria. In contrast to Japan, Korea's rulers, answering to the 500-year-old Yi

dynasty, tried to continue an isolationist policy. In 1882, however, they relented under pressure from all sides: from Japan, with which Korea had ancient cultural ties; from China; from the USA, which attempted to use force to make Korea open up, as it had done with Japan; and from Russia, which was trying to expand into southern Manchuria. Chinese and Japanese rivalry over Korea led to the brief Sino-Japanese War of 1894-5, decisively won by Japan. As part of the settlement, Japan was given Taiwan – the first major string to its imperialist bow. With China neutralised, Japan was also able to interfere in Korean domestic politics. It used its influence to drive through a raft of reforms in an attempt to modernise a country widely reviled for its backwardness – for example, slavery and child marriages were banned.

In Manchuria – officially a part of the Chinese Empire and the original homeland of its ruling Qing dynasty – Japan's chief rival was Russia. Russia had been gradually moving into the region since the mid 19th century. By 1898 it had more or less occupied Manchuria. Furthermore, the Russians had acquired from China a 25 year lease on Port Arthur (now Lüshun), strategically placed at the tip of the Liaodong (Liaotung) Peninsula. This irked the Japanese, who had also occupied parts of Manchuria but had been forced to withdraw after the Sino-Japanese War.

The Russo-Japanese War

In 1902 Japan enhanced its imperial prestige by entering into an alliance with Great Britain. By the following year, the Japanese and the Russians were spoiling for a fight. Rivalry reached fever pitch in December that year, when Japanese troops intervened on the Korean government's behalf to help to put down a domestic revolt. Russia bridled at this incursion.

Then on February 8, 1904, without warning and without a declaration of war, Japan launched a pre-emptive attack on the Russian Pacific Fleet in Port Arthur. Using the speed of their torpedo boats, the Japanese quickly sank two battleships; then a crippled Russian cruiser went down in the channel, blocking the entrance of the harbour. In a separate action off Chemul'po (Inchon), the Japanese sank two more Russian cruisers.

TWO-WAY FLOW: JAPAN IN THE WEST

While Japan was opening its doors to Westernisation, the West was opening its eyes in wonder at Japanese culture. By the 1880s, Japanese art had developed a cult following among the aesthetes of London, Paris and New York. By the time Giacomo Puccini wrote *Madama Butterfly* (1904) – in which the heroine, a geisha, is deceived by a US naval officer, with tragic consequences – Europe had a reasonably realistic understanding of modern Japan.

The unique sense of design, composition and colour in Japanese art had a long-term effect on Western art and design, seen for example in the work of the French post-Impressionists Edgar Degas and Toulouse Lautrec and in the Art Nouveau style. The influence of Japanese architecture took longer to emerge. The American Frank Lloyd Wright was already developing his radical style when he visited

Japan in 1905. He called his distinctive dwellings 'prairie houses' because their low rectangular forms and flat roofs recalled the landscape of the prairies. But their informal layout, simplified interiors, pared-down ornament and Wright's careful observance of 'spirit of place' also have much in common with the traditional Japanese approach to architecture.

VISIONS OF JAPAN Frank Lloyd Wright designed the Robie House in Chicago (below) following his first visit to Japan in 1905. Puccini's hugely successful opera *Madama Butterfly* tells a tragic tale of deception, set in emergent Japan.

THE COCKPIT OF THE FAR EAST A cartoon illustration from a contemporary book pictures the cock, representing Korea, crowing impotently at the rising sun of Japan.

With the Russian fleet blockaded in Port Arthur, the Japanese were able to operate with impunity. They landed 80 000 troops on the Liaodong Peninsula and the southern Korean coast, ignoring Korean protestations of neutrality. These forces swept north into Manchuria, where they inflicted a series of costly defeats on the Russian army. The Russians reversed their dismal fortunes in October with a victory on the River Sha-Ho, but at enormous cost: they lost 40 000 men, while the Japanese lost 20 000.

Throughout the conflict, the casualties on both sides were severe, numbering hundreds of thousands. However, the Japanese, bolstered by victory, took the losses in their stride. The Russians, with a strictly muzzled press, hoped to conceal their setbacks from their public – but news spread. As new conscripts and opponents of the war demonstrated in Moscow and St Petersburg, Russia's domestic politics began to unravel.

Their worst military setback was yet to come. In a 12 day battle for Mukden in February and March 1905, the Russian army under General Kuropatkin was all but annihilated. Fleeing a battlefield where the dead from both sides numbered some 200 000, the surviving Russian troops scurried northwards towards their border.

In the meantime, Tsar Nicholas II had dispatched his Baltic Fleet to the Far East to relieve Port Arthur. Since the ice-bound north of Russia was impassable, the 45 ships

had to travel by the southern route – a journey of 18 000 miles (28 000 km) that began in October 1904 and took over six months. Choosing to go round the Cape of Good Hope, rather than through the Suez Canal, Admiral Zinovi Rozhdestvenski had to stop at an island off Madagascar to repair engines faltering under the strain of the journey. At Cam Ranh Bay, in French Indochina, he was joined by a squadron under Admiral Nebogatov, which had been dispatched from the Baltic in January 1905, and had sailed via Suez. Together they steamed north.

Meanwhile, on January 2, 1905, Port Arthur had surrendered after an 11 month siege. By this time, some three-quarters of

MASTERS OF THE SEAS The lightning attack on Port Arthur (above) demonstrated the modern fighting strength of the Japanese navy. With a stranglehold around the crippled Port Arthur (below), Japan could easily supply its troops in Korea and Manchuria.

GRAVEDIGGING Despondent Russian troops bury the dead on a hilltop near Port Arthur in November 1904, the tenth month of the siege.

the 20 000 strong garrison were suffering from dysentery or wounds. The last remnants of the Russian Pacific Fleet at Port Arthur had been scuttled in the harbour.

The objective for the Baltic Fleet changed to Vladivostok, the Pacific coast terminus of Russia's Trans-Siberian Railway, now in its turn under siege by the Japanese. On May 27, 1905, as the fleet stole through the Strait of Tsushima separating Japan from Korea, it was ambushed by the Japanese navy under Admiral Togo. Outmanoeuvring the Russians, the Japanese opened their offensive with a devastating broadside. The Russian fleet, thrown into panic, was quickly put to rout: five ships sank as a result of the opening engagement; the remainder were chased northwards into the night, harried by torpedo boats. At dawn the main cluster of 12 Russian ships was forced to surrender. Only three vessels from the entire Baltic Fleet survived to reach Vladivostok. A total of 4830 Russian sailors had been killed, and 5917 wounded. The Japanese had lost just three torpedo boats and 117 men, with 590 wounded.

It was a humiliating disaster for the Russians, who urgently sued for peace. The Japanese, meanwhile, pressed home their advantage and stormed the Russian island of Sakhalin, to the north-west of Japan. The war was eventually brought to a close on September 5, 1905, when a treaty was signed at

ADMIRAL TOGO: RELUCTANT HERO

In many ways the hero of the Battle of Tsushima, Admiral Heihachiro Togo (1847-1934), was a typical product of his era. Born into the family of a modest samurai, he joined the embryonic Japanese navy and was sent to England in 1871 to study warfare. Here, he was deeply impressed by the British approach to naval affairs, and by the strength of its sense of tradition. His hero was Admiral Nelson.

Back in Japan, Togo worked hard to mould the Japanese navy along British lines as he gradually moved up the ranks. In 1904, after distinguishing himself in actions off Korea, he was placed in command of the Japanese navy.

Togo mixed two virtues: prudence and daring. His attack on Port Arthur and subsequent blockade was a stroke of strategic genius from which the Russians never recovered. When faced with the task of heading off the Russian Baltic Fleet, he had sufficient resources to cover only one approach to Vladivostok. Togo weighed the considerations that faced the Russian commander in chief, and guessed correctly that he would take the shortest route through the Tsushima Strait. It was a knife-edge decision, but the result was one of the greatest naval victories in maritime history.

Togo later became Chief of the Naval Staff and Admiral of the Fleet, and was ennobled to Count, then Marquis (Japan had adopted the European pattern of honours in 1884). But even in this exalted position, he remained modest and insisted on living in the same humble house where he had lived as a junior officer. When his admirers raised money to buy him a residence more suited to a national hero, he persuaded them to fund statues of the founders of Japan's navy instead.

Admiral Togo was awarded the British Order of Merit by King Edward VII in 1906. Lord Fisher, the British First Sea Lord, recalled that Togo insisted on wearing the medal back to front as he feared that the inscription 'For Merit' might appear boastful.

ROLE MODEL The Battle of Tsushima was hailed as the first major naval engagement of the modern era. The tactics used by Admiral Togo were closely studied by the European navies.

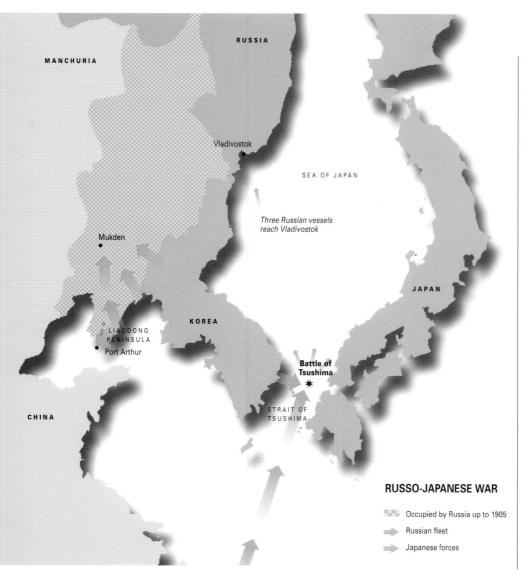

Three Russian vessels reach Vladivostok

RUSSIA
MANCHURIA
Vladivostok
SEA OF JAPAN
Mukden
JAPAN
KOREA
LIAODONG PENINSULA
Port Arthur
Battle of Tsushima
CHINA
STRAIT OF TSUSHIMA

RUSSO-JAPANESE WAR

Occupied by Russia up to 1905
Russian fleet
Japanese forces

resume its campaign of rapid modernisation and reform, and the Japanese resident-general (governor) soon began to appropriate responsibility for domestic affairs. To the Western powers, the Japanese policy of modernisation seemed commendable, but in Korea it caused widespread resentment.

One victim of this anger was Ito Hirobumi, among the great Japanese statesmen of the era. A visit to Europe when he was 22 had persuaded Ito of the benefits of the Western industrial economy and political structures; he had subsequently been responsible for many of Japan's crucial political and constitutional reforms. He was also prime minister in 1892-6, 1898 and 1900-1. After the Russo-Japanese War, Ito negotiated the partial transfer of Korean sovereignty to Japan, and he became the first resident-general in 1906. As the figurehead for the unpopular Japanese reforms, he was widely reviled in Korea, and was assassinated by a Korean patriot in 1909. The following year, Japan annexed Korea, thus extinguishing any pretence of its status as an independent nation. The 'land of the rising sun' was flexing its muscles as the new regional power of the Far East.

NEIGHBOURS Japan had the advantage of fighting a war on its doorstep, while the Russians were logistically at full stretch. Below: Japan's resident-general in Korea, Ito Hirobumi (on the left), is a model of dignity as he poses for the camera with his family.

Portsmouth, New Hampshire – a treaty brokered by US President Theodore Roosevelt, for which he won the Nobel peace prize.

From now on, the Western imperial nations had to respect Japan as a peer. Signs of this enhanced status were immediately apparent. The ink on the Treaty of Portsmouth was scarcely dry when Great Britain strengthened its alliance with Japan and sent its first ambassador to Tokyo.

Building on strength

Under the terms of the Treaty of Portsmouth, Japan won half the island of Sakhalin, rights of access to southern Manchuria, the lease of the Liaodong Peninsula, and – most important – unhindered influence over Korea. The Russians also had to pay an indemnity. Japan had fulfilled all its territorial ambitions of the war, but it had been brought to the verge of bankruptcy. This aspect of things left many at home deeply dissatisfied. Just as throngs

of people had turned out into the streets of Tokyo to celebrate the fall of Port Arthur with resounding cheers of 'Banzai!', they now marched in their tens of thousands to berate their government for its failure to obtain a larger Russian indemnity which would have covered the costs of the war. Such demonstrations were in themselves a sign of changing times. In Japanese politics, the people now had a voice which, half a century before, would have remained stoically silent.

Initially, Japan demanded only that it should take control of Korea's defence. But almost immediately it was clear that Tokyo intended to

REVOLUTIONARY FERMENT

RUSSIA WAS IN TURMOIL, A POWDER KEG OF SOCIAL INJUSTICE IN A TIME OF RAPID ECONOMIC CHANGE: IN 1905 THE FUSE WAS LIT

For many Russians, the humiliations of the Russo-Japanese War of 1904-5 were too much to bear. The war was unwarranted, ineptly handled, and had cost the lives of hundreds of thousands of Russian conscripts. But antiwar demonstrations mounted by students and middle-class protesters were just one ingredient in a cauldron of unrest that was already coming to the boil as the war got under way.

Discontent had been simmering in Russia for at least two decades, since the assassination of Tsar Alexander II in 1881. This had ended a programme of reforms, which had included overhauls of the educational and administrative systems and the emancipation of Russia's serfs. Under Alexander II's successors, Alexander III (reigned 1881-94) and Nicholas II (reigned 1894-1917), reform was replaced by repression enforced by troops and thousands of secret police.

Russia was an unreconstructed autocracy: the tsar ruled with absolute authority, assisted by an unelected government of ministers drawn from the nobility, and a huge and lumbering bureaucracy. His empire was vast, comprising half of Europe and half of Asia. By 1905 the bulk of the Trans-Siberian Railway had been completed, covering 5600 miles (9000 km), but even then it did not span the entire width of the empire. The Tsar ruled over 126 million people; of these, 80 per cent were rural peasants, while the ruling nobility comprised just 1 per cent.

By the standards of western European countries, Russia was backward – a feudal state in a time warp. Yet, at the turn of the century, it was undergoing a period of galloping economic advancement. Industrialisation, assisted by government funds and foreign capital, was transforming many of the western cities, notably Moscow and the capital, St Petersburg. The vast plains known as the steppes, stretching across the Eurasian landmass from south-eastern Europe as far as Siberia, had been opened up to grain farming, making Russia one of the world's leading wheat exporters. Blessed by all kinds of raw materials, Russia was just beginning to realise its economic potential.

But these commercial developments simply exacerbated the deep social injustices that dogged the nation. Only a small minority from the nobility and the entrepreneurial middle classes stood to gain, while the poor, often living in appalling conditions, and with no political power, watched their prospects deteriorate. Many peasants had seen their horizons expand when serfdom was abolished in 1861, but the redistribution of land to peasant communes, at high terms of payment and without any programme of agrarian modernisation, had introduced new frustrations and impoverishment.

Conditions in St Petersburg were an extreme expression of conditions across the country as a whole. On the one hand, there were the sensationally grand imperial palaces that lined the River Neva, the imposing cathedrals, the elegant private mansions, the Art Nouveau cafés and the plush restaurants – and the workshops of Carl Fabergé, where some 500 craftsmen produced exquisite bejewelled knick-knacks for the tsar and the nobility. On the other hand was the crushing poverty of the workhouses and industrial tenements, festering with disease and mental illness, home to distressed families and child labourers dependent for their survival on the soup kitchens of the Church missions.

VOLGA BARGEMEN Human haulers drag a barge along the River Volga. Poverty and primitive conditions existed alongside ostentatious wealth in a land rich in raw materials.

1901 Student riots over Tolstoy's excommunication

1902 Lenin's pamphlet *What is to be Done?* published

1903 Social Democrats split between Mensheviks and Bolsheviks

1904 Birth of Crown Prince Alexis

1905 'Bloody Sunday' and revolution

1906 Stolypin becomes prime minister

1907 Beginning of Rasputin's ascendancy at Imperial Court

It was clear that reform was desperately needed. Moderates hoped that Nicholas might be persuaded to oversee a programme of enlightened change; some hoped to see the introduction of representative government, and perhaps a constitutional monarchy in the style of many other European nations. But the tsar's intransigence frustrated such aspirations, driving many reformers to seek more radical solutions – such as revolution.

Student power

Despite constant attempts by the authorities to curb their activities, the universities were hotbeds of radicalism. Here, idealistic

APOSTLE OF LOVE Tolstoy sits with his family on his country estate, Yasnaya Polyana. The author of *War and Peace* had, since the 1870s, adopted a radical doctrine of Christian love.

youths were able to exchange ideas and information, and study the work of revolutionary thinkers, such as the Germans Karl Marx and Friedrich Engels. Russian students had a habit of erupting in noisy demonstrations. In March 1901, thousands of students across Russia reacted against government efforts to impose new, restrictive regulations. They were also showing their displeasure at the excommunication of one of the great Russian heroes, the novelist Count Leo Tolstoy.

Tolstoy had reached his literary apogee three decades earlier with the publication of *War and Peace* (1869) and *Anna Karenina* (1876). After 1876 he had undergone a spiritual transformation, espousing nonviolent politics, the renunciation of wealth and a vehement dislike of government institutions and organised religion. His book *What I Believe*, which was published in 1884, proved immensely influential, helping to

NICHOLAS AND ALEXANDRA

Nicholas II's cousin, Wilhelm II of Germany, perhaps summed him up with the most damning accuracy: 'The Tsar is not treacherous, but he is weak. Weakness is not treachery, but it fulfils all its functions.' In 1894, at the age of 26, Nicholas succeeded to the imperial throne. He had inherited a position of supreme power, and almost god-like status in the eyes of most of Russia's peasant population – but for all that, he had had very little education in the affairs of state. His overriding ambition was to preserve unchanged the tsar's role.

In the year of his accession, Nicholas married Alexandra Feodorovna, daughter of the Duke of Hesse-Darmstadt and granddaughter of Queen Victoria. It was an arranged marriage, but the couple showed a touching devotion to each other and were soon graced by four daughters. The tsar, shy and awkward in company, took refuge in the pleasures of family life. In 1904 the tsarina gave birth to a son, Alexis. Tragically, Alexis had inherited the genetic flaw of haemophilia. Since the slightest injury could be life-threatening, he led a dismal childhood, under constant surveillance.

In 1907 his mother began to put her faith in Grigori Yefimovich Rasputin, a disreputable 'holy' man whose alleged healing powers appeared to transform Alexis's outlook. When Nicholas went off to take command of the Russian troops in Europe at the start of the First World War, he left the affairs of state in the hands of Alexandra. The government was soon dominated by Rasputin and his cronies. Rasputin was assassinated by monarchists in 1916, and the tsar returned from the front. But it was too late. In 1917 the Russian Revolution swept the Romanovs from power, and the following year the royal family was executed in a shabby cellar in Ekaterinburg.

TSAR ON A BOX A portrait of Nicholas II adorns a jewelled enamel box by Fabergé.

SINISTER INFLUENCE Rasputin sits among court ladies. His drunken rampages in St Petersburg were widely known, though the Tsarina refused to believe such tales.

mould, for example, the political philosophy of Mahatma Gandhi.

Tolstoy commanded great respect – even from the peasant's cottage on his estate, to which he retired in the latter years of his life. His fame protected him from the government interference that was normally accorded to radical thinkers. Alexy Suvorin, one of Russia's most influential newspaper owners, commented in his diary: 'We have two Tsars: Nicholas II and Leo Tolstoy.

Which of the two is more powerful? Nicholas cannot do anything with Tolstoy, he cannot share his throne, whereas Tolstoy is undoubtedly shaking the throne of Nicholas and his dynasty.'

In 1900, however, Tolstoy published his provocative novel *Resurrection*. The story of a nobleman who seduces a young girl who is then reduced to prostitution, its narrative included attacks not only on Russia's system of justice, but also on the workings of the

1910 Tolstoy dies

1911 Assassination of Stolypin

1912 Lena River massacre

Russian Orthodox Church. As a result, the Church – a conservative organisation closely allied to the state – excommunicated Tolstoy. Students, rising to his cause in St Petersburg in March 1901, invaded Kazan Cathedral and called for the overthrow of the tsar, while in Moscow they mounted barricades, and a state of siege was declared before troops restored order.

Talk of revolution

Russia had a long tradition of political violence, which would bubble up again, still more strongly, in 1905. Its origins lay in a succession of revolutionary movements moulded in the pressure cooker of frustrated ambitions. In the 1870s the Populist Movement had been responsible for widespread unrest, but was discredited by the acts of terrorism of its

BLOODIED HAND A radical journal makes its comment (top) on tsarist repression by reproducing an imperial decree with a red-stained palm print over it. Demonstrators (above) march through Moscow in 1905.

extreme wing and the assassination of Tsar Alexander II, which heralded a period of concerted repression. The Populist tendency re-emerged as the Social Revolutionary Party in the 1890s, while the Social Democrats pursued a more orderly Marxist programme and attracted a broader range of activists. Both, however, came under the suspicion of the secret police.

One route to reform lay in worker solidarity. With growing industrialisation came increased demands for worker representation. But trade unions had to be organised clandestinely: the penalty for those caught trying to do so was usually a spell in prison and then several years of exile in Siberia. Nonetheless, industrial workers did organise, and the strike became an increasingly widespread method of showing dissatisfaction. In 1902 and 1903, the Russian Empire was rocked by a wave of strikes and civil unrest, at Rostov-on-Don, Odessa, Baku and other industrial cities. It was a sign of things to come.

Many of the most influential socialist agitators, however, were either already in Siberia or living in exile in Europe. These included Georgi Plekhanov, the founder of the Social Democrats; Vladimir Ilich Ulyanov, otherwise known as Lenin; and Leon Trotsky.

Lenin had left Russia in 1900, having spent three years in exile in Siberia. The son of highly cultivated middle-class parents – his father was a schools' inspector – he had studied law in St Petersburg, where he had been arrested for trying to set up an underground newspaper. His hardheaded radicalism could be traced back to his youth: in 1887 his elder brother Alexander, a zoology student, had been executed for his part in a bomb plot to assassinate Tsar Alexander III. Not only did this instil a searing resentment against the Russian authorities in the young Lenin, it also made him virtually unemployable by association.

Lenin took up the cause of Marxism, and lived and breathed radical politics. In exile he wrote a highly influential pamphlet called *What is to be Done?* (1902) and edited several radical newspapers, including *Iskra* (*The Spark*).

Lenin was convinced that the only way forward lay, not in evolutionary political change, but in the violent overthrow of the government to usher in the rule of the proletariat. In 1903 a Congress of Social Democrats was organised to hammer out future strategy.

DEATH STALKS THE BARRICADES
The caricaturist Boris Kustodiev offers his judgment (above) of the revolutionary events of 1905 in *Zhupel* (*Bugbear*), one of many satirical journals that flourished briefly during 1905. Below: Protesters man the barricades in St Petersburg, also in 1905.

SECRET POLICE Bowler-hatted members of the tsarist secret police pose, unusually, for the camera. They kept files on radicals, such as the writer Maxim Gorky (above).

It began in a run-down flour mill in Brussels, watched closely by secret agents of both the Russian and Belgian governments. When two delegates were arrested and expelled from Belgium, the congress moved to London.

Through a strained series of meetings, Lenin engineered a split between his more radical, uncompromising Bolsheviks and the Mensheviks, who proposed a more graduated attitude towards revolutionary change. The congress voted in favour of the Bolshevik approach, which also won the backing of figures such as the hugely successful playwright and novelist Maxim Gorky. However, the split caused some resentment. The Social Democrats' founder, Plekhanov, sided with Yuly Martov, leader of the Mensheviks, and managed to induce Lenin's resignation from *Iskra*. For a while, Lenin seemed to have succeeded, only to be sidelined.

Lighting the fuse

During 1904 Russia continued to be convulsed by strikes and student unrest. In January 1905 strikes involving 75 000 workers erupted across the country. A leading figure in the St Petersburg strikes was a young Orthodox priest called Georgi Gapon.

Father Gapon illustrates the degree to which ordinary people had been goaded into radical action. He was not a revolutionary, in that he did not believe in the violent overthrow of the government. Rather, he believed that the tsar was being shielded from the realities of Russian life by his ministers, and that he might be persuaded to introduce reforms if he could be exposed to the pleading of his loyal people.

To this end, on Sunday, January 22, Gapon, dressed in his priestly robes, led a peaceable demonstration of workers and their families through the streets of St Petersburg towards the tsar's residence, the superb Winter Palace. Singing patriotic songs, they carried flags, icons and portraits of their 'Little Father', the tsar. They hoped to present him with a petition asking, among other things, for a government elected on the basis of universal suffrage, an eight-hour working day, the separation of the Church from the State, and an amnesty for political prisoners. It included the desperate plea, written in archaic language: 'If thou refusest to hear our supplications, we shall die here in this square before the palace.'

That is, in effect, what happened. As they approached the palace, the demonstrators found their way blocked by Cossacks, loyal peasant troops from the Ukraine. Suddenly, without warning, the troops opened fire on the crowd, killing between 50 and 1000 people (estimates vary widely), and wounding many others.

This attack on unarmed and essentially good-willed demonstrators caused widespread indignation. The effect of 'Bloody Sunday' was to galvanise the opposition; more significantly, it demonstrated to the peasantry and to many in the armed forces – who had previously remained largely loyal to the tsar – that the 'Little Father' did not have his children's interests at heart after all. The tsar had clearly been in the enemy camp all the time.

Faced with a massive revolt, the tsar began to offer reforms, promising belatedly an enquiry into people's living conditions. But it was an inadequate response to the situation. Tension mounted as a wave of demonstrations followed Bloody Sunday. On February 17,

BATTLESHIP POTEMKIN In June 1905, mutineers on the *Potemkin*, Russia's most powerful battleship in the Black Sea, threw most of their officers overboard and raised the red flag.

BLOODY SUNDAY

A correspondent from the *Manchester Guardian* was in St Petersburg on Sunday, January 22, the fateful day that triggered the 1905 revolution. His report, which appeared on January 28, gives some indication of the menacing atmosphere and the shock of the tragic turn of events:

'The morning was very fine; the sun shone from a sky of pale blue in which there were faint traces of cloud. There was a bracing frost, and a light breeze blew from the north-west . . . I went out at about half-past eleven with Mr Dillon, the correspondent of the *Daily Telegraph*. . . .

'Down the Kromberg prospect, we suddenly came face to face with a black mass of people who were marching slowly along towards the garden. We watched them go by. The workers were marching to the Tsar to demand their rights, a grand and moving spectacle. They walked along with a shambling gait and smiled awkwardly at the bystanders, as though their sudden and unaccustomed conspicuousness made them shy. . . .

'We suddenly met a band of Cossacks on foot. A bugle rang out. We turned swiftly back and followed the fleeing crowd. By this time the workers' procession had entered the garden and was within 200 yards [182 m] of the Cossacks. Suddenly there was a rattle of rifles, one volley, followed by a second, and a third and a fourth; an interval of silence and then we heard the shouts and cries. We learned afterwards that several were killed or wounded.'

Grand Duke Sergei, the tsar's uncle and a key adviser, was assassinated – blown up by a nail bomb dropped into his lap as he sat in his carriage close to the gates of the Kremlin in Moscow. Evidence that the tsar was truly out of touch can be seen in his reaction to news of the killing: 'How can that be?' he asked in dismay. 'Everything is so quiet – the strikes are ceasing. The excitement is subsiding. Whatever do they want?'

As reports reached western Russia of the defeat by the Japanese at Mukden in March, and the annihilation of the Baltic Fleet at Tshushima in May, there were more strikes, assassinations and demonstrations, and a growing wave of violent nationalist rebellions in non-Russian parts of the empire – in Poland, Latvia, Georgia, Finland and Armenia. Rioting had now also spread outside the cities: peasants, desperate for food and settling old grievances, looted and set fire to country manor houses.

Bit by bit, concessions were squeezed out of the tsar, but at the same time instructions were issued to the Cossacks and other security forces to show no mercy in suppressing insurrection. In June, even the loyalty of the armed services came into doubt. Off the port of Odessa, a city in the grip of a general strike, the crew of the battleship *Potemkin* rose up in mutiny. A week later 50 000 loyal troops restored order in Odessa at the cost of 6000 lives, while the crew of the *Potemkin* sought sanctuary in Romania.

In August 1905 the tsar announced that he would agree to a parliament of elected representatives, the Duma, meaning 'deliberation'. This suggested a move towards constitutional monarchy. But the opposition remained unimpressed: it was to be only a consultative body. The tsar retained the power to dissolve it, and would be under no obligation to carry out its recommendations.

A new crisis loomed. During the autumn of 1905, Russia was threatened by famine. Towards the end of October, workers in St Petersburg organised a Soviet (council or parliament) under the leadership of Leon Trotsky. One of its first acts was to call a general strike: on October 30 Russia came to a standstill as 1.5 million workers closed factories, railways, telegraph offices, hospitals and schools. It was an impressive show of force, and of the St Petersburg Soviet's authority.

The premier of the tsar's council of ministers, Count Sergei Witte, sensing impending

LEON TROTSKY: 'THE YOUNG EAGLE'

For 50 days in 1905, Leon Trotsky had a foretaste of real power. While the government floundered, Trotsky headed the St Petersburg Soviet of Workers' Deputies, coordinating the strikes, overseeing the distribution of supplies, and delivering many of the services normally performed by government.

Trotsky was just 26 years old, but he was already a seasoned revolutionary. Born Lev Davydovich Bronstein in 1879, the son of a Jewish farmer from the Ukraine, he became an activist while still a teenager. He was arrested in 1898 for trying to promote the South Russia Workers' Union, and spent two years in prison in Odessa. He was then exiled to Siberia, where he was accompanied by Alexandra Lvovna, a fellow activist whom he had married in prison. Together they raised two infants. In 1902, with Alexandra's encouragement, he escaped in a haywagon. In southern Russia he was enthusiastically welcomed by fellow revolutionaries and dubbed 'the Young Eagle'. In fact, Lev had taken another name: he had a counterfeit passport into which he inserted an alias – Trotsky, the name of his jailer in Odessa.

Trotsky ended up with Lenin in London, although at the 1903 Congress, he sided not with Lenin but with the Mensheviks, and was critical of Lenin's dictatorial style. He was one of the first activists to return to Russia in 1905. When the revolution collapsed, Trotsky was arrested and sentenced to indefinite exile to Siberia – but he escaped from a train station on the way, and travelled to Europe. Over the following years, he moved from city to city – Vienna, Berlin, Zürich, Belgrade, Paris, Madrid – musing on the failures of 1905 and developing a theory of 'permanent revolution', which coincided increasingly with Lenin's Bolshevism. He headed back to Russia during the crisis of 1917, and assisted Lenin in bringing about the October Revolution. In the civil war (1918-22), he played a key role as Commissar for War. However, in the power struggle that followed the death of Lenin in 1924, Trotsky was ousted in favour of Stalin. He was dismissed from the party in 1927, and in 1929 exiled from the USSR. Even in exile, Trotsky's alternative strategy for Communism was perceived as a threat, and he was murdered with an ice pick by a Stalinist agent in Mexico in 1940.

REVOLUTIONARY In London, Trotsky, shown here with his wife, helped Lenin to edit *Iskra, 'The Spark'*.

THE WRECKAGE Officials gather at Stolypin's villa after it had been shattered by a bomb in August 1906. The blast killed 30 people, including Stolypin's daughter.

disaster, wrung more concessions from the tsar, who issued an *Imperial Manifesto* promising 'freedom of conscience, speech, assembly and association', and extended the power of the proposed Duma. He also granted amnesty to all political prisoners.

But peace was not to be won so cheaply. In November, troops and sailors mutinied at the key strategic port of Kronstadt on the Baltic coast and at Vladivostok. In the same month, the authorities declared martial law in Poland and closed all Russian universities. A week of violent confrontation between troops and demonstrators in Moscow brought the year to a close, at the cost of 1000 lives. It also marked the beginnings of a military clamp-down, through which the tsar's control was gradually restored. By April 1906 the events in the year since Bloody Sunday had claimed 15 000 lives and the authorities had made 70 000 arrests.

Lenin had remained outside Russia until November 1905, vainly trying to send arms to the insurgents. He later looked back on the events of that year as 'a bourgeois revolution achieved by proletarian means': in other words, its aims had been to achieve a Western-style parliamentary democracy – a bourgeois aspiration. It reconfirmed his conviction that violent revolution at the chosen moment, not evolution, was needed to achieve socialism. He settled in Switzerland in 1907, awaiting that moment.

The Duma

Elections for the Duma took place in April 1906, and the new parliament was inaugurated on May 10, amid much fanfare. Rather to the tsar's surprise, the peasants had voted for progressives, not conservatives, and almost immediately the parliament ran into trouble, as the delegates pressed the tsar for an amnesty for political prisoners. A period of tetchy give-and-take ensued, as the tsar tried to come to terms with this new infringement of his powers. He dismissed Witte as premier,

SIBERIAN EXILE Criminals and political dissidents alike were dispatched to Siberia. Many lived in relative comfort, though with strict limits to their freedom of movement.

and installed Piotr Arkadevich Stolypin, a hardliner with a reputation for brutal suppression of insurrection. The new prime minister tried to maintain a balance. Hundreds were executed under new powers granted to courts-martial, but he also understood the necessity of pushing through reform. On the other hand, he found the Duma too radical to work with, and it was dissolved after just 73 days. Some 200 of the delegates tried to continue its work in Finland, but their power leeched away, as Russia settled down, soothed by the prospect of reform under Stolypin, and as thousands of radical dissidents were exiled to Siberia.

There was also a vicious right-wing backlash. The Jews suddenly came under attack, notably in southern Russia and in the Baltic region, where large Jewish populations were concentrated. Thousands died in pogroms in Odessa, Bialystok and elsewhere – victims of anti-Semitism, which the police did little to discourage. Underlying these attacks was the widespread suspicion that the Jews were instigators of the revolutionary unrest. This assumption grossly overstated the case, though it was true that many Jewish intellectuals had been driven towards revolutionary politics by the restrictions imposed on them. Trotsky and Martov, for instance, both came from Jewish families.

Isolated terrorist attacks and assassinations continued. On August 25, 1906, a bomb blast wrecked Stolypin's home, though

BOLSHEVIKS, MENSHEVIKS

At the Congress of Social Democrats, or 'Second International', held in London in 1903, Lenin argued that the only way forward was to create a centralised party run by a core of dedicated, professional revolutionaries, whose aim would be to bring about the dictatorship of the proletariat, by whatever means. His opponents, led by Martov, proposed a more evolutionary approach, and a more relaxed party structure. In the debate, the charismatic rhetoric of Lenin proved persuasive. He won the majority, and his side took the name *Bolsheviki* (meaning the majority), while Martov's supporters accepted the label *Mensheviki* (the minority).

he survived. Elections for a new Duma took place in February 1907, but again produced a comparatively radical assembly which was dissolved after 102 days, amid threats to arrest Socialist deputies for incitement to violence. It was only with the third Duma, opened in November 1907, that Stolypin, through judicious gerrymandering, managed to achieve an essentially conservative and suitably compliant assembly.

The eye of the storm

In the period after the 1905 revolution, the middle classes drifted away from radical politics. Russia again began to demonstrate its huge economic potential, and another boom took place, dented only by a serious famine in April 1907. Many of the wealthy turned their attention to cultural pursuits, looking westwards towards Europe. It was during this period that the Ballets Russes was launched to rapturous success in Paris. Russian art collectors also began to amass a wealth of contemporary European art; the Moscow-based merchant Sergei Shchukin, for example, was one of Matisse's main patrons.

As Stolypin put it in 1909: 'Give the State 20 years of internal and external peace, and you will not recognise Russia.' But time was not in Stolypin's gift. His long-term plan was to reform the distribution of agricultural

DEATH ON THE GOLD FIELD Strike led to massacre on the River Lena. During the unrest of 1912, 270 striking gold-workers were mown down by infantry led by an officer who had been present at the Bloody Sunday massacre.

land to create a class of rich landowning peasants, who could be relied upon to vote for conservative candidates at the Duma. However, this policy also produced a vast class of landless peasants who drifted towards the towns. By 1911, radical discontent was growing once more. Stolypin – popular with neither the left nor the right – resigned in March 1911, and in September, at the age of 49, he was assassinated at the Kiev Opera, in full view of the tsar and two of his daughters. Stolypin had given the tsar a respite of no more than six years.

The following year, Russia was hit by a wave of strikes. In the gold fields on the River Lena in Siberia, soldiers massacred 270 strikers demonstrating against the arrest of their leader. Half a million workers came out on strike on May Day that year. Social unrest continued; by 1914 it had surpassed even the fever pitch of 1905.

In contrast to the tsar, the revolutionaries had not failed to learn the lessons of this troubled era. In 1917 they were to drive these lessons home.

FIGHTING FOR FREEDOM

REVOLT WAS A CONSTANT THREAT IN EUROPEAN COLONIES OVERSEAS, AS LOCAL FRUSTRATIONS CONVERGED WITH NATIONALIST ASPIRATIONS

Lord Curzon, Viceroy of India from 1899 to 1905, had no doubt about the subcontinent's importance to Britain. 'It is only when you get to see and realise what India really is – that she is the strength and greatness of England – it is only then that you feel that every nerve a man may strain, every energy he may put forward cannot be devoted to a nobler purpose than keeping tight the cords that hold India to ourselves.' Unless, of course, that man happened to be one of the 250 million Indians. Curzon was the embodiment of the arrogance of the European colonial powers: any question that India might be accorded autonomy or self-rule was simply not on his agenda. To its British rulers in 1900, it seemed that India would be – and should be – for ever British.

But the seeds of change had already been sown. For some decades the British had been encouraging aspiring Indians to go to Britain for university and professional training, as lawyers, doctors, administrators – a policy which coincided with Britain's self-image as a paternalistic colonial power. Education in Britain also, however, brought exposure to radical politics which questioned the basis of colonialism. Educated Indians often returned home with revised ideas about equality, liberty and self-rule, lending informed political skills to the kind of nationalistic fervour that had lain dormant since the eruption of the Indian Mutiny of 1857-8.

The British in India lived in the shadow of the mutiny – effectively a war of independence – in which thousands had died amid scenes of the utmost brutality perpetrated by both sides. They remained nervous and insular, constantly alert to any hint of sedition. Consequently, when the Indian National Congress Party – founded in 1885 to promote reform – began to press its case for self-rule

RUNNING THE RAJ On his rounds near Madras, a British district magistrate (below, seated) assesses a claim for a reward for killing a cheetah. Elsewhere, the British ruled through local princes, such as the Maharajah of Patiala, photographed (right) with Lord Curzon.

1902 The Ovimbundu kingdoms rebel against the Portuguese in Angola

1905 Bengal is partitioned The Maji-Maji Rebellion begins in Tanganyika

1906 The Muslim League is founded in India

1907 Restrictions on non-whites in Transvaal

continued on page 78

UNFAVOURABLE COMPARISON

Britain was running India 'like the Tsar runs Russia', commented the British Labour MP Keir Hardie as a result of a visit there in 1907. Riots broke out in Calcutta in early October that year, and many blamed them on what they saw as Hardie's inflammatory remarks.

at the turn of the century, the British kept it under a watchful and suspicious eye.

While moderates in the Congress contemplated a slow struggle, extremists launched into open revolt. Violent incidents pepper the decade. Police shot dead 27 rioters at Vizagapatam in 1900; widespread riots in Punjab marked the 50th anniversary of the Indian Mutiny in 1907; two bombs were thrown at Lord Minto, Curzon's successor as Viceroy, in a failed assassination attempt in 1909. The next viceroy, Lord Hardinge, narrowly escaped assassination when a bomb exploded inside his howdah (the canopied seat on the back of an elephant) during the durbar of 1912 to celebrate the transfer of capital status from Calcutta to New Delhi. While on the one hand the British promised reforms and an extension of democracy, on the other they tightened the laws on sedition, increased the penalties for those found guilty of it, and gradually clamped down on gatherings of any kind.

The situation was further complicated by Hindu-Muslim rivalries, which often flared up in violence. The British partitioned Bengal along Hindu and Muslim lines in 1905, which both fuelled nationalist resentment and helped to foster the creation of the Muslim League in 1906. This left the Congress as a predominantly Hindu body whose activities were eclipsed by Hindu extremists such as Bal Gangadhar Tilak, who ran a terrorist campaign in Maharashtra from 1905 to 1909.

Nationalism and revolt

This general pattern was emulated around the globe. While the imperial powers maintained their high-handed approach to colonial rule, the local educated elite within the colonies pursued a nationalist political agenda, and extremists made life precarious for Europeans

NEAR MISS Lord Hardinge of Penshurst, Viceroy of India, was wounded when a bomb was thrown into his howdah during his state entry into Delhi on December 23, 1912. An attendant was killed.

posted there. The Dutch in the Netherlands East Indies (now Indonesia) faced a series of costly revolts: insurgents in Aceh, on the northern tip of Sumatra, held them at bay until 1908 and continued their struggle for autonomy throughout the remaining years of Dutch occupation; disturbances in north central Java and a series of strikes organised by Islamic labour unions coalesced into an outbreak of serious revolts in 1914. Meanwhile, nationalist sentiment was channelled into embryonic political movements. The first was Budi Utomo (High Endeavour), founded in 1908; of greater lasting significance was Sarekat Islam (Islamic Association), founded in 1912, initially to protect the interests of the Indonesian textile trade against the

1912 The Islamic Association is founded in the Dutch East Indies (Indonesia). The South African National Congress (later the ANC) is founded

THE DELHI DURBAR OF 1903

It was billed as 'the biggest show that India will ever have had'. On December 29, 1902, before a crowd of a million, a parade stretching 3 miles (5 km) passed through Delhi – marching bands, soldiers in full and exotic costume, bejewelled maharajas and their retinues, horse-drawn carriages of visiting dignitaries. At the culmination of the parade came the viceroy, Lord Curzon, and his wife, carried in a magnificent howdah on the back of an elephant, followed by another equally resplendent elephant bearing the king's brother, the Duke of Connaught. This state entry marked the opening of the festivities around the Coronation Durbar: the public proclamation of the new king-emperor, Edward VII.

The durbar itself took place on the plains outside Delhi on January 1, 1903. From a red-velvet throne set on a dais, Curzon read the proclamation before a crowd of 16 000 invited guests, including all the ruling Indian princes, as well as British top brass and foreign dignitaries. On either side of this event was a fortnight of military parades, sports matches, galas and balls, exhibitions and firework displays. The guests and their attendants, numbering 150 000, were accommodated in 70 specially erected luxury camps, equipped with running water, lighting and telephones.

Over the last decades of the 19th century, the British had gradually taken over and surpassed the spectacular rituals of India's former Mughal emperors. In retrospect, the Coronation Durbar – the word was borrowed from the Mughal for a royal reception – can be seen as the crowning spectacle of this imperial pomp. Lord Curzon justified its huge expense by asserting its political value in, he claimed, underpinning the supremacy of Britain as colonial ruler. He personally organised the durbar down to the last detail, and took the limelight. He saw it as a triumph; others, in Britain as in India, took a different view. 'A mere piece of empty pageantry', commented the *Manchester Guardian*. Correspondents drew attention to the contrast between the lavishness of the durbar and the poverty of most of the Indian population excluded from it, many of whom had just suffered a major famine.

Another durbar was held in 1911 to mark the coronation of George V. In this case, the king-emperor himself attended, giving the event a greater stature. Just as spectacular, it received rather less trumpeting, as the British took a more considered view of the impression they made.

BY INVITATION ONLY In a carefully orchestrated display of rank and pomp, leading dignitaries arrived at the 1903 Delhi Durbar in a magnificent procession of richly apparelled elephants.

Chinese, but later becoming the focus of nationalist aspirations. By 1917 it had 800 000 members. In British-occupied Burma, nationalist aspirations focused on the Young Men's Buddhist Association, founded by London-trained lawyers in 1906.

The French in Indochina (now Vietnam, Laos and Cambodia) faced a series of minor revolts and the ever-present threat of guerrilla attack. There were concerted outbreaks of terrorism in Hanoi and Hue in 1906-8, while the insurgency campaign in Annam (northern Vietnam) led by De Tham lasted until 1913. That same year, the nationalist opposition set up the Viet Nam Quang Phuc Hoi (Association for the Restoration of Vietnam). In Tunisia, convulsed by Islamic revolts against French occupation since 1883, opposition formed under the banner of Tunis al-Fatat (Young Tunisian Party), a forerunner of Destour, the party which would eventually lead the country to independence in 1956.

THE GOOD LIFE With strict divisions between rulers and ruled, a Frenchman in Indochina (below) would expect to preserve his strength by using the muscle power of a 'coolie'.

LIFE FOR THE BAD Colonialism claimed to bring the benefits of European justice. But prisoners in French Indochina (above) show that some local traditions were preserved.

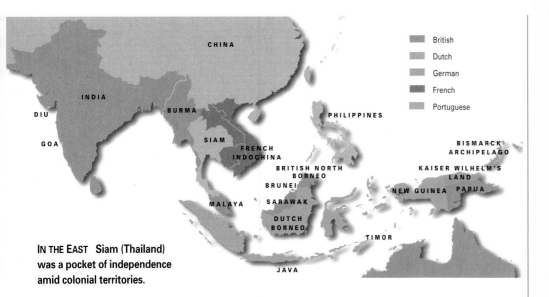

IN THE EAST **Siam (Thailand) was a pocket of independence amid colonial territories.**

British
Dutch
German
French
Portuguese

TRAGEDY IN BALI

INDONESIAN HEROINE Raden Adjeng Kartini was an eloquent critic of Dutch colonial rule.

For three centuries Bali had been a Hindu enclave in Muslim Indonesia. In September 1906, troops of the KNIL (Royal Nether-lands East Indies Army) landed at Sanur on its south coast and marched inland to Denpasar, capital of the Rajah of Badung. Until then the Dutch had left Bali's Hindu rajahs alone, but incidents such as a dispute over salvage rights had prompted them into action. The troops were greeted by silence, pierced only by the beat of a wooden *kulkul*, the sig-nal drum. Then the gates of the *puri*, the royal palace, were thrown open and 600 members of the court poured forth – bejewelled men, women and children dressed in white – led by the rajah on a lit-ter. He halted in front of the troops. A priest stepped forward. Suddenly he plunged a sacred dagger (*kris*) into the rajah's heart. The other Balinese followed suit, stabbing their children and themselves with *krises*, or rushing at the Dutch, forcing them to open fire. It was a massacre. The Rajah of Badung had car-ried out a *puputan* (a ritual mass suicide) in the face of overwhelming odds. Before the Dutch could claim Bali as theirs, there was another *puputan* at Pemecutan, and the Rajah of Tabanan and his son committed suicide. Two years later, a dispute at Klungkung led to another *puputan*. Shocked and shamed by these events, the Dutch introduced a new kid-glove approach to Bali termed 'ethical colo-nialism', under which the culture and way of life of the Balinese was respected and allowed to thrive.

The USA also had to contend with the dilemmas of colonial rule. In 1898, during the Spanish-American War, it had invited the assistance of Filipino insurgents led by Emilio Aguinaldo, who had fought against Spanish colonial rule. However, after the war ended, the insurgents found themselves excluded from Manila and soon realised that they were going to play no part in governing their country: they had fought the Spanish only to usher in colonialism under another flag. Aguinaldo took to the hills once more and continued the struggle until his capture in 1901, by which time his rebellion had cost the lives of 4200 Americans.

The abuses of the imperial powers did not go unnoticed by the more liberal or radical citizens in the colonial homelands. The doc-trines of colonialism were widely questioned, and home support for colonial actions abroad could never be taken for granted. One of the heroines of modern Indonesia was Raden Adjeng Kartini, the daughter of a noble family, who corresponded with Dutch liberals, expressing her resentment of discrimination, her desire for equal access to Western knowl-edge, and the need for reform. She died in childbirth in 1904 aged just 25, but her letters, published in 1911, had a considerable impact on colonial sensibilities in the Netherlands, and on the educated public in Asia.

Africa: a case apart

By and large, the colonial powers preferred to govern by indirect rule – by co-opting the support of local rulers, leaving their hierar-chies intact. The British had used indirect rule successfully in India, governing where possible through local princes. Africa, which had been subjected to a ruthless colonial scramble since the 1880s, presented a more complex quilt of possibilities, but indirect rule remained a viable option in many cases.

A key figure in shaping the British policy of indirect rule in Africa was Frederick Lugard. In the 1890s, representing the British East Africa Company, he had negoti-ated a mutually beneficial treaty with the Kabaka (king) of Buganda; under a 1900 agreement with the British, hammered out by the Kabaka's able chief minister Apolo Kaggwa, Buganda secured a position of political power and a degree of autonomy. Lugard further refined his doctrine of indi-rect rule when governor of Northern Nigeria in 1900-6 and again in 1912-14.

Indirect rule promised a com-paratively smooth and low-cost transition to a colonial regime. However, it was often achieved by meddling with inter-tribal rivalries – the old imperial princi-ple of 'divide and rule' – and deep-seated resentments were caused when unpopular minori-ties were given ascendancy by the colonial authorities.

Indirect rule was not always an option – especially when the colonists were confronted by out-and-out rebellion. Many tribes with a tradition of martial honour simply refused to be 'pacified'. Elsewhere, the gradual encroachment of white settlers

MASS SUICIDE **Bodies of the nobility of Denpasar surround the empty litter of the dead rajah.**

on traditional tribal lands made eventual hostilities inevitable. This occurred notably in eastern and southern Africa, where the savannah promised vast expanses of potential farmlands. The disruption of traditional trade links caused resentment – particularly with the rapid development of railways which began to thread deep inland after 1900.

Barely a year passed without a major revolt. In 1902-3, the Ovimbundu kingdoms rose up against the Portuguese in Angola. In 1905 a two-year revolt broke out against the Germans in Tanganyika (now Tanzania); it was known as the Maji-Maji Rebellion because it centred on a religious cult that distributed to its followers a potion called *maji*, said to act as a shield against bullets. The French faced many revolts in their diverse territories: a rising in Madagascar lasted six years to 1904; resistance by the Baule people

MEETING OF CULTURES The wives of this Nigerian potentate have adopted the dress of wealthy Europeans. Many African leaders displayed the trappings of Western power.

COLONIALISM UNDER ATTACK An illustration from the French publication *Le Petit Journal* depicts Herero warriors attacking a German garrison in Southwest Africa.

in Côte d'Ivoire continued until 1908; and Islamic revolts in Tunisia occurred throughout the period.

Some of the most shocking acts of oppression took place in German Southwest Africa (now Namibia). The Herero and Nama people had reached a measure of accommodation with German settlers and traders through a series of treaties, but these were enforced one-sidedly, and the Herero and Nama began to suffer a chain of indignities, including the confiscation of cattle and the loss of access to watering places. In January 1904, driven to despair, the Herero launched a revolt and killed 123 German settlers near Okahandja; however, English and Dutch missionaries and virtually all German women and children were spared.

The German response was led by General von Trotha, who was inclined to make remarks such as 'I know these African tribes. They are all the same. They respect nothing but force. To exercise this force with brute terror and even with ferocity was and is my policy. I wipe out

– were shot or expired of thirst in the desert. Meanwhile, von Trotha rounded up 17 000 outlying Herero and Nama (also in revolt) and placed them in crude concentration camps, where nearly half of them died. The revolts were suppressed, but at enormous cost. In 1904 there were 80 000 Herero and 20 000 Nama; by 1911 there were just 15 000 Herero and 10 000 Nama.

Forced labour

As Africa offered comparatively few possibilities for white settlement, the colonies there were seen primarily as a source of products and raw materials. Colonial governments reflected this in their structure: the number of administrators was directly related to the revenue accrued by the colony. This is why, in poorer colonies, officials were often spread very thinly, with vast areas of jurisdiction. In principle, only those colonies which produced a surplus could afford to invest in welfare and infrastructure projects, such as schools and medical facilities, beyond those provided by the missionaries.

Much of the revenue came from taxation, usually in the form of a poll tax. Africans were obliged to pay an annual sum of money to the authorities, or could provide labour instead. In French colonies, this amounted to some 12 days' work a year; in some British colonies, it amounted to two months a year. This forced labour often came on top of the number of days' labour which an individual owed his own chief or employer.

SCRAMBLE FOR AFRICA **By 1913 the whole of Africa, apart from Liberia and Ethiopia, had been seized by European colonial powers.**

Legend:
- British
- German
- French
- Portuguese
- Belgian
- Spanish
- Italian
- Anglo-Egyptian
- Independent

rebellious tribes with streams of blood and streams of money. Only by sowing in this way can anything new be grown, anything that is stable.'

However, von Trotha soon realised that, despite such comments, the Herero – armed with rifles traded by German merchants – were a force to be reckoned with. Avoiding pitched battles, von Trotha's troops all but surrounded the Herero stronghold, leaving one escape route into the desert. He also stationed troops at the water holes in the desert, with instructions to fire on any Herero who approached. In this operation countless Herero – men, women and children

EXPORT EARNERS **The tobacco farms of South Africa were typical of the drive to develop export-oriented economies. Such labour-intensive plantation crops could be raised successfully only if labour was cheap.**

THE ERUPTION OF MONT PELÉE

The clocks stopped at 7.50 am on May 8, 1902, in Saint-Pierre on Martinique. They melted beneath a volcanic heatwave reaching 815°C (1500°F), which raced down the flanks of the volcano Mont Pelée and engulfed the town, baking alive a population of 36 000. In five minutes, the 'Paris of the West Indies' – an elegant port of boulevards, mansions, government offices, a theatre and botanical gardens – was devastated.

Mont Pelée had been sending out warnings of its increased activity for a year. By early 1902, its rumblings began to disturb the citizens of Saint-Pierre. But an election was due and, concerned that their vote might dwindle, the governor of Martinique and the mayor of Saint-Pierre issued messages of reassurance. In April the mulatto quarter was ominously invaded by highly poisonous fer-de-lance snakes, driven out of vents on the mountainside: 50 people, and hundreds of domestic animals, died of bites. Election day, May 8, dawned. A fisherman out at sea described what he witnessed: 'We saw in the north a cloud that was red, red, red. There were explosions as of cannons. Soon all the sky was in flames. A great wave came and left fish thrashing on the sand. Then, darkness; in full day it was night. We could see nothing. All the fishermen cried out. "It is the end of the world," they screamed. "What have we done?" '

There were just three survivors: a shoemaker, a girl who had fled to a coastal cave and a prisoner called Sylbaris. Protected by the walls of his small underground cell, Sylbaris suffered burns, but lived to be dug out three days later. He was speedily pardoned, and spent the rest of his life as a curiosity, travelling the USA with the Barnum & Bailey Circus, and exhibiting himself in a replica of his Saint-Pierre cell.

INSTANT DESTRUCTION   Skeletal outlines of buildings are all that remain of Saint-Pierre (below). Auguste Sylbaris (left) survived, thanks to thick jailhouse walls.

The unpleasant job of tax collection was usually handed to locally recruited agents, who became as much the objects of hate as their European bosses. Poll tax, raised by all the colonial powers, was the direct cause of several revolts. The French in Côte d'Ivoire faced a series of poll tax rebellions.

The exploitation of raw materials was largely handled by private companies, and swathes of Africa were handed over by the colonial powers to commercial enterprises. The British South Africa Company ran a concession covering what is now Zambia until the territory was taken over by the British government (as Northern Rhodesia) in 1924. French Equatorial Africa (now Chad, Gabon, the Central African Republic and Congo) was similarly leased out in 30 year concessions; in the German Cameroons, concessions were offered for eternity. In such decisions lay the fate of millions of Africans.

These companies had exclusive rights to land, raw materials and labour in their area, and operated with virtual autonomy. The system was open to abuse, particularly in equatorial Africa. The Congo Free State – so called because its doors were open to virtually any European company which wished to exploit it – was the personal fiefdom of the Belgian king, Leopold II. Its vast area was assigned to commercial companies, which operated regimes of ruthless exploitation, mainly to extract ivory and rubber – now, with the demand for motor-car tyres, an increasingly valuable commodity. Although Leopold had announced the abolition of slavery in the 1890s, most of his subjects in Africa remained in conditions of virtual slavery under the companies, enforced by whippings, mutilation and summary execution. Following an international outcry, the Belgian government took over from the king in 1908 and applied direct rule. The Congo Free State became the Belgian Congo (it won independence in 1960 and later became Zaire and then, in 1997, the Democratic Republic of Congo), but few of the Congolese noticed the difference. By 1919 the African population of the Belgian Congo stood at half of what it had been in 1880.

Passive resistance

Despite all the revolts and rebellions against the colonial powers, and despite the rise of nationalism and the growing political pressure for self-rule, no country won independence – or even any great concessions – from the imperial powers during this era. For imperialism, bolstered by overwhelmingly superior military power, it was still full summer; for the nationalist movements, on the other hand, there were just the very earliest signs of spring, shoots that would bud in the interwar years and blossom after the Second World War.

In the long term, some of the most significant developments were taking place in South Africa. The South African National Congress, later the ANC, was founded in 1912 as a response by black Africans to increasing racial segregation. The Indian population likewise found itself subjected to discrimination. One of the first acts of the new Transvaal government of 1907 was to impose restrictions on its non-white population. One of these, the Asiatic Law Amendment Ordinance, obliged all Indians in Transvaal to carry a certificate of registration, obtainable only by submitting to fingerprinting. In response, the Indians began a campaign of civil disobedience.

The man behind this protest was an English-trained lawyer, Mohandas Karamchand Gandhi, who had been born in India and came to Transvaal in 1893. Gandhi developed a theory that the best way to oppose

NEW KIND OF REBEL Gandhi adopted simple, traditional Indian dress for his *satyagraha* campaign of noncooperation in South Africa. He was about 44 at the time of this photo.

imperialism was *satyagraha*, nonviolent noncooperation. He was sentenced to two months' imprisonment in 1907, but released after negotiations with General Smuts, then a minister in the Transvaal government.

Gradually the stakes grew higher. In November 1913 Gandhi led a protest against a new law which restricted Indians to the province in which they were resident. The 2500 marchers deliberately flouted the law by crossing the border from Natal into Transvaal, where they were arrested and sent back into Natal. Gandhi's subsequent imprisonment for the nonpayment of a fine sparked off widespread rioting in Natal, in which police opened fire on demonstrators, causing two deaths.

In 1915 Gandhi returned to India. As leader of the Indian National Congress, and known as Mahatma ('the great-souled one'), he played a crucial role in achieving Indian independence in 1947 – something that Lord Curzon could never have contemplated when the century began.

THE MAN WHO BLEW THE WHISTLE ON THE BELGIAN CONGO

Of all Africa's colonial regimes, the Congo Free State had the worst reputation. In 1903 the British consul there drew attention to the abuses of its forced labour schemes, and the neglect of the Belgian administration. His report caused an international outcry, forcing the Belgian king, Leopold II, to set up an inquiry. The consul was Roger Casement. After Africa he was posted to Peru, and in 1910 reported on atrocities committed by the Peruvian rubber trade. He was knighted the next year, and on retirement returned to his native Ireland. Here, he took up the cause of Irish nationalism. During the First World War, he was sent by the Irish Republican Brotherhood on a secret mission to Germany to arrange arms shipments, and to try to recruit Irish prisoners of war to the nationalist cause. He returned in a German submarine, but on April 19, 1916, was captured by the British after landing in County Kerry. His arms shipment was also intercepted. Casement was tried in London and hanged as a traitor: he paid the penalty of bringing his sense of justice too close to home.

EUROPEAN BARBARISM Severed hands, amputated by Congo Free State troops, are evidence of the atrocities perpetrated there. It was this kind of outrage that Roger Casement (above) exposed.

THE STRUGGLE FOR IDENTITY

MINORITIES WITHIN NATIONS AND NATIONS WITHIN EMPIRES BEGAN TO MOBILISE FOR EQUALITY, JUSTICE AND SELF-DETERMINATION

By the turn of the 20th century, many countries had developed a strong sense of nationalism. The imperial powers prided themselves on their national traits as they claimed superiority over their rivals; they paraded to the sound of rousing national anthems beneath national flags. But this emphasis on nationalism was a comparatively new phenomenon, a product of the politics and sensibilities of the 19th century. The word itself was less than a century old.

On the one hand, nationalism promoted concepts of racial, linguistic and geographical identity; on the other, it had a complementary effect on those who felt excluded by it. Across the empires, ethnic minorities and subject nations felt that their own cultures and identities were swamped, and so they fostered their own sense of nationalism.

Finland had been under Russian control since 1809, although as a Grand Duchy it had substantial autonomy and its own parliament.

A DANGEROUS TUNE

Music played its part in nationalism as composers researched their people's folk music. The Finn Jean Sibelius wrote *Finlandia* (1900) for an anti-Russian stage performance about Finnish history. It was an instant success and adopted as a nationalist anthem. Anyone whistling it in public faced arrest by the Russian authorities.

It also had its own army, though many leading Finns volunteered to serve as officers in the Russian army. Russian nationalists, however, found the autonomous status of Finland offensive, and pressed their rulers to have Finland fully integrated into Russia. They found a sympathetic listener in Tsar Nicholas II, who in 1901 disbanded the Finnish army and required all young Finnish men to serve in the Russian army. The following year, he insisted that Russian should be the official language of Finland, and then he withdrew Finnish self-rule; from now on, he would rule directly through a governor-general.

The tsar's measures were met with outrage. Patriotic Finns began a campaign of passive resistance: many civil servants refused to carry out any of his orders, deeming them 'illegal', and obstructed the operation of conscription. The tsar responded by appointing a hardliner, General Bobrikov, as governor in 1903: he was assassinated the following year. As the tsar became increasingly distracted by the Russo-Japanese War of 1904-5, and

NATIONAL FEELING   This Armenian magazine (above), promoting nationalist sentiments, started to appear in 1906. Below: A leader of Finland's national strike of 1905 under arrest by the Russian authorities.

STOP AND SEARCH Security troops frisk a suspect on the streets of Warsaw. The Russians strove to stamp out nationalist identity in Poland, but increasingly oppressive measures proved counterproductive.

Russia itself teetered on the brink of collapse with the revolution of 1905, the Finns began a general strike. The tsar was forced to revoke his repressive measures, self-rule was restored, and the suffrage extended to include all men and women over the age of 24 – the first time in Europe that women were given the vote. The ground had been prepared for Finnish independence, which was finally achieved during the turmoil of the First World War.

A similar but more anguished sequence of events occurred in Poland which, following partition in the late 18th century, was shared out among the Russian, German and Austrian empires. Only in the Austrian sector was Polish culture tolerated. In the Russian and German-ruled areas, systematic attempts were made to eradicate it. The schools were at the front line of this particular conflict. In 1902, for example, schools in the Russian sector were closed as Polish pupils dug in their heels and refused to sing the Russian national anthem.

The Russians had imposed direct rule under a governor-general in the wake of a Polish uprising in the 1860s. Rebellion, however, was never far from the surface, and in November 1904 fierce anti-Russian riots in Warsaw resulted in the deaths of 49 demonstrators. More riots and deaths followed in 1905, as revolutionary activity – much of it

coordinated among Russian, Polish, Armenian and Georgian revolutionaries – swept across the tsarist empire. More than 100 demonstrators were killed in Warsaw on May Day. A general strike was called in August, and the disruption continued for a further year, culminating in the imposition of martial law in August 1906. The Poles managed to extract some concessions from the tsar, such as permission to teach Polish in schools, but disturbances continued sporadically into the First World War; Poland finally won its independence in 1918 in the aftermath of the Russian Revolution and the First World War.

Where imperial ambitions were not called into question, nationalist aspirations were allowed to flower in comparative peace. At the turn of the century, Norway was part of a union with Sweden, but the Norwegians' sense of their own identity had produced a fervent groundswell of nationalism. In 1905, Norway separated and became an independent kingdom, ruled by a Danish prince who came to the throne as Haakon VII.

The Balkan cauldron

By contrast, where imperial ambitions clashed, a cauldron of conflicting interests could produce a volatile brew, and nowhere more so than in the Balkans. Here, the interests of the Austro-Hungarian Empire, the crumbling Ottoman Empire and the Russians – claiming Pan-Slavic sympathies with a spread of Balkan peoples – came face to face over a complex jumble of national, ethnic and religious enclaves. Serbia, Romania and Greece were independent; Bulgaria was effectively so, though it did not cut its last ties with the Ottoman Empire until 1912. All four countries had strategic interests and

FIRST BLACK HEAVYWEIGHT CHAMPION

On December 26, 1908 – in Sydney, Australia – the Canadian Tommy Burns, heavyweight boxing champion of the world, was knocked out in the 14th round of a severe and punishing fight. The victor was the Texan-born son of a bareknuckle fighter, Jack Johnson – the world's greatest heavyweight before the television age, and also the first black champion.

It was not just Burns who had been floored: thousands of white supremacists were unable to stomach the victory of a black boxer. For seven years, Johnson remained world champion, facing a series of white opponents who fought under the banner of 'The Great White Hope'. Johnson, however, did himself few favours with his arrogance. He was a controversial figure, and his relationship with white women incited fervent resentment among Southern bigots. Race riots greeted his victory over the former champion, Jim Jeffries, in a comeback fight in Reno, Nevada, in 1910. Three years later, Johnson was arrested and convicted under the Mann White Slave Act, which made it illegal to cross state lines with a white woman 'for immoral purposes'. He fled to Europe, and in 1915 travelled to Cuba, for a fight

against another Great White Hope, a huge cowboy from Iowa called Jess Willard. Billed as a contest of 45 rounds, it took place in the open air, under the bright Havana sun. In the 26th round, Johnson began to wilt and was felled by Willard and counted out. It was the end of his career. He returned to the USA in 1920 and was promptly imprisoned for the earlier conviction. In 1928, aged 50, he made a doomed attempt at a comeback. He died in a car crash in 1946.

BLACK AND WHITE Jack Johnson's 1908 victory (left) made him the first black heavyweight champion of the world. His private life regularly provoked scandal – for example, after the suicide of his first wife (above) in 1912.

THE SCAPEGOATS OF SOCIETY

Anti-Semitism in Europe has a long history, stretching back beyond medieval times, when the Jews, already marginalised by discriminatory laws, were singled out for repeated acts of violent persecution by fanatical Christians. Massacres often occurred in the train of malicious rumours of Jews killing Christian children for blood with which to perform clandestine ceremonies. There were haunting echoes of the medieval past in the massacre of Jews in April 1903 in Kishinev, Bessarabia (now in Moldova), part of the Russian Empire. The two days of murder, rape and torching were triggered by accusations that two children had been killed for their blood by the Jews.

The Kishinev massacre was the first in a series of increasingly vicious attacks on the Jewish population of Russia. The authorities did little to intervene; they may even have instigated the attacks, with the tacit blessing of Tsar Nicholas II, who had developed an irrational loathing for his 5 million Jewish subjects. The Jews had become the targets of Russian nationalist propaganda, which accused them of being responsible for labour unrest and revolutionary terrorism, and spoke of a worldwide Jewish conspiracy to win domination through business and banking.

The Russian oppression of the Jews attracted international criticism – but this was casually waved aside by the tsar. During the Russian Revolution of 1905, the beleaguered authorities found that anti-Semitism provided a welcome distraction, and an effective means of channelling the counterrevolutionary fervour of the nationalists. In November 1905, 1000 Jews were massacred in Odessa in the Ukraine by a mob of 50 000, who went on the rampage clutching icons and portraits of the tsar. Other outrages occurred elsewhere in Ukraine, and also in Poland – in Bialystok and Siedlce.

At this time, a new word entered the English language: 'pogrom' – a Russian word meaning 'devastation', but which had come to denote an organised massacre, especially of Jews.

SAVAGERY AND BEWILDERMENT
The century opened with a pogrom at Kiev in 'Little Russia'. Kiev lay at the eastern extremity of the vast area of central and eastern Europe where Ashkenazi and Hassidic Jews had settled in the 18th and 19th century.

satellite populations in places such as Austrian-ruled Bosnia Herzegovina and in Ottoman-dominated Macedonia. Ethnic confrontations exploded into a series of violent confrontations, for instance around Monastir in Macedonia. Here, in April 1903, a massacre of 165 Muslims by Bulgarians elicited a crushing response from the Turkish army. Ottoman troops slaughtered some 50 000 Bulgarian men, women and children.

The Turks were ruled by the autocratic and paranoid Sultan Abd al-Hamid II, who took a similarly uncompromising attitude towards the Armenians, a Christian people whose territory spanned the frontier between the Russian and Ottoman empires. Armenian nationalism was brutally crushed on both sides of the border; the Ottoman Sultan, for his part, pursued a deliberate policy of extermination which was responsible for the deaths of half a million Armenians – a foretaste of an even bloodier Turkish decimation of the Armenians in 1915.

Stateless Jews

Macedonians, Estonians, Welsh, Basques – a spirit of nationalism, with varying degrees of fervency, was engendered in countless parts of Europe. For the Jews, nationhood was a more complex issue. Since the Diaspora, which had begun in Roman times, Jews had settled all over

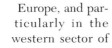

Europe, and particularly in the western sector of the Russian Empire, in a broad arc from Warsaw to Kiev. Many towns had high Jewish populations, such as Kishinev in Moldova, where 50 per cent of the inhabitants were Jewish. Jews usually remained outside the ambit of nationalist ideology, and became instead the victims of it, the target of nationalist vengeance, which could be whipped into a frenzy for cynical political ends, notably in Russia.

Anti-Semitism was also common in Britain, Germany, the USA – and most famously in France. The Dreyfus case – in which a Jewish officer serving in the French army had been falsely convicted in 1894 of passing secrets to Germany – had severe repercussions in French politics. Although

RICH MAN, POOR MAN   A Jewish water-carrier in Minsk and potsellers in Poland give the lie to Russian propaganda that portrayed all Jews as wealthy parasites and agitators.

Dreyfus was pardoned in 1899 and fully exonerated in 1906, the damage had been done. To the liberal or left-wing supporters of Dreyfus – the Dreyfusards – the establishment, which had supported the military in this embarrassing episode, had exhibited a combination of dangerous and distasteful tendencies: monarchist, chauvinistically Catholic and rabidly anti-Semitic.

Many of the Dreyfusards saw a burning need to eradicate such tendencies. They decided to target first of all the church schools, in an attempt to limit the influence of the Church on public education. This was the spearhead of a series of deeply divisive anticlerical actions. In 1902 the new French prime minister, Emile Combes, set about closing some 3000 church schools. In addition, various monasteries, convents, church-run hospitals, orphanages and mental asylums were forced to close by the removal of public funding. So, too, was the 900-year-old monastery of La Grande

FORMAL ENTRY   Jewish rituals – such as this *bar mitzvah* ceremony photographed in Poland in 1906 – served to bond the community, but were also portrayed as sinister and threatening by anti-Semitic agitators.

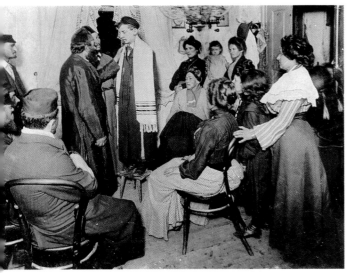

Chartreuse, near Grenoble, motherhouse of the Carthusians, which was admired by locals for its good works, and by the world at large for its famous liqueur.

Meanwhile, the Dreyfus case had another important effect. A Hungarian Jewish journalist covering the case, Theodor Herzl, was so appalled by the proceedings, as well as by other examples of anti-Semitism, that he decided to set up a movement – Zionism – to press for an independent Jewish homeland. He hoped that the Jewish people might be restored to the Holy Land – Palestine, then part of the Ottoman Empire. As with other nationalist movements, language was to play a key role in establishing an identity. In this case, the language was Hebrew, revived in the 1880s as a spoken language after centuries of dormancy.

Language also played its part in Ireland.

KICKING THE HABIT   In a French magazine of 1903, Liberty, symbol of Republican France, remonstrates with a monk who has had to pack his bags. Many saw monks as unfortunate victims of the drive towards secularising state institutions.

The first Anglo-Norman invaders had arrived there in 1068, and the whole island had come under direct English rule in Tudor times; in the 300 years since then, Ireland's distinctive Celtic traditions had been constantly denigrated and demeaned. The Gaelic League, founded in 1893, retrieved the Gaelic (or Irish) language from the brink of extinction, and was part of a general revival of Irish culture. All this conferred a

Ulster in the north, where a largely Protestant population had pushed forward a programme of industrialisation, bringing prosperity to Belfast and Londonderry and their surrounding areas.

The main focus of Irish political aspirations was Home Rule – the re-establishment of an Irish parliament in Dublin under the English Crown. This was promoted by many of the Irish MPs in London, and Home Rule Bills had been presented to parliament – and defeated – twice, in 1886 and

Orange over the Catholic James II at the Battle of the Boyne in 1690.

While there seemed to be some prospect of Home Rule, nationalist politics in the south remained comparatively calm. But the repeated frustrations of the Home Rule movement had awakened more radical instincts. The Irish Republican Brotherhood (IRB) re-emerged around 1910. Also known as the Fenians, this radical nationalist movement had originally been set up and funded in 1858 by Irish American emigrants; now it revived under an influx of younger members. Meanwhile, a journalist named Arthur Griffith published a newspaper called *United*

OURSELVES ALONE   The Sinn Fein envisaged by Arthur Griffith (above) promoted non-violent agitation for an independent Ireland. Demonstrators (right), reciting the rosary for Sinn Feiners in Dublin's Mountjoy Prison, are confronted by armed British troops.

new dignity on what it meant to be Irish. This was underpinned by an emergent set of Irish writers of international standing, such as the poet W.B. Yeats – who would win the Nobel prize for literature in 1923. A parallel renaissance was effected in the field of sports, where the Gaelic Athletic Association, founded in 1884, set about reviving traditional non-English sports such as hurling.

Home Rule

Ireland's long history of political, religious and cultural oppression left its mark in dire poverty and the persistent neglect symbolised by its absentee landlords. A series of reforms in the late 19th century had gone some way to redressing this, notably the Land Acts, by which tenant farmers were able to buy land of their own. This was enhanced by the Land Purchase Acts of 1903 and 1909. In the 1870s, just 3 per cent of the population had owned 95 per cent of the land; by 1916, 64 per cent of the population was landowning. Yet living conditions in much of Ireland remained primitive – particularly in Dublin, whose slums ranked among the worst in Europe. An exception to this rule was in

1893. Lined up in opposition to Home Rule were the Ulster Protestants, who had no desire to be ruled by the poorer, mainly Catholic and agrarian south. Their ingrained anti-Catholic culture was expressed in the traditions of the Orangemen, who ostentatiously celebrated the victory of William of

Irishmen, and then after 1906 another called *Sinn Fein* (meaning in Irish 'Ourselves Alone'). This was also the name of his Irish nationalist party, founded the previous year and pledged to bring about a parliament in Ireland through non-violent means; Sinn Fein later became the public face of the IRB.

In 1910, in a pair of indecisive elections, the combined British and Irish electorate voted in equal numbers for the Conservatives and Liberals, handing the balance of parliamentary power to the Irish Nationalist MPs, led by an old Home Rule campaigner, John Redmond. At the second election, the Liberal Herbert Asquith was able to retain his position as prime minister with the support of

HOME RULE   A cartoon from *Punch* in 1909 depicts the Irish Nationalist MP John Redmond canvassing local support for Home Rule in Ireland.

the Irish MPs. His government soon succeeded in passing the Parliament Act, which – to the outrage of many peers – greatly diminished the House of Lords' power of veto; previously, Home Rule Bills had been vetoed by the House of Lords.

In January 1913 parliament passed the third Home Rule Bill. The Irish Nationalist MPs believed that they had triumphed at last, and there were joyous street celebrations in Dublin. By contrast, in the north, the militant Ulster Volunteer Force went on parade, declaring that they would resist the imposition of Home Rule to the last drop of blood. The Asquith government was paralysed by the dilemma, unable to act without incurring the wrath of one side or the other. Germany looked on with interest, believing Ireland to be on the verge of civil war; Lord Hardinge, Viceroy of India, warned that if a solution could not be reached in Ireland – at the heart of the British Empire – there would inevitably be trouble in India.

Faced with Ulster's intransigence, the government came up with an awkward compromise: the six Protestant-dominated counties of Ulster would be excluded temporarily from the Home Rule Act and would remain, for six years, under direct rule from London. This did not have the desired palliative effect: the nationalists condemned it as a travesty; the Ulstermen would not abide the idea of an arrangement labelled temporary.

The process all took time. In fact, it was not until September 1914, after the First World War had started, that the Home Rule

FORCE OF ARMS Ulster Volunteers demonstrate their determination to resist Home Rule in a show of strength, which includes a mounted machine gun. By 1914 their armoury consisted of some 40 000 rifles.

SIGNED IN BLOOD

'With the help of God, you and I joined together . . . will yet defeat the most nefarious conspiracy that has ever been hatched against a free people.' With these words, the Dublin MP and barrister Sir Edward Carson addressed a crowd of 50 000 in northern Ireland in September 1911. With the political parties in London at loggerheads, and the balance of power held by Irish Nationalists pressing for Home Rule, the future looked bleak for the Protestants of Ulster. They were implacably opposed to being governed by Dublin, and were prepared to fight for their right to remain directly linked to the British Crown. To this end, they drew up a Solemn League and Covenant, signed by 250 000 men – many of whom wrote their names in blood. This was backed by a similar supporting document signed by over 200 000 women. Immediately, a corps of Protestant volunteers and Orangemen began drilling practice using wooden rifles. In January 1913, the Ulster Volunteer Force was established – 100 000 disciplined and well-armed men. Although illegal, their show of strength was applauded by many in the Conservative opposition in London, including the Conservative leader, Bonar Law, as well as by high-ranking officers of the British army. In April 1914, a shipment of 24 000 rifles, brought in secret from Germany, arrived for them. In response to these events, the southern Irish in Dublin created the Irish National Volunteers, an army of 180 000 men. Although equipped with only 1500 smuggled weapons, their determination was not in doubt. In March 1914,

British officers stationed in Ireland met at the Curragh, near Dublin, and declared that they would be unwilling to use force against the Ulster Volunteers. This declaration, called exaggeratedly the 'Curragh Mutiny', demonstrated the impotence of the British government. Home Rule for Ireland might have been the will of parliament, but the government was unable to enforce it throughout Ireland against the wishes of the Protestant minority.

FACE OF INTRANSIGENCE Sir Edward Carson, figurehead of the anti-Home Rule Movement in Ulster, addresses a meeting in September 1913.

VOLUNTEERS IN UNIFORM **Although illegal, the Ulster Volunteer Force had a uniform. Its commander was a retired English general of the Indian army – evidence of the tacit backing of the British establishment.**

Bill eventually received royal assent. However, a Suspending Bill was attached to the effect that the Act would not be enforced until the end of the war – predicted, at the time, to last but a few months.

Meanwhile, in August 1913, the Irish Transport and General Workers' Union had begun a strike against the company that ran the Dublin tramways. The employer, Walter J. Murphy, proved intractable and instituted a lockout of the 24 000 workers, which eventually broke the strike after eight months of bitter hardship. Murphy, it turned out, was a supporter of Home Rule. The conclusion for the Irish worker was that the leaders of the Irish nationalist cause – the middle classes and entrepreneurs – did not necessarily have all the aspirations of ordinary Irish people at heart. By the time the strike had ended the Irish had acquired a new sense of militancy.

Impatience with the progress of Home Rule led to the Easter Rising of 1916. The resulting polarisation of loyalties catapulted Ireland into civil war and an unsatisfactory political division that remains unresolved.

Birth of the blues

One of the crucial influences on events in Ireland came from the American Irish communities. The USA had received immigrants from just about every nationalist minority in Europe – many of them emigrating because

STRIKE BOUND **The British authorities arrest James Larkin, leader of the Dublin transport strike in the summer of 1913.**

nationality was a cause of discrimination against them.

The one sector of the population which did not benefit from the American Dream was the former slaves. The American Civil War (1861-5) had been fought over the issue of slavery, but the subsequent reconstruction programme, which was meant to enforce the benefits of emancipation in the South, had collapsed in 1877. After that, the Southern

THE PLOUGH AND STARS Operating under their flag (far left), members of the small Irish Citizen Army (below) offered some protection to the 1913 strikers. Dublin's O'Connell Street (above) was the focus of mass meetings by the trades unions.

states had done what they could to restore white supremacy, introducing surreptitious legislation to disenfranchise the blacks and – through the notorious 'Jim Crow' laws – to institutionalise segregation. By 1900 many black Americans had been reduced to pover-

SCRAPING A LIVING Ox-carts, unmade roads and primitive housing were common features (right) of the turn-of-the-century American South. Music (below) provided one of the few legitimate outlets for expressing grievances.

ty and dependency by a new equivalent of slavery: share-cropping. When the big plantations were broken up, land was available for sale, but few blacks had enough capital to buy it. Instead, they had entered agreements whereby landlords rented farmland to them – along with a hut, seeds, a mule and some basic food – in return for a share of the crop

produced. High interest rates, fluctuating crop prices and discrimination in favour of poor whites soon revealed the iniquities of this system.

Segregation, officially condoned by federal government legislation if 'separate, but equal' (it never was), affected the railways, housing, work, education and places of entertainment, as well as the voting system and access to justice.

In their work, black people were usually restricted to labouring jobs, operating factory machinery, maintaining the railroads and working in the cotton fields. Violent confrontation was systematised by racist organisations such as the Ku Klux Klan, founded just after the Civil War.

Many blacks responded by leaving the South and heading for the industrialised northern cities, where continued poverty condemned them to life in the growing ghettos. Northward migration increased in the early years of the 20th century.

This disillusioning experience was to force black Americans to review their own identity, and to make a virtue of their separateness. It was at this point that the blues came to maturity in the hands of performers such as Huddie Ledbetter, alias Leadbelly, and to reach a wider audience with W.C. Handy, whose 'Memphis Blues' in 1912 became the first published blues song. Meanwhile, ragtime and danceband music was adapted in New Orleans into the early manifestations of jazz.

Black Americans also created their own institutions, notably churches but also schools. Booker T. Washington fought hard for black education, and – with the backing of the philanthropic tycoon Andrew Carnegie – he established the leading black educational institution at Tuskegee, Alabama, in 1881. Washington took a conciliatory attitude towards race relations; others, such as W.E.B. Dubois, took a more strident view. Educated at Harvard, and a teacher of economics and history at Atlanta University in Georgia, Dubois was one of the first black activists to call for full racial equality. In 1909 he helped to found the National Negro Committee, which the following year became the National Association for the Advancement of Colored People, a pressure group calling for the end of racial inequality and segregation – and above all to lynching (but that was not achieved until the 1950s).

Vindictive violence remained a feature of the black American experience, and often accompanied any indications of black advancement. In October 1901, for example, Booker T. Washington was invited to dine at the White House by President Roosevelt. News of this inspired a series of race riots in which 34 people died. The struggle for racial equality was just beginning.

WORKERS OF THE WORLD

FOR INDUSTRIAL WORKERS LOCKED INTO LIVES OF DRUDGERY AND SQUALOR, TRADE UNIONS HELD OUT THE HOPE OF A BETTER DEAL

With telephones, wireless radio, electricity, motor cars, relativity and Cubism, the period 1900-14 appears to have had its feet planted firmly in the modern world. Yet most people were still living and working in conditions reminiscent of the darkest days of the Industrial Revolution – the kind of grim early Victorian world that Charles Dickens had portrayed in *Oliver Twist*.

The industrial cities had grown at an exponential rate during the 19th century. By the turn of the century there were 66 million more people in Europe than there had been in 1815. Berlin had a population of 173 000 in 1800; by 1900 it had nearly 1.9 million. There were similar rises in other capital cities, and even more dramatic increases in the new industrial centres. Middlesbrough in north-eastern England was an example: with a population of 6000 in 1842, it had ballooned to 105 000 in 1907, growing on the back of its

steel industry. Roubaix in France, Essen in Germany – all witnessed similar expansion.

Row upon row of cramped, shoddily built and decaying housing clustered around the factories in the centres of these towns. Here, families of up to a dozen people or more lived in three-room houses, without running water, sharing earth privies in the yard with a handful of other houses, and breathing air laden with the smoke of burning coal – their only source of energy.

Even for those in full employment, money was desperately short. In coal-mining towns, the womenfolk would regularly pawn

DAY'S END Workers at Harland & Wolff's shipyard in Belfast stream homewards. Employed in a prospering industry, these skilled workers could walk forth with pride and confidence. To the rear rises the *Titanic* under construction.

DIRTY, NOISY AND DULL Men and women operate assembly lines in a factory producing agricultural machinery (below). Back home, technology remained basic. With no running water or bathroom, a miner gets clean with a rub-down next to the stove (above).

the family's Sunday clothes on Monday, and redeem them on Saturday when the weekly pay packet came in. Any member of a family who could work tried to do so, including wives and children. Pregnant women worked virtually up to their confinement, and returned to work just four weeks after giving birth. Babies were often brought up by elder children, bottle-fed in unsanitary conditions – a major contributory factor to the high infant mortality rates. About one in five babies born into working-class families died in their first year.

Malnutrition was commonplace. Whole families would survive on a diet of little more than bread and dripping, tea and occasional strips of bacon. Work-related illness and diseases such as tuberculosis and rickets were rife, and went largely untreated; cholera epidemics were still common. Many

WORKERS' FRIEND Seebohm Rowntree sought to alleviate poverty as well as describe it. For example, he established a pioneering pension plan for workers in the family cocoa firm.

people drowned their misery by spending what little they had on alcohol; alcoholism was so prevalent that many middle-class observers believed it to be the cause of poverty, rather than a symptom of it.

Working hours were extremely long. In the USA, women and children were still working up to 14 hours a day in textile mills until 1914. Sunday was often the only day of rest, although around the turn of the century many workers were granted Saturday afternoon as well. The larger factories and the mines operated round the clock in shifts.

1900 Strikes take place in the mining areas of Belgium, Germany and Austria

1904 Martial law is imposed in Spain following industrial unrest

1906 The Labour Party is formed and wins 29 seats in the British General Election

Working conditions were dangerous and dirty, with the unregulated use of noxious chemicals and machine rooms full of dust that caused lung diseases.

Pricking consciences

In the 1880s Britain's Social Democratic Federation published a report in the *Pall Mall Gazette* in which it claimed that a quarter of Londoners lived below the bread line.

HARD AT WORK A German cartoon pokes fun at the working life of the bosses, upon whose casual discussions rested the livelihoods of the thousands of workers toiling in the factory in the background.

This struck a prosperous shipowner named Charles Booth as a propagandist lie, and he set out to disprove it. He began an exhaustive 17 year survey of East London, with teams of researchers going from house to house, asking detailed questions and collecting statistics. It soon became clear that conditions were in fact rather worse than even the Social Democratic Federation had suggested. Booth's monumental *Life and Labour of the People of London* (published in instalments between 1899 and 1903) showed that 30 per cent of Londoners were living in dire poverty, with an income that was inadequate to provide the bare necessities. Of these, 10 per cent – mainly families of the unemployed or the occasionally employed – lived in extreme distress.

Another survey undertaken in York by Benjamin Seebohm Rowntree, a scion of the wealthy cocoa-processing family, showed that London was not an exception. His *Poverty: A Study of Town Life* (1901) described some of his findings in graphic detail: 'House No. 4 two rooms, seven inmates. Walls, ceiling and furniture filthy. Dirty flock bedding in living room placed on a box and two chairs. Smell of room from dirt and bad air unbearable . . . Children pale, starved-looking, and only half-clothed, one boy with hip disease, another

THE COURRIÈRES COLLIERY DISASTER

'The Greatest Mining Disaster on Record' read the headlines: a terrible coal-mining tragedy had happened at Courrières in the Pas-de-Calais, northern France. At about 7 am on Saturday, March 10, 1906, an underground explosion triggered a massive fire. It spread through three pits, and claimed the lives of 1290 miners – overcome by heat and fumes in the cramped shafts and tunnels, and crushed in collapsing galleries.

At the surface, the first sign of the disaster was the lick of flames at the mouths of the three interconnected pits. Engineers, officials and miners just ending their shift immediately volunteered to go to the rescue but, despite great bravery, they were forced back by the intense heat. It was several hours before rescue operations could begin in earnest, and they continued through the night and into Sunday. Some 250 miners – half the full complement – were brought up alive from one pit. In the other two, rescuers found only a handful of survivors, many of them badly injured. As the hours proceeded, their efforts met with diminishing returns, even with the assistance of specialist mining firemen from Westphalia in Germany, who arrived with the newest breathing apparatus. As they wormed deeper underground in very unstable conditions, they encountered only the appalling spectacle of more collapsed galleries piled high with bodies. By Monday it was clear that there could be no more survivors.

Meanwhile, family members had gathered around the mines, desperate for news. As the *Illustrated London News* reported: 'The scenes around the pit-mouths as the bodies were brought up by slow degrees were, as may be imagined, extremely painful. The women whose husbands and sons are missing are almost beside themselves with grief, unable to tell if their loved ones are among the crushed and blackened forms which the police have arranged in long lines in one of the sheds.' Most of the dead came from Billy-Montigny, a village of 4500 inhabitants. It was a close-knit community in which virtually every family was employed by the mine – men underground, women and children at the surface. Just about every family lost one or more of their menfolk in the disaster, and some lost them all. One survivor lost three brothers, five brothers-in-law and four nephews.

TRAGIC BURDEN A pathetic bundle is all that remains of one of the victims carried out from the Courrières pithead. The dead were buried in mass graves in the local cemeteries.

with sores over face.' It was Rowntree who introduced the concept of the 'poverty line' – the level of income beneath which adequate subsistence is impossible.

It was a great shock for middle-class Britons to have these facts laid before them. And photography, with the assistance of the hand-held camera, made the grim realities undeniable. Here, in the motherland of a great empire, more than a third of the people were living in conditions more readily associated with the most wretched corners of

power of collective action. As a last resort, they could go on strike – but at the risk of losing income or even their jobs.

Many trade unions had developed along the lines of medieval guilds: initially they were designed to protect the interests of specific trades and professions, frequently against competing sets of workers. The unions would bargain over pay and working conditions on behalf of members, and provide them with

OBSTRUCTIVE ACTION French strikers blocked railway lines with engines to stop all traffic during a railway strike in October 1910.

financial assistance in times of ill-health or distress. Such unions tended to represent skilled artisans. But a major change occurred in the late 19th century when the mass of unskilled workers began to join unions. A series of strikes in the London docklands in the 1890s – which won concessions, including increased pay – demonstrated the immense potential of such unions. This 'new

ALL OUT Marching strikers became a familiar sight in the industrialised world. In Boston, uniformed public transport workers parade their grievances alongside a streetcar (left), while strikers in Mons, Belgium, march to the rhythm of a brass band (below).

the colonies. Britain was not alone; throughout the industrialised world, wherever there had been rapid industrial expansion, parallel conditions existed.

By the late 19th century, various social reformers – drawn mainly from the middle classes – were pressing for change. But political power lay largely in the hands of the wealthy, who were easily swayed by the arguments of the industrialists that any concessions or intervention would affect competitiveness in world trade. Essentially, the workers understood that change was not going to come from above: they had to bring it about themselves.

Unions: a force for change

The one trump card held by the workers was strength in numbers. By organising themselves into trade unions to defend their common interests, they could exert the

unionism', embracing the unskilled worker, changed the face of industrial relations.

By the turn of the century, industry had become a battleground, with the strike as the workers' principal weapon of negotiation. Strikes occurred regularly across the industrialised world. In 1900 there were strikes in the mining regions of Belgium, Germany and Austria. In 1902 King Alfonso XIII of Spain declared martial law in the face of widespread industrial unrest. A railway strike in Hungary in 1904 led to riots. In 1907, violent disturbances broke out in Antwerp, Belgium – British 'blacklegs' (non-union workers) were shipped in as strikebreakers in the docks.

The power of the unions had become a major political issue. Governments of all persuasions saw them as a threat, and responded according to their powers. In authoritarian regimes, such as Russia, all union activity was repressed, and strikes were met by a show of force, which often led to riots and death. Concessions were achieved in Russia only after the revolution of 1905. In more liberal countries, such as Britain and France, unions themselves may have been tolerated, but strike action often led to bitter confrontation.

One of the main weapons of the employers

THE BELLE ÉPOQUE

HERE'S TO US   A lunch party on board a private American yacht celebrates happy days with champagne.

The heyday of the Edwardian era, the belle époque is remembered as a time of glittering prosperity, sensual elegance and luxurious tranquillity. Across Europe, royalty, nobility, great landowners and the captains of industry enjoyed a hectic calendar of balls, summer garden parties, dinners, concerts, theatre trips, outings to the race courses. In Mayfair in London, in the Faubourg Saint-Germain in Paris, in Newport, Rhode Island, in Vienna, Brussels and Berlin, they stuffed their palaces and mansions with fine paintings, richly upholstered furniture, costly knick-knacks, towering ferns, tiger skins, Indian rugs and other trophies of foreign travel. They employed hosts of butlers, housekeepers, valets, footmen, maids, chauffeurs and nursery staff to smooth the wrinkles of their busy lives. To relax, they cruised the Atlantic in liners, sailed the Mediterranean in their private yachts, gambled in Monte Carlo, Cannes or Biarritz, shot big game in Africa. Then they worked off some of their bloated lifestyle with a cure at the fashionable spas made famous by royalty, such as Marienbad in Bohemia or Bad Homburg in Germany. At weekend house parties in country mansions, away from the public gaze, the night-time click of bedroom doors discreetly signalled their private disregard for the buttoned-up morality of the era, and brought solace to many trapped in the deserts of arranged society marriages. It was a time of massively self-indulgent spending – on clothes, jewellery, motor cars, entertainment. Although ostentation was frowned upon as the sin of the newly rich who had been admitted with reluctance to the ranks of 'Society' – the press-barons, property tycoons, millionaire shopkeepers and the like – it was a common defect.

But running parallel to this ostentation was a growing sense of anxiety, distantly echoing the unsettling doubts of the middle-class reformers, the widespread industrial unrest, the socialist revolutions and the anarchist assassinations across the Western world. It was as though participants in the belle époque – a thin layer of spume upon the ocean of humanity – somehow perceived the onset of a distant storm. As the Liberal politician and social historian C.F.G. Masterman put it in his book *The Condition of England* (1909), people looked forward 'with foreboding, wondering how long the artisan, the shop assistants, the labourers, the unemployed will be content to acquiesce in a system which expends upon a few weeks of random entertainment an amount that would support in modest comfort a decent family for a lifetime'. In any case, visions of the belle époque, gilded by nostalgia, have probably exaggerated the high-life pleasures of what was in fact a deeply troubled era. In *The Edwardians*, the English writer J.B. Priestley – a child of the era – described this as the 'Edwardian myth', a myth conjured up by the well-to-do after the trauma of the First World War: 'They are remembering the time before the real wars came, before the fatal telegrams arrived at every great house. The Edwardian was never a golden age, but seen across the dark years afterwards it could easily be mistaken for one.'

was the lockout: faced by the threat of unwelcome union action, they closed the factory gates, safe in the knowledge that this would harm the workers' pockets more than their own. In the event of a strike, it was usually possible to engage blacklegs, although such high-handed behaviour could backfire; instead of humbling the strikers, it often made them more embittered and militant. Nonetheless, while the unions remained localised and limited to particular crafts, they were vulnerable to 'divide and rule' tactics. Trade unions could be truly effective only if they covered entire industries, and if possible related industries as well. Thus a strike by dockers, supported by all transport workers, could bring the country to a standstill.

A political agenda

Many of the early union leaders were socialists. They believed that the key to a more egalitarian world lay in the ownership of the means of production – the factories, the mines, the transport, the capital. If this could be wrested from the bosses, and placed in the

EMBLEMS OF SOLIDARITY Lavish banners, with edifying mottoes, became the symbols of unions and their branches, such as the British National Union of Railwaymen (above left) and the German Workers' Union (above right).

hands of the state representing the many, the wealth of the nation could be shared fairly. Where it seemed feasible, many socialists and labour activists sought to bring about change through existing democratic structures. In countries such as Britain, the electoral franchise had been gradually broadened to include more and more working people, so it seemed entirely likely that increasing numbers of members of parliament would come to represent the working class.

The picture in Britain, as elsewhere, was complicated by the different, overlapping groups standing for labour interests. There

THE VOICE OF LABOUR The veteran Labour MP James Keir Hardie took to the podium in Hyde Park to address striking tailors in May 1912. He had been the first chairman of the Independent Labour Party, which celebrated its 21st anniversary in 1914 (left).

had been a small group of working-class MPs, the 'Lib-Labs', elected with the support of the Liberal Party though not members of it, since the 1870s. The first working-class member elected without the support of the Liberals was James Keir Hardie, the son of a ship's carpenter, who entered parliament in 1892. The next year he founded the Independent Labour Party (ILP). In 1900 Hardie, various trade unions, members of the Social Democratic Federation and the reformist pressure group called the Fabian Society came together to form the Labour Representation Committee, which in 1906 became the Labour Party, effectively absorbing the earlier ILP. In the 1906 general election, campaigning for full employment, a maximum 48 hour week and a state pension scheme, the new Labour Party won 29 seats in parliament.

INDEPENDENT · LABOUR · PARTY

FOUNDED AT BRADFORD JAN 13th 1893 COMING OF AGE CONFERENCE AND CELEBRATION BRADFORD APRIL 11th 1914

THERE IS NO WEAL SAVE COMMONWEAL

Collaborating with 25 Lib-Lab MPs, it influenced the passage of reforms undertaken by the Liberal government of the day.

Even so, the road to change through established political structures was slow and frustrating. In Britain, the unions found the path blocked on two landmark occasions. In 1901 a small railway company in Taff Vale in Wales successfully sued the Amalgamated Union of Railway Servants for losses and damages after a strike in which union pickets were said to have tried to 'molest and injure' employees continuing to work. Following a judgment by the House of Lords, the highest court in the land, the union had to pay compensation of £23 000 to the company. This judgment showed that unions could be held financially liable for strike action: strikes became potentially ruinous, and the workers thereby lost their weapon of last resort. The Liberal government elected in 1906 was quick to rescind this judgment: in the Trade Disputes Act of 1906, unions were absolved of financial responsibility for strike action. After this, in economic conditions of increasing employment but static wages and a rising cost of living, union membership rose dramatically, doubling between 1906 and 1913.

The Labour Party was largely funded by

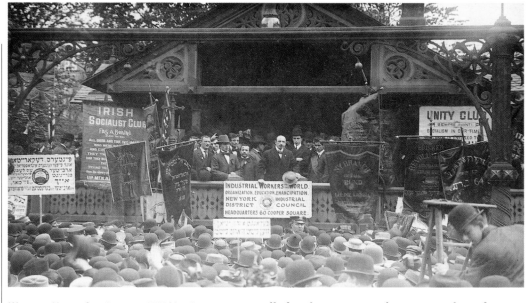

WORKERS UNITE Speakers at a 1908 May Day rally of the International Workers of the World (IWW) in New York face a large and attentive crowd. Impatient with the democratic process, IWW leaders believed in militant class warfare.

the trade unions, which used a portion of the members' weekly contributions for political purposes. When W.V. Osborne, an official in the Amalgamated Society of Railway Servants, complained about this practice in 1909, his objection was upheld. In the so-

called Osborne Case, the House of Lords ruled that it was illegal for unions to raise a political levy. This meant that the Labour Party lost most of its financial backing. At this time, members of parliament received no salary at all, but the Liberal government again came to the rescue by introducing an allowance for all MPs; this permitted the Labour MPs to survive. The Osborne judgment was reversed in 1913; after this, trade unions could use their funds for political purposes, provided that they had the agreement of the majority of their members.

In the USA, meanwhile, the development of unions in the final decades of the 19th century had been hampered by rigorous opposition from the employers, using tactics such as lockouts, infiltration and law suits. The most ruthless employers were the corporate 'trusts' – huge, monopolistic industries that dominated the US economy, in particular the railroads, steel and petroleum. These wielded considerable power in politics, and also over the conditions of their workers; some were guilty of blatant misdemeanour, such as price-fixing, conspiracy and corruption. One of President Theodore Roosevelt's key contributions to domestic politics was to initiate 'trust-busting' legislation to limit the powers of these organisations and to loosen their grip on the economy.

In contrast to the bullying, well-organised employers, US unions tended to be localised and craft-based, and as a result lacked muscle.

THE LION-TAMER A US cartoon of 1904 embroiders on President Roosevelt's reputation as a game-hunter to depict him boldly taming the monopolistic trusts.

All the same, the USA suffered a series of bitter local strikes in the early 1900s, notably in the mining industry. The five-month strike by 200 000 Pennsylvanian anthracite miners in 1902 was one of the most severe. Led by John Mitchell, the United Mine Workers demanded a maximum nine-hour day and increased wages. As with many US mines, the owner was a railroad company, whose president advised workers not to listen to 'labour agitators' but to trust in 'the Christian men to whom God . . . has given control of the property interests in this country'. The dispute was eventually resolved with the help of Roosevelt, who set up a commission to enquire into the miners' grievances.

For many people in the industrialised world, existing political structures seemed unable to deliver change fast enough. For them, political and economic inequalities called for more radical action. Many adopted a credo called syndicalism. The goal was to create huge industry-wide unions ('one industry one union') capable of exerting enormous pressure, and then to call strikes at every opportunity in order to bring about the economic chaos and paralysis needed to usher in a new political order. The trade union would thereafter be the basic unit of government.

Power in syndicates

Syndicalism was widely embraced in Germany and France, while in the USA a similar stance was taken by Industrial Workers of the World (IWW, otherwise

UP IN ARMS Troops were called out in Liverpool as tensions rose during the 1911 transport workers' strike. The dockers' leader Ben Tillett (left) played a key role in the strike.

known as the 'Wobblies'). This was founded in 1905 by the Marxist Daniel de Leon to represent the unskilled workers excluded by most existing US unions. 'The working class and the employing class,' blazed de Leon, 'have nothing in common. There can be no peace so long as hunger and want are found among millions of working people and the few, who make up the employing class, have all the good things in life . . . These conditions can be changed and the interest of the working class upheld only by an organisation formed in such a way that all its members in any one industry, or in all industries if necessary, cease work whenever a strike or lockout is on in any department, thus making an injury to one an injury to all . . . By organising industrially we are forming the structure of a new society within the shell of the old.'

For a time, syndicalism seemed to offer a new dawn – and, to those who opposed it, a real threat of revolution. In Britain it was adopted by the radical union leader Tom Mann; in 1910, Mann put forward his views in a monthly journal called the *Industrial Syndicalist*. That same year, the charismatic dockers' leader Ben Tillett amalgamated the dockers' and seamen's union to form the Transport Workers' Federation (TWF) – achieving the kind of all-inclusive scale deemed desirable by the syndicalists.

In January 1911, Britain's Union of Sailors and Firemen called a strike, after months of disputes in the docks and shipyards. The employers brought in blacklegs. Now other transport workers – including Ben Tillett's TWF – came out in sympathy. This brought the Port of London to a standstill. The strike spread to the docks of Southampton, Manchester and Liverpool. Miners in South Wales were also engaged in a ten-month strike. When the railway workers, now amalgamated as the National Union of Railwaymen, joined the strike in support of the dockers, Britain was paralysed. The Liberal government tried to resolve the strikes by setting up special commissions, but no sooner was one dispute settled than another blew up. Meanwhile, police and troops were sent in to maintain order and to provide essential services. During an unusually hot summer, tempers flared; there were riots and looting; trains were set on fire. Nine people were killed in rioting in Llanelli, South Wales, in July 1911. Public transport stopped as petrol ran out, leaving the empty streets to soldiers marching beside armoured cars. Industries closed for want of coal. Shops and markets were bare, and there was talk of starvation.

The disputes rumbled on. Another coal strike in February 1912 resulted in a million workers being laid off. This was resolved by April when minimum-wage legislation was presented to parliament – an unprecedented demonstration of the government's willingness to intervene in wage negotiations. In May the TWF called a national transport strike to force the Port of London Authority to recognise the union and accept a 'closed shop', giving the TWF power over recruitment; by the end of the month, 100 000 dockers were on strike. But other unions backed away, fighting shy of the syndicalist agenda. In June the dock strike collapsed: Tillett had overreached himself. The nation – and the Trades Union Congress representing the majority of unions – proved less radical than he.

The economic fallout of such action was evident. Between 1901 and 1907, up to 4 million working days had been lost to strikes each year in Britain. In 1912, the total amounted to 41 million. To some, the country seemed to be on the brink of catastrophe. In January 1914, union leaders created what employers feared most: the 'Triple Alliance' between the TWF, the National Union of Railwaymen and the Miners' Federation. Tom Mann argued that this would bring about 'the elimination of the employer'. It seemed that the unions held the employers in the palm of their hand. But before the Triple Alliance could be put to the test, the First World War intervened.

HEALTHY PURSUITS

With shorter working hours, and Saturday afternoon off work to add to Sunday, many ordinary people found that they had more time on their hands than ever before. The late 19th century had seen an unprecedented flourishing of sports, which carried over into the new century. Basketball was invented in the USA in 1891 and soon became a major school and college sport. In Britain, soccer became the great working man's game, with teams of professional players vying for the national cups watched by thousands of spectators. In France, as in Britain, rugby was a major school sport, played at many of the lycées, notably in south-west France. The prevailing ethos was that school sport was healthy for both physical and mental development, good for resolving conflict and for engendering a sense of team spirit.

Lawn tennis had been launched in 1873, and caught on with extraordinary speed. Championships have taken place at Wimbledon every year since 1877. Although it was not a working-class game, the championships aroused great public interest. Ladies' tennis in particular helped to develop a new image of women – independent, athletic and determined. Britain's great women's star at the turn of the century was Charlotte Sterry, who won the Wimbledon championship in 1895-6, 1898, 1901 and 1908. In 1900 she won the mixed doubles with the leading British men's player of the era, Hugh Doherty, who went on to win the men's championship five times in a row (1902-6).

Cycling had reached a peak of popularity in the late 19th century, when technology was perfected with the classic diamond-frame machine. Cycling clubs were popular, and opened their doors increasingly to ladies. Cyclists venturing abroad could always rely on a friendly welcome and assistance from a chain of national touring clubs that covered much of the globe. The first Tour de France was held in 1903: 60 cyclists took part, but only 20 finished after a gruelling race lasting 19 days. Cycling, walking, mountaineering, angling and camping – promoted particularly by the Scout movement – all helped to extend public access to the 'great outdoors'. No country did more to promote a sense of the value of natural beauty and landscape than the USA, where Yellowstone became the world's first national park in 1871. The USA was fortunate to have a great champion of this movement as president, at a critical moment when the environment was under intense pressure from farming, mining and forestry interests. During his term of office (1901-9), Theodore Roosevelt helped to establish five new parks, and the first 18 national 'monuments' – areas of outstanding landscape set aside for scientific and historic preservation. Inspired by naturalists such as John Muir and John Burroughs, Roosevelt also created 50 wildlife refuges, starting with Pelican Island in Florida.

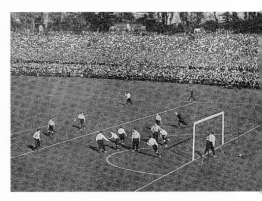

CUP FINAL FEVER A record 114 815 people watched the 1901 FA Cup Final at Crystal Palace. Non-league Tottenham Hotspur drew 2-2 with Sheffield United, but went on to win the replay at Bolton, 3-1.

VICTORY IN PARIS A mixture of relief and exhaustion shows on the faces of the competitors in the first ever Tour de France as they reached the finish line in Paris on July 19, 1903.

TOWARDS THE WELFARE STATE

A FEW COUNTRIES RESPONDED TO PRESSURE FOR SOCIAL CHANGE BY INTRODUCING GOVERNMENT-FUNDED SCHEMES TO RELIEVE DISTRESS

TEMPORARY SHELTER A London night refuge for women is pictured in the French journal *Le Petit Parisien* in 1902. The accommodation amounts to little more than coffin-like cots.

David Lloyd George, the British Liberal politician, used highly coloured images to describe the wealthy adversaries who stood in the way of his proposed social reforms. He contrasted them to 'the old workman having to find his way to the gates of the tomb, bleeding and footsore, through the brambles and thorns of poverty'.

In virtually all the industrialised countries, sickness and old age were akin to destitution. Some workers were provided for by funds distributed by their trade unions; a few were given pensions, even retirement homes, by enlightened employers; others might be accommodated in almshouses.

But most poor workers, once they were no longer employable, had to depend for survival on the good will of their family – or otherwise upon soup kitchens, the Salvation Army and handouts from charities and the Church. In Britain the Poor Law, in operation since Tudor times, offered assistance administered through the parish, but this was extremely rudimentary: it included accommodation in workhouses, where orphans would be mixed in with the aged, the sick and the mentally ill.

The basic ethos at the turn of the century was that if you were poor and unemployed you were either feeble or unworthy. Public assistance ran not far short of punishment. But this attitude was changing. Many people began to acknowledge that luck came into the equation, and that the poor were at the mercy of the fickle turns of the economy.

The US movement called 'progressivism' demonstrates the direction of this changing attitude. Social reformers such as Jane Addams working in the slums of Chicago and

SIT UP TO SLEEP For a penny a night, the Salvation Army offered the homeless food and 'sit-up' accommodation in their shelter at Blackfriars, London.

Lillian D. Wald in New York began to press for government action to relieve urban distress. They saw that government or municipal funding, drawn from income raised through taxes, was the only way to initiate the kind of coordinated renewal programmes and reforms that the dire circumstances called for. Robust government action was also needed to limit the power of the big corporate trusts and to push through legislation to reduce working hours, secure pensions and so forth.

Among the leading progressive politicians was the Republican governor of Wisconsin and US senator, Robert M. La Follette, who drove through a number of important reforms at municipal and federal government level. Many of the policies of President Theodore Roosevelt were likewise considered progressive – such as his Pure Food and Drug Act of 1906, designed to curb abuses in the food and pharmaceutical industries.

Roosevelt thought that his chosen successor, William Howard Taft, would show a similar enthusiasm for reform, but he soon became disillusioned with Taft's performance. He stood against Taft in the 1912 election, representing the Progressive Party. The result, however, was to split the Republican vote and to put the Democrat Woodrow Wilson into the White House. As it turned out, Wilson pushed through a raft of progressive measures, including antitrust acts and laws to control child labour, though much of the social change called for by the progressives did not take place until the New Deal in the 1930s.

A similar pattern could be traced in other industrialised countries, where democratic governments came under the combined pressure of social reformers, trade union agitation and growing political representation by social democratic and labour parties. As in the

HOME SWEET HOME In the overcrowded tenements of Berlin it was not uncommon to find a family of eight sleeping in one room (below). Some of the German unemployed, however, were the lucky beneficiaries of purpose-built welfare 'colonies' (bottom).

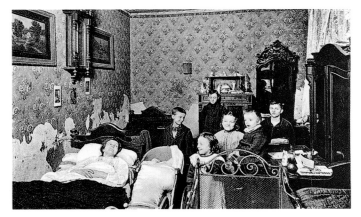

USA, municipal authorities began to take over responsibilities for the public good. Efforts were made in France, Germany and Britain to clear the worst slums, thus creating the beginnings of public housing schemes.

Political stagnation

But reform, by definition, meant a change to the status quo. It was bound to be controversial, meeting resistance from those – such as taxpayers – whose interests were dented in favour of those who benefited. Successful reform was possible only where government had both the will and a stable enough grip on power to see legislation through. In Germany rapid industrialisation had created a large urban population living in overcrowded tenements around the city centres. No head of government, however, could fill the shoes of Bismarck, German chancellor from 1871 to 1890. Among other achievements, he had driven through reforms in the 1880s, introducing an old age pension scheme and sickness and accident insurance. Subsequent governments were fragile coalitions dominated by the old landowning Junker class

CRIME AND BIRDSONG IN LONDON'S EAST END

Working-class districts of major industrial cities may have been grim, but they were also colourful concentrations of vigorous humanity. The *Strand Magazine* ran a series of articles called 'Trips About Town' by George R. Sims, recounting his forays into the East End of London. In this article of 1905 he visited the Sunday market in Bethnal Green, where caged birds were sold:

'And now we plunge into Sclater Street . . . At first you see nothing but the avenue of bird-cages. The crowd in the narrow street is so dense that you can gather no idea of . . . what the mob of men crowding together in black patches of humanity are dealing in.

'You press your way in and find that the shops are mostly packed with linnets, canaries, love-birds, Japanese nightingales, parrots, bird-cages and fittings, and all the necessaries and luxuries of pet land . . .

'But it is in the roadway, in the densest part of the crowd, that you find the dominant note of the day's dealings. There you see everywhere little groups of men, each with a bird in a small cage tied up in a blue bird's-eye pocket handkerchief. The tying is all to a pattern. One side of the cage is open to the light, and the bird within is being eagerly examined by quiet connoisseurs . . .

'Here is a typical unemployed. The poor fellow stands, the picture of hopelessness, offering his empty bird-cage for a few pence. There is a suggestion of Dickensy pathos about the shabby, gaunt-looking, but clean-faced man trying to sell the cage of the pet poverty has compelled him to part with . . .'

1908 The Old Age Pension Act introduced in Britain

1909 Royal Commission recommends the introduction of insurance schemes to cover sickness and unemployment

1912 The Democrat Woodrow Wilson wins the US presidential election

EIGHT HOURS Paris Métro workers lobby for an eight-hour day in 1913. Support for workers' rights even appeared on soap labels (right), but socialist politicians such as Aristide Briand (left) had limited impact as reformers.

and the Kaiser. The landowning classes refused to contemplate additional taxation and death duties to fund further reforms; in any case the German budget was increasingly overshadowed by deficits from the cost of naval construction. Such an atmosphere left little room for extending the welfare state.

In France, too, unstable coalitions hindered reform. The most stable period was 1899-1905, when the government was dominated by the 'Bloc Républicain' of left-wing and centre parties. Here, the reforms were driven largely by anticlericalism, in which the state took over Church-run institutions, but this brought chaos in the wake of change. After 1905 the Socialist Party withdrew from the Bloc, refusing to compromise its ideals by taking part in any more coalitions. The result was instability in government, while many of the working class, alienated from parliamentary politics, opted for the confrontational and revolutionary tactics of the syndicalists. After 1906 the first government of Georges Clemenceau, leading a Radical Bloc, attempted moderate reforms, such as introducing an eight-hour working day and income tax, but these were mostly blocked by parliament. The signals were in any case confusing: both he and his successor Aristide Briand, who was prime minister from 1909 to 1912, imposed draconian measures on strikers. Thereafter rearmament in the face of the growing threat from Germany dominated the political agenda. France had to wait until 1930 for its first government-sponsored social insurance.

Pressing for change

The two-party system in Britain proved a more solid base from which to launch reforms. Both parties contained a fairly broad range of opinion, and where they overlapped there was consensus that reform was needed. An important source of political pressure was the Fabian Society, a left-wing group that advocated evolutionary (as opposed to revolutionary) social change. Founded in 1884, its early members included a host of influential writers and intellectuals – figures such as the playwright George Bernard Shaw, the political reformer and later theosophist Annie Besant and, above all, the hard-working husband-and-wife team of Sidney and Beatrice Webb. The Fabian Society pressed for government intervention in social affairs, insisting that the state should 'guarantee to every worker, in all the contingencies of life, an unbroken sufficiency of the means to a healthy existence'.

PARTED BY THE WORKHOUSE

Conditions in British workhouses were distinctly harsh and heartless. For example, old and impoverished married couples, after many decades living and often working together, were obliged to go into separate men's and women's accommodation.

Beatrice Webb was appointed to a Royal Commission set up in 1906 to look into the workings of the Poor Law. This reported in 1909, and recommended the introduction of insurance schemes against sickness and unemployment and the establishment of state-funded labour exchanges – previously a service provided by trade unions. It also recommended that municipal boroughs and parishes should be empowered to treat the old, the sick, the insane and the very young in separate institutions. The Commission, however, remained divided over several issues, including the causes of poverty. The majority blamed factors such as personal weakness and alcoholism; the minority, led by Beatrice Webb and the future Labour MP George Lansbury, blamed economic causes beyond the control of the individual. The minority report went on to recommend the abolition of the Poor Law in favour of separate committees to look after its charges, such as Health Committees for the sick – but the Poor Law stumbled on until the 1940s.

In Britain, it was perhaps among the young that reforms in this era had the greatest impact. In 1904 the Inter-Departmental Committee on Physical Deterioration reported on its survey of the general health of the population – commissioned in part as a response to the alarming evidence witnessed by army recruitment offices during the Boer War. It recommended school medical inspections, the provision of state-funded meals for needy children and the introduction of physical exercise as part of the school curriculum. Local authorities were empowered to provide free meals for schoolchildren in 1906, and a year later the School Medical Service was established.

Previously, members of the working class saw very little of the medical profession. Doctors tended to be called only when the sick were at death's door, and the family lived in hope that the doctor might kindly 'forget' to send his bill. Health facilities remained scant for most of the population: even in 1913, there were just 21 health visitors in Birmingham, serving a population of 525 000. After 1907, however, school medical staff were at least able to monitor the young.

Their initial findings were alarming: half had bad teeth; a third were unhygienically dirty; and many suffered from ring worm, poor sight and partial deafness.

The Liberal reforms

A major turning point in Britain came in 1906, when the Liberals led by Henry Campbell-Bannerman won a landslide victory over the Conservatives, fatally split over trade tariffs. Campbell-Bannerman selected a dynamic cabinet of reformers, including Herbert Asquith, David Lloyd George, Winston Churchill and the working-class activist and Independent Radical John Burns. In 1908 they introduced the Old Age Pension Act, which provided a pension of five shillings a week for anyone over the age of 70, provided that he or she had an income of less than £31 10s per annum – a figure bordering on the poverty line. Married couples received seven shillings and sixpence a week. This provision was considered almost revolutionary at the time. Many opponents disagreed with the use of government funds to sponsor such a costly venture, and suggested that it would bankrupt the country – even though the Germans had had old age pensions since 1883.

MEDICAL EXAMINATION For many children, their first encounter with a doctor came at school. Checkups performed by the School Medical Service in Britain provided a vital safety net for the health of the nation.

WELSH WIZARD: DAVID LLOYD GEORGE

Energetic and a brilliant orator, David Lloyd George (1863-1945) was a key member of the reforming Liberal governments led by Henry Campbell-Bannerman and Herbert Asquith. His parents were Welsh, of modest means, and although born in Manchester, he retained a close affinity with his Welsh origins. He was christened David George, but his father died when he was an infant and he was brought up by his mother and her brother, Richard Lloyd, whose name he adopted.

Having trained as a solicitor, Lloyd George switched to politics in his mid-twenties. He came to prominence during the Boer War with controversial support for Boer independence. He served as President of the Board of Trade from 1906 until promoted to Chancellor of the Exchequer when Asquith took over as prime minister in 1908. This gave Lloyd George the financial power to push through the social reforms close to his heart. The rejection of his 'people's budget' by the House of Lords in 1909 resulted in a constitutional crisis, but Lloyd George was in his element during such confrontation; he famously dismissed the Lords as '500 men chosen accidentally from the unemployed'.

His popularity was dented by the whiff of 'insider dealing' surrounding his purchase of Marconi shares in 1912. Nonetheless, he took over as prime minister on Asquith's resignation in 1916 during the First World War to head a coalition government. Returned to power in 1918, he saw his position eroded by economic depression which failed to deliver his promise 'to make Britain a fit country for heroes to live in'. His coalition with the Conservatives collapsed in 1922, and he stepped down as prime minister.

Although married, Lloyd George lived openly with his secretary Frances Stevenson, whom he married after his wife's death in 1941. This aroused much gossip, but he seemed oblivious.

FAMILY MAN? David Lloyd George stands with his wife Margaret and daughter Megan.

JUST LOOKING Winston Churchill (centre) and his wife line up behind Prime Minister Herbert Asquith to inspect the operation of a new labour exchange in south London in 1910. National Insurance stamps (inset) were introduced the following year.

In 1908 Campbell-Bannerman had to retire on the grounds of ill-health, and Asquith took over as prime minister. The reforms continued. In 1909 Winston Churchill, now President of the Board of Trade, introduced publicly funded labour exchanges, following the recommendations of the Poor Law Commission. Again, this was on the German model. Also that year he introduced the Trade Boards Bill, setting up trade boards to fix minimum wages for the sweated industries – the thousands of small businesses employing mainly women to produce clothing, cardboard boxes and so on, for low pay and in wretched conditions. This was an issue close to the heart of the Women's Trade Union League led by Mary Macarthur, who had set up the National Anti-Sweating League in 1906.

New taxes were needed to fund the Liberal reforms – especially the old age pension – as well as the rearmament of the British navy. So in 1909 Lloyd George, as Chancellor of the Exchequer, introduced a radical budget, raising income tax for higher wage-earners, applying a super-tax for incomes over £5000, imposing a motor tax on cars and petrol and increasing death duties and taxes on tobacco and alcohol. He called this his 'people's budget' – 'to wage warfare against poverty and squalidness'. The House of Lords, however, refused to pass it, thereby putting further reforms on hold. The Liberals were indignant; as one of their MPs, Augustine Birrell, wittily put it: 'The House of Lords represent nobody but themselves, and they enjoy the full confidence of their constituents.' Reform of the House of Lords then became a burning issue, resolved in the Parliament Act of 1911, by which the power of the Lords was curtailed and it was no longer able to reject finance bills.

In 1911 the Liberal government introduced the National Insurance Act. All workers and their employers had to pay weekly insurance contributions into a national fund, and the government undertook to pay benefit in times of sickness and unemployment. This effectively expanded to a national level the insurance schemes previously arranged by friendly and provident societies. The benefits were limited in scope – and the scheme was highly controversial. The British Medical Association (BMA) rejected it, mainly on the grounds that funding was inadequate to meet doctors' wages; but they abandoned their boycott in January 1913. One source of complaint came from ladies with a large domestic staff; as employers, they now had to pay insurance contributions, registered in the form of stamps. They found this 'stamp-licking' demeaning and objectionable.

Even so, from these small beginnings developed Britain's welfare state that came into full flourish after the Second World War.

THE STIRRINGS OF SOCIALISM

CHANGE WAS IN THE AIR, BUT FOR MANY SOCIALISTS THE ONLY SURE WAY TO ACHIEVE THEIR GOALS WAS THROUGH ARMED STRUGGLE

The big newcomer to the political arena was socialism. In the 1880s, socialism was in its infancy; by 1914, every industrialised country had a major socialist presence – either in mainstream politics, as in Germany or France, or in subversive underground movements, as in Russia.

The socialists were often the first political activists to go among the working class. They brought with them new hopes and aspirations, and a sense that something could be done to alleviate oppression through the collective discipline of the party, or through a trade union. Socialists were at the forefront of the 'new unionism' aimed at unskilled labour. They began at the grass roots level among people who were not yet politicised, but whose growing resentment could easily be channelled into political action.

Through the growth of mechanisation and unskilled labour in the most recent phase of industrialisation, the classes had become increasingly divided. As a result, many in the working classes never had any contact with members of the employer classes that ruled their lives – and they often had only brief contact with the educated middle classes through schools, or through experiences on the wrong side of the law. This separateness helped to identify the working class – an important distinction in the socialist vision of the future.

Most socialist theory focused on the proletariat, the urban

CITY LIFE AND RURAL DREAMS
Rural resettlement projects in Germany (right) strike a vivid contrast with the alleyways of Whitechapel, London (below). In the German scene, the building in the foreground is for poultry.

industrial working class. But it was clear that those working the land still represented a large proportion of the population. In France in 1900, 43 per cent of the population earned their living from the land; in Germany 36 per cent. Although traditionally conservative in outlook, many rural people were trapped into poverty, and were a potential source of support for the socialists.

Following the lead of Karl Marx, socialists believed that class, not nationality, was the basis for struggle. Socialism, therefore, was an international movement: it called for all workers of the world to recognise their common interests, and to struggle to overthrow capitalism and take hold of the means of production for their own benefit. Embodying these international aspirations was the federation of socialist parties and trade unions

LEADERS OF THE LEFT   A rare woman among the leaders of the Second International, meeting in Amsterdam in 1904, Polish-born Rosa Luxemburg was a prominent figure in Germany's Social Democratic Party.

known as the Second International, founded in Paris in 1889 – the 'First International', or International Working Men's Association, had been set up in 1864, with Marx himself as one of its leading lights, but had become hopelessly bogged down in internal disputes.

Revolution or evolution?

Some socialists, such as the British Fabians, strongly opposed violent revolution. For others, this was the only means. At the critical 1903 Congress of the Russian Social Democratic Workers' Party held in exile in Brussels and London, Lenin forced the party to split into the Bolsheviks and Mensheviks over this very question: revolution or evolution?

The answer was never cut-and-dried. Socialism attracted impassioned social reformers angered by the capitalist system, whose iniquities were clear for all to see in the working-class districts of any industrialised town. Anger and impatience for change quickly spilled over into talk of violent revolution. Events in Russia in 1905 demonstrated the vulnerability of existing government structures to revolutionary insurrection, if carefully planned and carried through.

What was taken as read by all socialism's adherents was that it would triumph over capitalism: this had been satisfactorily demonstrated by 'scientific' historical analysis of the class struggle since feudalism, as propounded by Marx and others. The collapse of capitalism was an inevitable part of this evolution; the only question was when. The more cautious recognised that violent confrontation could lead only to immense disruption, which might actually delay the realisation of the socialist dream. This was the view of men such as the French socialist politician Jean Jaurès and the German Eduard Bernstein. In their minds, the path to socialism required more measured steps – in pushing for universal suffrage, for example. Giving the vote to working-class people, who would inevitably, it was believed, vote for socialist candidates, meant that socialism could be achieved within existing political

VOICE OF MODERATION   The German socialist Eduard Bernstein advocated reformism, or revisionism. He believed that Marxist socialism could evolve out of capitalism, without the trauma of revolution, provided the electoral system permitted change.

structures. This 'gradualist' approach was criticised by radical socialists as eating at the table of the enemy. Many socialists, however, took a flexible view, believing that approaches should be tailored to national circumstances.

The socialists were not simply pressing for political change, nor indeed social reforms; they wanted to bring about a change in attitude, to sweep away the hidebound traditional institutions of the past and replace them with efficient, representative organisations that corresponded to the needs of the modern world. They were committed to reason, education, enlightenment and science. Religion, often tied closely to the state, evoked the old world of ignorance and superstition – hence many socialists, notably in Germany and France, were strongly anticlerical.

The effect of the cause

Despite exerting pressure for change, the socialists could claim few tangible gains in this period. Their time was to come during and after the First World War; meanwhile, where reforms were achieved, they were largely carried out by liberals and progressives in government.

Nonetheless, socialist parties grew rapidly in strength: in Scandinavia, for instance, socialists were polling a third of the vote. By

1912-14, socialist parties in the USA were able to command a million or more votes; likewise in Italy. In 1914, a third of the voters in France opted for the socialist candidates led by Jean Jaurès, and 103 socialist deputies were returned to the National Assembly. But the socialist party with the most significant parliamentary influence was in Germany where the Social Democratic Party (*Sozial-demokratische Partei Deutschlands*, SPD), founded in 1875, presented a disciplined front and became the largest party in the Reichstag in 1912. However, even then it did not form part of the government.

Confronting the SPD was a combination of capitalist and imperialist interests, led by the Kaiser, and appealing to patriotism and traditional bourgeois instincts for wealth and comfort. In contrast to the socialists' internationalism, their opponents tended to be nationalistic, xenophobic and anti-Semitic. The situation propelled some notable personalities to the fore, including Rosa Luxemburg. Born in Russian Poland to Jewish parents, she became a Marxist while a student in Switzerland; later she moved to Germany, where she became a leader of the German SPD in 1898. She was arrested in Berlin during the Spartacist Uprising in 1919, and was cruelly murdered by members of a right-wing paramilitary group, the Freikorps.

Britain had had a Social Democratic Federation since 1881 but, compared with the continent, radical socialism and Marxism played a less significant role in mainstream

JEAN JAURÈS: APOSTLE FOR PEACE AND SOCIALISM

The French socialist Jean Jaurès cut an unusual figure for a politician in his day: stocky, broad-shouldered and with an impish grin, his very demeanour suggested that he was a man of the people, and a fighter. He used a political language to match: fiery and impassioned. He began his career as a university lecturer in Toulouse, but an interest in politics led to his election, at the age of 26, to the National Assembly in Paris. This proved a disillusioning experience and pushed him farther towards radical politics. He returned to Toulouse University, where his speeches on social welfare and reform attracted enthusiastic audiences. By 1890 he had converted to socialism, declaring a deep-seated hatred for the injustices of capitalism: 'The domination of one class is an outrage against humanity', he declared. In 1894 he was returned to parliament on a socialist ticket. As an evolutionary socialist, he advocated negotiation and arbitration in place of revolution. After 1904 he conveyed his brand of socialism through *L'Humanité*, a daily newspaper he founded with fellow politician Aristide Briand. The next year, he became the leader of a unified Socialist Party.

It was clear to Jaurès that the forces of capitalism and imperialism were pushing the world towards war: 'The fever of imperialism has become a sickness,' he declared. 'It is the disease of a badly run society, which does not know how to use its energies at home.' During the Balkan Crisis of 1912, he called an Emergency Socialist Congress in Basle, Switzerland, and for a time it seemed that international socialism – through strikes and political action – might make war impossible. As the storm clouds gathered, however, socialist solidarity evaporated. On July 31, 1914, Jaurès met with colleagues in a café in Rue Montmartre, Paris. A disturbed patriot, his head full of the glories of a war with Germany, leant through the window and shot Jaurès dead. Four days later, war was declared.

IN FULL CRY Jaurès addresses a crowd in Paris in 1913. The skills of oratory were even more important in the days before the microphone.

1911 The Sidney Street Siege

1912 In Germany the Social Democratic Party (SPD) is the largest party in the Reichstag

1914 Jean Jaurès is assassinated in Paris

LAND AND LIBERTY: REVOLUTION IN MEXICO

For over 30 years, starting in 1876, Mexico was ruled by Porfirio Díaz. The country prospered under his ruthless regime, but only a narrow band of society enjoyed the profits. By 1910 he had become deeply unpopular among the poor and the dissenting middle classes of his country. A number of radical groups had sprung up, many inspired by the European syndicalist and anarchist movements.

A reforming politician, Francisco Madero, opposed Díaz in an election in 1910 and was defeated; he then took up arms and triggered a nationwide revolt, overthrowing Díaz in 1911. Disgruntled factions congregated around rebel leaders, such as Francisco ('Pancho') Villa in the north and Emiliano Zapata in the rural states of the centre and south. In 1913 Madero was the victim of a right-wing coup by General Victoriano Huerta; imprisoned, he was killed 'while attempting to escape'. In 1914 Huerta was in turn overthrown by a rebel coalition led by Venustiano Carranza, assisted by General Alvaro Obregón. Zapata and Villa also formed part of this coalition, but soon fell out with Carranza and Obregón, and formed their own alliance to fight a guerrilla war against them. Mexico was now in a state of civil war – a war that would cost 250 000 lives. Zapata, a farmer, of Indian blood, had been goaded into revolutionary action by the iniquitous behaviour of sugar planters in Morelos State. Fighting under the slogan 'Land, liberty, and death to the landowners!', his prime concern was agrarian reform, redistributing confiscated estates among peasants. Villa was more of a firebrand, a former bandit roaming the north, the scene of most of Mexico's economic development.

After 1915 Carranza started to squeeze the rebels into their homelands. He also brought about a number of reforms, introducing a new constitution and state education, and restricting the power of the Roman Catholic Church. Mexico's giant neighbour to the north, the USA, with huge investments in the country, remained aloof until 1916 when Villa crossed the border into New Mexico and killed some American citizens at Columbus. It sent in forces to bring him to justice, but after 11 months of fruitless pursuit, Villa was still at large. In 1919 Zapata was lured into a trap by a traitor and murdered. Some of his demands were met by the government after 1920, when Obregón ousted Carranza, who was subsequently murdered. During Obregón's four-year presidency, the revolts began to subside. Villa was murdered in 1923. This fate also lay ahead for Obregón, assassinated after being elected for a second term in 1928. The dust kicked up by the Mexican Revolution began to settle only in the 1930s.

politics. Reforms, largely inspired by the genuine and urgent concerns of middle-class activists such as the Fabians, and backed by prominent writers, artists and even industrialists, were enacted by the Liberal governments of Campbell-Bannerman and Asquith. And to many opponents, their government seemed virtually revolutionary. A.J. Balfour, the leader of the Conservative Party in opposition, declared: 'Campbell-Bannerman is a mere cork, dancing on a torrent, which he

REPRESSION AND REVOLUTION Porfirio Díaz held power through brutal suppression and the firing squad (below). This helped to unite a broad opposition behind revolutionaries such as Pancho Villa (bottom, seated, at the centre) and Emiliano Zapata (seated, with sombrero), photographed in 1914 in the presidential palace in Mexico City.

cannot control, and what is going on here is a faint echo of the same movement which has produced massacres in St Petersburg, riots in Vienna, and socialist processions in Berlin.'

The British Labour Party was never wholly socialist; it had even deliberately omitted the word 'socialist' from its constitution. After 1906, however, through its 29 MPs, it could claim to be making gradualist progress alongside the Liberal government, which in any case shared many of its concerns. Parallel political developments took place in Australia, where the Labor Party actually formed the federal government in 1912.

Nevertheless, a more radical strain of socialist activism did emerge in Britain after 1906 under the title 'Guild Socialism'. This was a peculiarly British movement based loosely on the ideals of the medieval guilds. Its leading lights, such as G.D.H. Cole and Arthur J. Penty, envisioned a world governed by large worker-controlled guilds representing the major industries. In fact, Guild Socialism was similar to syndicalism, but less militant. They shared with the anarchists a hostility to the idea of the state, and all its manifestations, such as bureaucracy. Although politically insignificant, the Guild Socialists at one stage looked set to take over the Fabian Society.

THE INTERNATIONAL

Most socialists and communists were inspired by a vision of global socialism, in which justice and equality would be extended to all workers around the world under the banner of a giant federation called the International. However, this concept was perpetually undermined by the inability of workers to unite. Old national and ethnic squabbles, religious disputes, rivalries between unions representing different crafts and trades – all stood in the way of universal harmony. Nonetheless, the dream of international socialism remained alive, and it was reinforced in the socialist anthem 'The International' (or 'Internationale'). Written by a French transport worker in 1871, it was sung at all the major socialist meetings of this period:

'C'est la lutte finale.
Groupons-nous, et, demain
L'Internationale
Sera le genre humain.'

('This is the final conflict.
Let us form up, and, tomorrow
The International
Will be the human race.')

Many went on to form the Communist Party of Great Britain after 1917.

Throughout the industrialised world radical groups were thus constantly refining and defining their outlook in contrast to others. By this means, each sought the way forward towards its vision of the future.

Against war

The leading socialists maintained a strong sense of the international dimension of their movement, and held regular meetings to discuss global issues. They were also ready to welcome foreign comrades, notably those fleeing from Russia. Trotsky, for instance, called on the leader of the Austrian Social Democrats, Victor Adler, when he first arrived penniless in Vienna in 1902.

The most pressing issue facing international socialism was war. In contrast to those proposing revolution, many moderate socialists were pacifists, and struggled to unite all socialists in opposition to war – or at least international war fought in the interests of capitalism and imperialism. This concern had been voiced as early as 1900, at the Fifth Congress of the Socialist International in Paris, when delegates from 21 countries passed a resolution to oppose militarism and war. By 1910, this concern was beginning to seem ever more pressing. A meeting of international socialists in Basle, Switzerland, that year drew up the following resolution: 'If war threatens to break out, it is the duty of the working classes and their parliamentary representatives in the countries involved,

MOBILISING LABOUR A Labour Party candidate campaigns in Yarmouth (top) during the British general election of 1906. By 1910 Labour had 40 MPs and could campaign effectively for the reform of the House of Lords (above).

supported by the coordinating activity of the International Socialist Bureau, to exert every effort in order to prevent the outbreak of war by the means they consider most effective . . . In case war should break out anyway, it is their duty to intervene in favour of its speedy termination and with all powers to utilise the economic and political crisis created by the war to arouse the people and thereby to hasten the downfall of capitalist class rule.'

This proved a vain hope, but the sentiments expressed indicated the belief that socialists, through combined international action, could change the world in a vital way. When war did come in 1914, nationalism was the stronger force. Men like Keir Hardie, first leader of the British Labour Party, were bitterly disappointed that the Socialist International failed to mount a general strike to avert war, and this was said to have contributed to Hardie's death the following year.

THE AGE OF THE ANARCHIST

ANARCHISTS RANGED FROM THOSE FIGHTING TO OVERTHROW CAPITALISM BY VIOLENT MEANS TO BELIEVERS IN A UTOPIAN VISION OF COMMUNITY AND COOPERATION

For any head of state, this was a dangerous time to be alive. Assassinations occurred with shocking regularity, often carried out by determined individuals who cared nothing for their own survival. Some of these were the by-product of palace coups, or the work of nationalist factions. For instance, King Alexander and Queen Draga of Serbia were shot dead by disaffected army officers in 1903; a similar fate befell King Carlos I and Crown Prince Luis of Portugal in 1908.

One cause repeatedly blamed for assassination was anarchism. There had been several attempted anarchist attacks on Queen Victoria; President Carnot of France was assassinated by an Italian anarchist in 1894; and another killed the Empress of Austria in 1898. In July 1900, King Umberto I of Italy was assassinated by an anarchist. In September 1901 President William McKinley of the USA was shot by an anarchist called Leon Czolgosz in the Temple of Music at the Pan-American Exposition in Buffalo, New York; he died eight days later. In 1906, an anarchist threw a bomb hidden in a bouquet of flowers at the carriage of King Alfonso XIII of Spain and his bride on their wedding day; it killed 18 people, but not the royal couple.

Anarchists were also widely blamed for outbreaks of violent crime and civil unrest. A famous case occurred in the East End of London in December 1910. Three unarmed policemen were shot and killed during what appeared to be the burglary of a jewellery shop in Houndsditch. Following a tip-off, the police raided another house and found arms, ammunition and the ingredients for explosives. This, they believed, was the lair of 'Peter the Painter', nickname of Peter Straume, a signwriter and self-confessed anarchist from Riga in Russian Latvia. The culprits were tracked down to a house at No. 100 Sidney Street, in nearby Stepney, and in the early hours of January 3, 1911, the area was cordoned off by

POINT BLANK   A French illustration of 1900 depicts the death of King Umberto of Italy in Monza. The assassin, Angelo Bresci, was avenging the suppression of a workers' revolt in Milan in 1898.

MARRIAGE MAYHEM   King Alfonso XIII of Spain and his bride, Ena, had a narrow escape when an anarchist bomb exploded during their wedding procession in Madrid in 1906.

armed police. When shots were fired at the police from an upper window, military reinforcements were summoned; by midday there were 750 police at the scene, as well as an attachment of Scots Guards armed with Maxim guns. Winston Churchill, the new Home Secretary, arrived to review proceedings. At 1 pm smoke was seen seeping from the windows of the house. Churchill ordered the attendant fire engine to stay away, and the house burned to the ground. Inside were two charred bodies, identified as those of Fritz Svaars and Jacob Vogel. There was no sign of 'Peter the Painter', who had vanished into thin air. The story fostered a growing xenophobia in Britain towards refugee communities, who were seen as a potential anarchist threat from within.

The term 'anarchist' was often applied by the press to any violent dissident. In fact, it had a clear-cut meaning. Building on the work of

19th-century radical thinkers – such as the French Pierre Joseph Proudhon, who had declared that 'property is theft' – the anarchists believed that society would be best ruled without any form of government at all. (The word anarchy comes from the Greek *anarkhos* meaning 'without a ruler'.) They believed that hierarchies of government and institutions were inherently evil and led to oppression and inequality. Anarchists advocated a world ruled by thousands of local, volunteer organisations which had the interests of all individuals at heart. The end product envisaged by anarchism was similar to that of socialism – with one major difference. Socialists wanted the state to take over the means of production on behalf of the people; anarchists wanted the people themselves to own the means of production, without any state structure at all. Like socialism, anarchism was divided into two camps. There were those who felt that anarchism could be achieved by gradual evolution – the 'euthanasia of government'. And there were those who could not wait, believing that the conditions for anarchism had to be manufactured through 'direct action': strikes, insurrection, revolution – and the assassination of rulers. In reality, anarchism never achieved much political clout, although it did have a broad following among union activists in Italy, Spain and Portugal.

The more benign anarchists earned some sympathy among the broader public. Among these was Piotr Kropotkin, who spent two years in Russian prisons before fleeing to the West. In his latter

'MOST DANGEROUS WOMAN IN AMERICA' Emma Goldman espoused free love and birth control as well as anarchism.

years he settled in Britain, and wrote an influential book, *Mutual Aid* (1902), advocating cooperation in place of confrontation. More controversial was Emma Goldman, the daughter of Lithuanian immigrants to New York. A rousing public speaker, she was a vehement critic of social injustice and an advocate of women's rights. Her open attitude to free love was the subject of much censure, but she reached the nadir of her political life after the assassination of President McKinley in 1901. Because his assassin had attended one of her lectures in Chicago, the US authorities tried unsuccessfully to connect her to the crime. In 1903 a law was passed that enabled the US authorities to deport anarchists of foreign extraction; Goldman founded the Free Speech League to oppose this, and later created the American Civil Liberties Union. During the First World War, she was deported to Russia for her vocal opposition to military conscription. However, she found Bolshevik Communism distasteful, and continued to travel and lecture, and died in Canada in 1940, at the age of 70.

STRONG ARM TACTICS Home Secretary Winston Churchill (right, in top hat) sent more than 1000 armed police and soldiers to root out a handful of anarchists during the Sidney Street Siege in 1911 (below).

VOTES FOR WOMEN

AS THE NEW CENTURY GATHERED PACE, THE CAMPAIGN FOR VOTES FOR WOMEN EXPLODED INTO ONE OF THE GREAT ISSUES OF THE ERA

Women in Colorado, USA, had been able to vote in state elections since 1893, and their right to do so seemed entirely logical to local people: 'Woman Suffrage in Colorado . . . has more than demonstrated its justice,' declared Judge Lindsey of Denver in 1906. 'No one would dare to propose its repeal; and if left to the men of the State, any proposition to remove the right bestowed upon women would be over-whelmingly defeated.' Colorado women were not the first in the United States: Wyoming was the true trailblazer, giving women the vote in 1869. Utah and Idaho followed suit in 1896, and by 1913 they had

been joined by Washington State, California, Oregon, Kansas, Arizona and Alaska. As a result, the USA can justifiably be called the pioneer of votes for women.

But it was a different matter at national level. In a country founded on a Declaration of Independence that stated 'We hold these truths to be self-evident, that all men are created equal', giving women equal voting rights to men had an undeniable rationale; and by the turn of the century, it had a new urgency. Social workers such as Jane Addams, working among the poor of Chicago, felt a sense of burning indignation that women – as wives and mothers, and now as an increasingly important part of the work force, let alone as individuals – had unequal rights with men when it came to property, divorce and representation in government.

It was a global issue. The *Adelaide Observer* in Australia might have been speaking for all disenfranchised women when

STATE BY STATE American campaigners gather in Washington DC in 1913. Left: Male supporters do their bit for the US 'Woman Suffrage' campaign around 1906.

it announced: 'It has always been an anomaly in the colony [of South Australia], that while the most drunken, ignorant man in the community possessed the technical qualifications to vote for members of parliament and to be a member himself, the most intellectual and noble woman has not enjoyed such rights.' Australia took the lead from its neighbour, New Zealand, which had given national voting rights to its women as early as 1893. South Australia and Western Australia followed suit during the 1890s, and one by one, over seven years following the creation of the Commonwealth of Australia in 1901, all the states gave the national vote to their women.

Feminists in the rest of the world were still locked in struggle. They set up national women's suffrage movements, and also pooled their experiences through organisations such as the International Woman Suffrage Alliance. By 1910, the vote had been given to women in Finland (1906), and to the 300 000 women in Norway who paid stipulated levels of tax (1907). Pressure for the vote varied from country to country. France, for instance, had had a vociferous – but unsuccessful – feminist movement virtually since the revolution of 1789. As in the rest of French politics, the movement was split by religious, regional and class affiliations. A women's suffrage bill was introduced in the French parliament in 1901, but it was rejected – the fate of all such bills until as late as 1945.

The women of Germany were comparative latecomers. As Alice Zimmern put it in her *Women's Suffrage in Many Lands* (1909): 'The status of woman as the home-maker and *Hausfrau* was so firmly established, the intellectual superiority and absolute predominance of man so much taken for granted by both sexes, that the mere desire to revolt against their subjection would not have been sufficient to inspire large masses of German women.' In any case, German women were restricted by laws of association which prohibited them from forming political groups or attending public meetings, particularly in Prussia and Bavaria. These were lifted by the Reichstag in 1908, and thereafter the women's

1903 Women's Social and Political Union (WSPU) founded by Emmeline and Christabel Pankhurst

1905 Suffrage bill fails to get through the House of Commons

suffrage movement grew rapidly. However, German women won the right to vote only after the collapse of the Second Reich at the end of the First World War.

The suffragettes

Nowhere was the struggle for votes for women more vigorously and publicly fought than in Britain. There had been a strong movement for women's rights in Britain since the 1860s. In 1897 the National Union of Women's Suffrage Societies was formed, led by Millicent Garrett Fawcett, and dedicated to peaceable and law-abiding lobbying.

One of its activists was Mrs Emmeline Pankhurst, who, like many in the women's movement, had become increasingly frustrated by the lack of progress. As long ago as 1867, the first bill for extending the franchise to women had been presented to, and rejected by, the House of Commons. In 1903 Mrs Pankhurst and her eldest daughter, Christabel, formed the Women's Social and Political Union (WSPU), dedicated to taking a strong, militant line of action under the motto 'Deeds Not Words'. In the early years, they worked from a base in Manchester, holding meetings and distributing leaflets at factory gates. The temperature increased, however, in 1905, after a suffrage bill was talked out by MPs. In October that year, Christabel Pankhurst was arrested for assaulting the

police after repeatedly interrupting a Liberal Party meeting in Manchester. Instead of paying a fine, she and her co-defendant Annie Kenney opted for a seven-day prison sentence. In its coverage of the story, the *Daily Mail* branded the women 'suffragettes', and that is the name the WSPU adopted.

At this point, Mrs Pankhurst moved to London, and set up the WSPU headquarters in the Strand. Assisted by a large number of mainly middle-class recruits – Annie Kenney was a rare working-class exception – the

POLITICS OF PERSUASION 'Women want to vote', proclaims a French banner (top). French demonstrators march for the vote in 1914 (above). The British suffragette Una Dugdale (below) takes the argument to male workers in Newcastle during a by-election in 1908.

MARTYRS TO THE CAUSE Christabel Pankhurst (centre) and Emmeline (right) on trial after an attempt to 'rush' the House of Commons in 1908; they were given prison sentences. The WSPU awarded medals to suffragette hunger strikers (far right) to engender a spirit of pride.

WSPU launched a nationwide campaign. They printed and distributed leaflets and posters, they held thousands of public meetings, they walked the streets bearing placards, they chained themselves to railings and disrupted political meetings. They also held large demonstrations, and on several occasions stormed – or 'rushed' – parliament. Confrontations became increasingly antagonistic, and resulted in mass arrests. On most occasions, the suffragettes chose to go to prison instead of paying a fine, thereby attracting greater publicity and sympathy for the cause. After 1909, suffragette prisoners

TEA AND CAMPAIGNING This china tea set is decorated with a logo, designed by Sylvia Pankhurst, incorporating the WSPU initials and an angel.

adopted a strategy of noncooperation: they refused to eat. The government authorised prison staff to force-feed hunger strikers, applying primitive methods used in lunatic asylums. When news of this practice reached public ears, there was an outcry.

But the Liberal government remained intransigent – particularly the prime minister, Herbert Asquith. Even ministers who had initially been sympathetic, such as Winston Churchill and David Lloyd George, were becoming hardened against the suffragettes by the continual campaign of harassment. Public sympathy was hard to gauge. The suffragettes had many supporters among both men and women. They also had detractors, and the air was thick with sexist theory – such as the idea that women had smaller brains then men, or were too emotional to be entrusted with the responsibility of voting.

There were many high-profile women opponents. Mrs Humphrey Ward, a popular novelist, vehemently disapproved, although she was a noted social worker and philanthropist. Marie Corelli, another extremely successful novelist, couched her antipathies in these terms: 'If the mothers of the British race decide to part altogether with the birthright of their simple womanliness for a political mess of pottage then darker days are in store for the nation than can yet be foreseen or imagined. For with women alone rests the Home, which is the foundation of Empire. When they desert this, their God-appointed centre, the core of national being, then things are tottering to a fall.'

OFFENSIVE ACTION

November 18, 1910, was the suffragettes' 'Black Friday'. Indignant that the Conciliation Bill, offering a limited franchise to women, had been irrevocably delayed by the dissolution of parliament, over 300 delegates of the WSPU decided to march on the House of Commons. The police treated the marchers on this and two subsequent days with a level of brutality not before encountered. The WSPU set up a committee to investigate police behaviour and produce a report:

'For hours I was beaten about the body ... Often [I was] seized by the coat collar, dragged out of the crowd, only to be pushed helplessly along in front of one's tormentor in a side street ... while he beat one up and down one's spine until cramp seized one's legs, when he would then release one with a vicious shove, and with insulting speeches, such as "I will teach you a lesson. I will teach you not to come back any more ..." Once I was thrown with my jaw against a lamp-post with such force that two of my front teeth were loosened...

'... Several times constables and plain-clothes men ... passed their arms round me from the back and clutched hold of my breasts in as public a manner as was possible ... My skirt was lifted up as high as possible, and the constable attempted to lift me off the ground by raising his knee. This he could not do, so he threw me into the crowd and incited the men to treat me as they wished.'

Such sentiments were shared by many women. Equally, however, the WSPU could itself call upon the support of large numbers of women of all backgrounds. The breadth of this support was demonstrated by the success of two great showpieces of the movement: a huge rally in Hyde Park in June 1908, and a spectacular Women's Coronation Procession in June 1911, to mark the accession of King George V. After the Hyde Park rally, which

BUTTONHOLING THE PM With little security surrounding public figures, suffragettes could badger politicians in the street. Here Herbert Asquith is flanked by two activists, Olive Fergus and Mrs Frank Corbet.

was attended by 200 000 supporters, a reporter on the *Daily Mail* wrote: 'I am sure a great many people never realised until yesterday how young and dainty and elegant and charming most leaders of the movement are. And how well they spoke – and with what free and graceful gestures; . . . earnest, but happily humorous as well!'

But events soon began to take a more sinister course. Frustrations seethed as another franchise bill sank without trace in parliament. The WSPU took a more militant turn.

DERBY DEATH Few in the crowd seem to be aware of the tragedy as the suffragette Emily Davison collides with the king's horse, Anmer, at the 1913 Derby.

On March 1, 1912, suffragettes in the West End of London suddenly drew hammers and stones from their muffs and broke scores of shop and office windows. Over 120 women were arrested. A 'guerrilla campaign' ensued: telegraph wires were cut, letterboxes were set on fire, government ministers' houses were bombed (although without loss of life). In 1913 Mrs Pankhurst was sentenced to nine months' imprisonment for incitement to cause damage; to avoid such charges, Christabel fled to Paris. Mrs Pankhurst's second daughter, Sylvia, took over the leadership in Britain.

Public revulsion to the policy of force-feeding induced the government to take a new line after March 1913. In the Prisoners (Temporary Discharge for Health) Act, soon dubbed the 'Cat and Mouse Act', women prisoners were released if they became dangerously ill or weak in prison – but if they had not completed their sentences, they were liable to rearrest on recovery.

On June 4, 1913, a suffragette ran onto the racecourse during the Derby, where she was bowled over by the king's horse and knocked unconscious. She died four days later from head injuries. Her name was Emily Wilding Davison, an Oxford English graduate and veteran of nine imprisonments. It seems that her act was intended not as suicide but simply as a publicity stunt – to stop the king's horse in a race that had the eyes of the world upon it. The result, however, was that Davison became the suffragettes' first and only martyr. Her funeral procession through London was attended by thousands.

SUFFRAGETTE COLOURS

Black and white photographs fail to show that, after 1908, members of the WSPU would demonstrate wearing clothes in configurations of the movement's three colours: purple, white and green. Emmeline Pethick-Lawrence, the WSPU treasurer, explained that purple symbolised dignity, white was for purity, and green for fertility and hope. Posters, sashes, badges, insignia and a vast range of other merchandise – stationery, playing cards and tea sets – similarly incorporated this 'tricolour' scheme, making their cause instantly identifiable.

In March 1914, a 31-year-old suffragette, Mary Richardson, entered the National Gallery, produced a meat cleaver and slashed the *Rokeby Venus* by Velasquez. 'I have tried to destroy the picture of the most beautiful woman in mythological history in protest at the government's destruction of Miss Pankhurst, the most beautiful character in modern history', declared 'Slasher' Richardson, in reference to Sylvia, repeatedly harassed under the Cat and Mouse Act. Other paintings were attacked elsewhere.

VOTING RIGHTS AROUND THE WORLD

Women's suffrage has now been achieved in most countries. But it was a long process, and often it came with restrictive qualifications. For example, women might qualify to vote only by being house-holders, or taxpayers, or by passing literacy tests. The dates below show only the bald details of when women were first able to vote in each country. Among them are some surprising latecomers.

New Zealand	1893
Australia	1902-8 (in the various states)
Finland	1906
Norway	1907 (higher taxpayers); 1913
Denmark	1915
Soviet Union	1917
Britain	1918 (aged over 30); 1928
Germany	1918
Poland	1918
Netherlands	1919
USA	1920
Ireland	1922
South Africa	1930 (Whites)
Turkey	1934
France	1945
Italy	1945
Japan	1945
China	1949
India	1949
Switzerland	1971

Public sympathy for the suffragettes began to melt away, and the WSPU also lost the support of many of its leading lights, such as the husband-and-wife team, Frederick and Emmeline Pethick-Lawrence. They argued – with good reason – that these militant tactics were counterproductive, and only seemed to vindicate the government's tough line.

Nevertheless, suffragette protests continued until the eve of the First World War. On May 22, 1914, despairing of ever winning their case with the government, a big demonstration was held outside Buckingham Palace in which an attempt was made to deliver a petition directly to the king. Fifty-seven protesters were arrested, including Mrs Pankhurst.

But she was not to be outplayed. When war was declared in August 1914, she opted to drop the votes-for-women issue and gave her full backing to the patriotic war effort. Christabel returned from Paris to assist her, and the WSPU swung into action to support

FINAL FLING Police out in force at Buckingham Palace in May 1914 to prevent the suffragettes delivering a petition to George V. Right: Protesting to the last, Emmeline Pankhurst is arrested under the 'Cat and Mouse Act' and carried away.

the thousands of women now drawn into work. Not all suffragettes agreed with this policy, however; like the socialists, many were deeply opposed to the war. They included Sylvia Pankhurst, whose left-wing, pacifist stance caused a deep rift with her mother.

In any case, partly as a reward for women's contribution to victory in the war, and partly out of political expediency, the coalition government of Lloyd George gave the vote to women aged 30 and over in 1918. Equal franchise with men aged over 21 was finally achieved in 1928.

THE REPUBLIC OF CHINA

WITH THE MAJOR POWERS SQUABBLING OVER CHINA'S CARCASS, LOCAL REPUBLICANS SWEPT ASIDE 4000 YEARS OF IMPERIAL HISTORY

The new century started on a sombre note for China. In August 1900, the Boxer Rebellion was quashed by an impromptu alliance of foreign troops. Soldiers from Britain, France, Germany, Japan, the USA and Italy all lent a hand in restoring order in the north. China was forced to pay a large indemnity to the hated foreigners, who won the right to station troops in Beijing (Peking) for the first time.

It was yet another humiliation to add to the pile of indignities that had already been heaped upon the court of the Chinese emperors of the 256-year-old Qing dynasty. After a century and more of violent uprisings, foreign incursions and one-sided trading treaties, it was no longer clear quite who ruled China.

In 1898 the Guangxu (Kuang-hsü) Emperor – emperors were referred to, not by their personal names, but using special 'reign names' that they assumed on coming to the throne – had belatedly attempted to introduce reforms to provincial government, the educational and legal systems, and the civil service. These were modest enough, but they represented a considerable leap forward for a deeply traditional regime, steeped in ritual practices and operated by a rigidly conservative bureaucracy.

LIVING IN THE PAST   The Empress Dowager Ci Xi (right) lived in utmost luxury, sealed off from the realities of China. A photograph taken in Beijing in 1910 (below) reveals few signs of the 20th century.

They also had a fearsome opponent in the Empress Dowager Ci Xi (Tz'u-hsi). A favourite concubine of the last-but-one emperor who had died in 1861, she was the mother of his only son and successor, and an arch manipulator; she had manoeuvred her way into becoming the real power behind the Chinese throne during the last years of the 19th century. As an ultra-conservative, she would not hear of reform, so in 1898 she re-emerged from retirement in her Summer Palace to engineer a minor military coup. She outmanoeuvred the Guangxu Emperor so

PEKING TO PARIS BY CAR

It was the French newspaper *Le Matin* that laid down the challenge. On January 31, 1907, it thundered: 'What needs to be proved today is that as long as a man has a car he can do anything and go anywhere. Anywhere. Yes, anywhere. . . . Is there anyone who will undertake to travel this summer from Paris to Peking by automobile?' Some 10 000 miles (16 000 km) separated Paris and Beijing, mostly without roads. Yet there was no shortage of takers, and the challenge soon evolved into a race. In the event, the high cost of taking part whittled the contestants down to just five cars and, to avoid seasonal rains in the East, the route was reversed; the cars would be shipped to Beijing and head west to Paris. Four of the cars were sponsored by manufacturers: two De Dion-Boutons from France, a Dutch Spyker driven by the mercurial Frenchman Charles Godard, and the smallest car, a Contal three-wheeler. The largest was a 40-horsepower Itala, driven by the flamboyant Prince Scipione Borghese, who entered the race at his own expense.

The five cars set out from Beijing on June 10, 1907. The contestants had agreed to travel in convoy as far as Irkutsk in Russia, with supply dumps prearranged to assist them over this first section of the journey, which included the Gobi Desert; after Irkutsk they could begin the race. Their troubles began early. The Contal had engine difficulties, and then ran out of petrol in the Gobi Desert. Efforts by the other contestants to send back petrol failed, and its driver Auguste Pons and his mechanic came close to death from dehydration, until rescued by nomads. On June 18, Borghese, with his mechanic Ettore Guizzardi and the writer Luigi Barzini, grew impatient with the convoy and sped ahead. After that, Godard and his passenger, Jean du Taillis – a journalist for *Le Matin* – ran out of petrol. Left behind by the De Dion-Boutons, they survived by drinking the radiator water and getting a tow from camels. Unlike the Contal, they were able to continue.

Conditions improved when the cars reached the route of the Trans-Siberian Railway, although Borghese, in the lead, found he had to recruit horses and oxen to pull the Itala through several wide rivers. The Itala forged on until on August 10, 62 days after leaving Beijing, Borghese and his companions made a triumphal entry into Paris. The remainder of the convoy was still in Russia. Godard was held up when his Spyker developed engine trouble; by the time he restarted, he was 19 days behind the De Dion-Boutons, but he drove huge distances for long hours and caught up. The three teams now decided to continue in convoy, and to share the glory of coming second together. This did not please the director of *Le Matin*, who wanted the De Dion-Boutons to blaze into Paris waving the flag for France. The result was a bizarre sequence of events. Godard, ever impoverished, had borrowed money from Dutch officials in China against fraudulent promises of repayment by letters of credit. He was convicted in his absence of obtaining money on false pretences, and *Le Matin* had him arrested in Germany, thus taking him out of the race. Du Taillis continued in the Spyker; but at Enghien, outside Paris, Godard emerged from the crowd, jumped into the driver's seat and demanded to take the car to the finishing line. He was removed by members of *Le Matin*'s staff.

PIPE DREAMS To help the imperial government to raise money for capital projects, foreign entrepreneurs issued bonds with the promise of high interest, like this one of 1903 for 500 French francs. Many such bonds ended up in picture frames, as curios not worth the paper they were printed on.

decisively that thereafter he remained a virtual prisoner in the Forbidden City of Beijing. Only the intercession of French diplomats saved him from death.

It was against this background that the Boxer Rebellion took place. To the indignation of the foreign powers, the imperial court in Beijing refused to condemn the Boxers; indeed, it lent them military support. When the Boxers were quashed by the international troops, however, the empress dowager had to retreat and make conciliatory noises to the foreigners, as well as grant them further trade concessions. She also began to hold out the promise of reforms very much along the lines of those proposed earlier by the Guangxu Emperor; she permitted the creation of elected provincial assemblies, though she delayed consideration of far-reaching constitutional changes. Unfortunately, the moment for such piecemeal reforms had passed: they were too little, too late.

Against the Manchus

The Boxer Rebellion revealed the fragility of the Qing dynasty. The uprising had taken place mainly in the north. In the south, where many provincial governors had refused to go along with the imperial government's pro-Boxer edicts, the local authorities had already tasted a degree of independence from Beijing.

For centuries, there had been sporadic anti-government rebellions. The Qing dynasty

MAKING TRACKS Rural China had virtually no made-up roads. Here, Charles Godard welcomes a tow.

were not Chinese but Manchus – that is, they were invaders, originating in Manchuria. Ever since they seized control of China in the mid 17th century, they had appointed fellow Manchus to the key positions at court. The Manchus had never integrated fully with the Chinese; in fact, until 1902 they were forbidden to intermarry with the Chinese. They also maintained separate traditions: their women, for instance, did not practise the painful Chinese tradition of footbinding, which broke aristocratic women's feet in childhood, imprisoning them in disability for the sake of a sense of beauty.

In the wake of the Boxer Rebellion, China seethed with anti-Manchu and republican sentiment. Clandestine opposition organisations, providing a focus for dissidents, sprouted both in China and among emigré communities abroad. One of the leading dissident activists was a medical doctor called Sun Yat-sen.

Sun Yat-sen was a Christian Chinese, who had received his medical training in Hong

PAYING PENANCE Prince Chun, brother of the Guangxu Emperor, visited Berlin in 1901 after the Boxer Rebellion. The kaiser, sitting next to the coachman, parades his bewildered guest like a spoil of war.

Kong. In 1894 he had set up the Revive China Society, and instigated a failed uprising in Guangzhou (Canton) the next year. After this, he began long years in exile, travelling to the USA, Britain and Japan. An abortive attempt by Chinese government agents to kidnap and imprison him in London in 1898 projected his name into worldwide fame. In Japan, in 1905, he founded the Tong Meng Hui (Revolutionary Alliance) and he developed the socialist-republican doctrine of Three Principles – to promote nationalism, democracy and the people's livelihood.

The end of a dynasty

The empress dowager died in 1908, a day after the Guangxu Emperor. The new emperor was a two-year-old infant, and the country was governed by the conservative duo of his father, Prince Chun, as regent and the new empress dowager, Long-yu, a widow of the former emperor and niece of Ci Xi. This regime brought no prospects of change.

What seemed at first a trivial incident resulted in the collapse of the dynasty. The imperial government wanted to hand over two railways in central China to foreign powers in exchange for loans, but this caused strikes and riots which the government tried to crush with the army. A disaffected military

THE LAST EMPEROR

EMPEROR IN WAITING The infant Puyi stands at the knee of his father Prince Chun.

Just before she died on November 15, 1908, the Empress Dowager Ci Xi engineered her final coup. One day before, the Guangxu Emperor had died without an heir. Given Ci Xi's reputation for ruthless scheming, it is not surprising that people surmised that he had been poisoned at her instigation – her deathbed wish to ensure the succession of a ruler of her choice. This choice was the late emperor's two-year-old nephew, Puyi, who came to the throne as the Xuangtong Emperor.

Isolated in Beijing's Forbidden City, Puyi grew up in a world of arcane ritual, while China was ruled by his father and the Empress Dowager Long-yu. He was five years old when the general, Yuan Shikai, persuaded Long-yu to accept abdication on his behalf. On February 12, 1912, she set her seal to the document that put an end to the Qing dynasty. Puyi stayed in the Forbidden City, with most of his privileges intact, bar real power, living in a strangely irrelevant world, like a once-magnificent but disused theatre.

After 1918 he gained some knowledge of the outside world through a British tutor, Reginald Johnston. It was Johnston who helped to whisk Puyi into Japanese hands when he was finally ejected from the palace in 1924. Under the influence of the Japanese, Puyi was transformed into a Westernised playboy, and in 1932 he was installed as regent, later emperor, of a Japanese puppet state in Manchuria. At the close of the Second World War, he was captured by the Russians, and in 1959 deported to China. After years in prison undergoing communist 're-education', he worked in a botanical garden, and died virtually forgotten in Beijing, aged 61, in 1968.

1908 Death of
the Empress
Dowager Ci Xi

1912 The emperor
Puyi abdicates. China
becomes a republic

1913 Sun Yat-sen
forced into exile after
the failure of his revolt

FORCING A PATH TO THE ROOF OF THE WORLD

IN JUNE 1903 A BRITISH EXPEDITION MARCHED INTO THE MYSTERIOUS HIMALAYAN MOUNTAIN KINGDOM OF TIBET, RULED BY ITS PRIEST-KING THE DALAI LAMA

In the late 19th century, the British were convinced that Russia had designs on their empire in India. This inspired a cloak-and-dagger spying campaign known as the 'Great Game', played out across the mountainous borderlands of Afghanistan, the Hindu Kush, the Himalayas and beyond.

A blank area remained on the map between the two empires: Tibet. Nominally a part of China, it had long excluded all foreigners from its territories. However, Lord Curzon, Viceroy of India, believed that Russia was making overtures to its rulers, and won permission from London to send a mission there to negotiate an agreement to keep the Russians out. To lead it, he chose an Indian-born army officer and veteran of the Great Game, Francis Younghusband.

In June 1903, Younghusband and 200 Indian troops marched into Tibet. A delegation came to meet him, but prevaricated endlessly. Younghusband withdrew and reported to Curzon, who won permission to mount a much larger expedition. So in December 1903, Younghusband returned with

UNEQUAL Swords and matchlock guns were no match for British artillery. This soldier's leg was shattered by a shell.

FOLLOWING THE FLAG An Indian soldier raises the British flag on the Tang La Pass in January 1904, a month after entering Tibet.

a force of 1000 mainly Sikh and Gurkha troops under Brigadier-General James Macdonald. The Tibetans refused to parley, and Younghusband advanced, until on March 31, 1904, the Tibetans made a stand. About 15000 troops, armed with matchlock rifles and swords, hid behind a high wall that blocked a valley. General Macdonald sent in his troops, but the Tibetans failed to fire, even when their general was captured. After some hesitation, Macdonald ordered his men to disarm the Tibetans. As they did so, the Tibetan general exploded with fury, opened fire with a revolver and shot off the jaw of an Indian soldier. At this point, Macdonald's troops opened fire with their Enfield rifles and Maxim machine guns. Within four minutes, 700 Tibetans lay dead or dying. Horrified, the British took the wounded to their field medical station, for which the Tibetans proved touchingly grateful.

Younghusband moved on. On August 3, the British reached the capital Lhasa, having fought off stiff pockets of resistance with heavy Tibetan losses. Younghusband was anxious to negotiate a treaty and get back to India before the onset of winter; but the Dalai Lama had fled, leaving an old lama in charge with little authority. Younghusband nonetheless hammered out an Anglo-Tibetan Convention, which included an agreement that Tibet would not enter negotiations with any other power, apart from China, without British permission. Then, on September 23, Younghusband and his expedition withdrew.

After the collapse of the Qing dynasty in 1912, Tibet declared independence, which it maintained until it was invaded by China in 1950. Younghusband, for his part, had undergone a profound mystical experience there. In 1910 he retired to devote himself to religion, and founded the World Congress of Faiths in 1936.

garrison nearby in Wuchang, Hubei province, began a mutiny in 1911. The action of the mutineers was supported by the provincial assembly, which then declared independence from the imperial government. Suddenly, like falling dominoes, China's provinces followed suit, so that within six weeks most had declared independence.

The imperial court responded by sending in loyal troops, which in November massacred republicans at Wuhan (Hankow) and Nanjing (Nanking) in central China. But in December, republican forces retook Nanjing. A provisional national government was then set up there, and Sun Yat-sen – having carefully canvassed the support of sympathetic governments abroad – returned from exile to assume the role of provisional president.

Meanwhile, the regent, Prince Chun, reluctantly called on the support of the seasoned military strongman, Yüan Shih-kai, who commanded the loyalty of the 30 000-strong Northern Army. The last vestige of imperial power now rested with this force. Yüan Shih-kai, a schemer, saw the hopelessness of the situation, but also an opportunity. After negotiations with Sun Yat-sen, he persuaded the regent to resign, and the empress dowager to allow the infant emperor to abdicate. This

END OF PIGTAILS The Manchu emperors insisted that their Chinese subjects should wear their hair in a pigtail as a symbol of servitude – as seen among imperial troops on manoeuvres in 1909 (above). Republican soldiers cut off pigtails (right) during the 1911-12 revolution.

THE JAPANESE EXAMPLE

Japan's defeat of Russia in 1904-5 impressed reform-minded Chinese. With a constitutional monarchy, Japan had been able to modernise. If only China could throw off an antiquated autocratic government, it too could achieve similar feats against the Western powers.

was achieved on February 12, 1912, and China became a republic.

As part of the payoff for arranging this deal, Yüan Shih-kai was to become president. Sun Yat-sen, recognising the limitations of his own military support – and that confrontation would provoke civil war – ceded his position.

Within a few years, Yüan Shih-kai was becoming increasingly dictatorial. In 1913 seven southern provinces loyal to Sun Yat-sen's Nationalist Party, the Guomintang, tried to secede, but the revolt was crushed

and Sun Yat-sen was forced once more into temporary exile, in Japan.

Following the tradition of army strongmen who had founded new dynasties in China's past, Yüan Shih-kai now proposed to declare himself emperor. When the southern provinces showed themselves to be vehemently opposed to this, he demurred; but then, in June 1916, he suddenly died before he could fulfil this ambition. And China descended into increasing lawlessness.

FLYING THE FLAG A Chinese patriot holds up the flag of the new republic (left). Sun Yat-sen (far left) was the driving force behind the 1911-12 revolution, but it was the former imperial strongman Yüan Shih-kai (below, seated) who become the first president after the emperor's abdication in February 1912.

THE PRELUDE TO WAR

WITH THE CLASH OF IMPERIAL AMBITIONS, THE INTERNATIONAL ALLIANCES THAT HAD PRESERVED PEACE LOOKED INCREASINGLY FRAGILE. THE GREAT POWERS PURSUED A RUINOUSLY COMPETITIVE ARMS RACE, AGAINST A BACKDROP OF NATIONALIST PROPAGANDA. SEVERAL SMALL INCIDENTS DEMONSTRATED THAT IT WOULD TAKE JUST ONE SPARK TO CAUSE A CONFLAGRATION. IN THE END AN ASSASSINATION IN SARAJEVO KINDLED THE WAR THAT SO MANY PEOPLE SAW AS INEVITABLE.

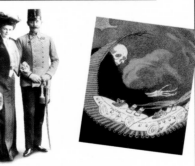

THE EUROPEAN ALLIANCES

WITH THEIR COMPLEX ALLIANCES, THE EUROPEAN POWERS WHO RULED MUCH OF THE WORLD BELIEVED THEY COULD FORESTALL A MAJOR WAR

Marshal Hubert Lyautey, a respected French colonial administrator, had an exalted vision of his calling: 'I had a dream of creating, of raising into life countries which had been asleep from the beginning of time, and showing them these riches of their own of which they are ignorant . . . In Madagascar I made towns grow up . . . And in Morocco, amongst these ancient lands of lethargy, what a rich joy there has been in giving them desire, in quickening the blood in their veins . . . There are people who regard colonial enterprises as barbarian. What stupidity! Wherever I have gone, it has been to construct; and whichever country I had to destroy I built up again later, more solidly and durably.'

The rights and wrongs of colonial rule were debated as fiercely then as they are now in hindsight; but in the opening years of the 20th century, the snowball of imperialism had its own momentum, accelerated by such sentiments as Lyautey's. Today, they seem highly Eurocentric and the product of selective memory; then, they appeared commendably enlightened. There was a general attitude that colonies spread the benefits of Western industrialised civilisation to the benighted and undeveloped world.

It was Britain that had the world's largest empire; in 1906 government sources claimed that it covered one-fifth of the world's land area and contained 400 million subjects.

TAMING EVEN THE WILDLIFE Army officers in German East Africa, photographed in 1913, riding two zebras they have trained.

Daylight fell somewhere on the British Empire constantly as the globe turned – so it was an empire upon which 'the sun never set'. The French Empire stretched from the Caribbean, across much of northern Africa, to Indochina; the German Empire consisted of large chunks of Africa and many of the Polynesian islands. In the closing years of the 19th century, Japan had joined the imperial nations by acquiring Taiwan; the Russians had pushed into Manchuria; the USA had taken over the Philippines and other Spanish possessions. Only the Dutch seemed content with their geographical status quo, simply consolidating their grip on the thousands of islands of the Indonesian archipelago – as well as parts of the Caribbean.

The balance of power

The shape and colour of the imperial possessions seemed more or less settled. There was always a lurking fear, however, that local conflicts in the colonies would give rise to a clash of imperial interests. This made the structure of alliances forged within Europe in the 19th century the more important to keep the powers in a state of equilibrium. A Triple Alliance of Germany, Austria-Hungary and Italy was balanced by an alliance between Russia and France. Britain

AND THE BAND PLAYS ON French satirical statuettes portray the monarchs of the Triple Alliance nations as street musicians: (left to right) Franz Josef of Austria-Hungary, Wilhelm of Germany and Victor Emmanuel of Italy.
Top: The Entente Cordiale depicted as a romp between a tubby British tar and a scantily clad Liberty, symbol of republican France.

1901 Germany seeks British support for the Triple Alliance in return for help against Russia

1902 Britain forms alliance with Japan to curb Russian ambitions in the Far East

1904 Britain signs Entente Cordiale with France

1907 Russia becomes part of a 'triple entente' with Britain and France

BLÉRIOT CROSSES THE CHANNEL

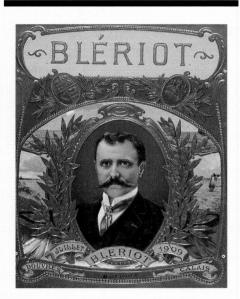

LABELLED A HERO Blériot's cross-Channel flight made him a household name, fêted in special issues of merchandise such as this box of cigars.

Suddenly, the fragile aircraft flew in from over the sea, out of the cold, grey morning sky. 'There was something almost uncanny about the sight of this remarkable machine', reported the *Daily Graphic*. It fluttered in the turbulent updraught of the white cliffs of Dover, then homed in on a lone man waving a French flag in open land close to Dover Castle. It circled in the tricky winds, then bumped down on the dewy grass. It was 5.17 am on July 25, 1909, and the Frenchman Louis Blériot had become the first person to cross the Channel in an aircraft. He had flown the 23½ miles (38 km) in 36 minutes to claim a £1000 prize offered by the *Daily Mail*.

The significance of Blériot's hop across the Channel was immediately appreciated. Many expressed concern that Britain's island defences had been so casually breached. As for Blériot himself, he was rewarded by acclaim and honours, and wealth. Already the successful manufacturer of a patented automobile lamp, he went on to become a leading aircraft manufacturer.

remained aloof at the start of the century; by siding with neither bloc, the British liked to think that they held the balance of power.

By virtue of this arrangement, many people thought that Europe – if not its satellites – would never again suffer the ravages of war. As late as 1914 the journalist H.N. Brailsford wrote: 'It is as certain as anything can be that the frontiers of our modern national states are finally drawn. My own belief is that there will be no more wars among the Six Great

Powers.' For others, however, such certainties had been undermined by the growing power of Germany. Unlike Bismarck, the German chancellor until 1890, Kaiser Wilhelm II had little time for the niceties of the alliance system. He wanted Germany to be an imperial power with large overseas territories. He succeeded in this ambition with remarkable speed in the last two decades of the 19th century, acquiring for his country its 'place in the sun that is our due'. He was essentially playing the same game as Europe's other imperial nations, but his antics began to unsettle them.

The balance shifts

In 1901 Britain tried to recruit Germany's help in curbing Russian ambitions in the Far East. Germany, however, would comply only if Britain promised to come off the fence and support the Triple Alliance – a price Britain would not pay. Instead, in 1902 it entered into a rather surprising alliance with Japan, with the same end in mind of curbing Russia.

Then, in 1904, Britain signed the Entente Cordiale with France – a medium-strength arrangement, less binding than an alliance. Edward VII played a hand in this, following a bridge-building visit to Paris in the aftermath of the Boer War. Apart from expressions of mutual support, the British agreed to allow France a free hand in Morocco.

It was the kind of arrangement guaranteed to irritate Germany. The kaiser insisted *continued on page 130*

A PLACE IN THE SUN In March 1905 Kaiser Wilhelm upset international opinion with a visit to Tangier (below). It was generally agreed that France and Spain should have the run of Morocco, to the exclusion of Germany.

THE RACE TO THE POLES

BY 1900 THERE REMAINED ONE LAST GREAT CHALLENGE FOR EXPLORERS: THE FEARSOMELY INHOSPITABLE REGIONS LYING AT THE EARTH'S NORTHERN AND SOUTHERN EXTREMITIES

Scientific enquiry and the quest for fame spurred on polar explorers at the start of the century. Little was known about either the Arctic or the Antarctic – it was not fully understood, for example, that the North Pole lay over a frozen ocean and the South Pole over a frozen continent.

Many expeditions had ventured into the Arctic in the late 19th century, and many had come to grief. Among the men who led them none was driven more by the naked ambition to win fame than the US naval officer, Commander Robert Peary. Controversially, he had adopted Inuit (Eskimo) means of travel, using huskies and sledges, and wearing Inuit fur clothing. Many considered this downright unsporting: they believed in the superiority of the manufactured textiles and equipment of the industrial world, and set great store by the team spirit of physically man-hauling sledges and provisions.

Peary made his first, unsuccessful, attempt on the North Pole in March 1900. By the time of his fifth attempt, he was 53 years old. His expedition started out from its base camp in northern Canada on March 1, 1909. He was supported by a team of 23 men, mostly Inuits from Greenland, and 19 sledges pulled by 133 dogs. Most went ahead to set up a series of relay stations. Peary followed, moving swiftly to the last station, before he, his long-standing black assistant, Matthew Henson, and four Inuits pushed on to the final goal. They reached the Pole on April 6, 1909. 'The Pole at last!!!' wrote

FOR GLORY AND SCIENCE The Poles remained the ultimate goal for men like Robert Peary (above). The Frenchman Jean Charcot's *Pourquoi Pas?* is pictured (below), beset by ice during his 1908-10 Antarctic expedition.

Peary in his diary. 'The prize of 3 centuries [of Arctic exploration], my dream & ambition for 23 years. Mine at last.' It should have been his crowning triumph, but when he returned south, he discovered that fellow American Frederick Cook – his companion on an earlier Greenland expedition – had just posted a rival claim. Cook declared that he had reached the Pole on April 21, 1908 – the previous year. Thwarted by adverse weather, his team had taken over a year to return to Greenland.

A bitter dispute ensued. Cook's records were lamentable. It was probable that he had been to the far north, but he provided little in the way of navigational or astronomical evidence that he had reached the Pole. When he was found to have falsified an earlier claim to have reached the summit of Mount McKinley in Alaska, Cook seemed discredited. In 1911 a committee of the US House of Representatives came out in Peary's favour. As it happened, however, Peary's records also proved wanting. There were a number of mysteries, including a blank page in his diaries covering the vital 30 hours spent at the Pole, notes for which were inserted on a loose sheet of paper. His journey to and from the Pole also seemed to have been achieved with unusual speed. Had he falsified his record? Had he deluded himself? Had he really been to the Pole? The debate has still not been resolved.

The events in 1909 had a decisive effect on the plans of another Arctic explorer, the Norwegian Roald Amundsen. He had spent many years in the northern ice, and like Peary had adopted Inuit methods of survival and travel. He was planning to conquer the North Pole himself when the news of Cook's and Peary's rival claims came in. He secretly changed his plans. In 1910 he set off with his expedition in their ship, the *Fram*, and waited until they were in the middle of the Atlantic to drop the bombshell: he was not going to lead them to the North Pole after all, but to the South Pole – the last remaining polar prize. His team accepted the new challenge, but the news came as a shock to Captain Robert Falcon Scott, the leader of a concurrent British Antarctic Expedition. At Melbourne, Australia, heading south on his ship, the *Terra Nova*, Scott was handed a telegram: 'Beg leave to inform you *Fram* proceeding Antarctic. Amundsen.'

The Antarctic had by now become a region of huge international interest. Scott had led an expedition there in 1901-4, reaching the farthest point south to date. The French doctor Jean Charcot carried out important scientific research in the Antarctic in 1903-5 and again in 1908-10. One of Scott's 1901-4 party had been Ernest Shackleton. Having fallen out with Scott, Shackleton led his own expedition. In 1908 he came to within 97 miles (156 km) of the South Pole before turning back, fearing

STORY OF TRIUMPH Amundsen wrote up the account of his journey during a stay in Argentina before returning to Norway in 1913. It was called simply *Sydpolen* (*The South Pole*).

that his team would run out of supplies. As he observed to his wife: 'I thought you would prefer a live donkey to a dead lion.' Scott now believed the way was open to him to claim the South Pole for himself – and for England. 'What matters now is that the Pole should be attained by an Englishman', he wrote with jingoistic fervour typical of the day. So when he heard of Amundsen's bid, he felt he was being challenged by an unscrupulous opportunist.

But Amundsen was much more than this. A meticulous planner, who minimised risks, he plotted his route to the Pole and back via carefully laid stores depots. On October 20, 1911, Amundsen, four Norwegian colleagues and 52 huskies started out from their base camp at the eastern edge of the Ross Ice Shelf. They reached the Pole on December 15. Then they set off for the return run, reaching their

base camp on January 25, 1912, precisely the day that Amundsen had forecast. It was a great triumph for newly independent Norway.

Scott's team set out from their base camp at the western edge of the Ross Ice Shelf on November 1, 1911. They were accompanied by ponies, dogs and two motor sledges, but they abandoned these as impractical on the ice shelf. After climbing Beardmore Glacier, Scott selected a team of four to accompany him to the Pole, and they headed on into the plateau, man-hauling their equipment. They were already suffering from exhaustion and scurvy when they found the Norwegian flag at the South Pole on January 17, 1912. It was a crushing moment, and as they trailed back towards their base camp in appalling conditions, they perished one by one. The bodies of Scott and his last two companions were found in their tent – along with their diaries, photographs and final letters home – by a search party in November 1912.

It made a sensational news story in Britain. Scott and his team became national heroes, who had made the ultimate sacrifice. The British press dismissed Amundsen as an egotistical upstart, who had won the race on unequal terms by using dogs – most of which he had heartlessly killed and eaten en route. The fact that the same fate befell Scott's ponies was conveniently forgotten. But perhaps Amundsen's greatest fault was one that besets many of the best explorers: he had made it look too easy.

BEATEN TO IT They have reached the South Pole, but disappointment is written on the faces of Scott's team: (left to right) Wilson (who holds the string to release the camera shutter), Scott, Evans, Oates and Bowers. Right: Scott wrote the final entry in his diary on March 29, 1912.

we shall stick it out to the end but we are getting weaker of course and the end cannot be far.

It seems a pity but I do not think I can write more –

R Scott

Last entry –

For Gods sake look after our people

THE AGADIR INCIDENT: TEETERING ON THE BRINK

DISMEMBERING MOROCCO
A French cartoon of 1903
foreshadows the
contention over Morocco
that would build up to the
Agadir Incident.

As an independent sultanate, Morocco in 1900 was one of the few pieces of Africa not claimed by a European power. It was generally agreed, however, that the north coast fell within the Spanish sphere of influence and the rest within the French. This did not please the Germans who claimed commercial interests in Morocco. In 1905 the kaiser made an unexpected visit to Tangier, met German businessmen there, secured a contract to build a new port facility and announced that 'the sovereignty and integrity of Morocco will be maintained'. Tension was eased after three months of negotiations at Algeciras in Spain in 1906: the French and Spanish retained their spheres of influence, but Morocco remained officially independent.

In early 1911, Morocco was hit by uprisings, and the French sent troops to Fez and Casablanca, apparently at the sultan's request. The Germans objected that France was seeking to establish a protectorate and in July sent a gunboat, the *Panther,* into the port of Agadir. Berlin claimed that it was defending its nationals and commercial interests in a time of unrest; the French suspected that it wanted to establish a military base. Britain supported its entente partner France, and an international showdown was averted only by a treaty signed on November 4: Germany left Morocco to France and received land on the borders of the German Cameroons.

which effectively tore up the Algeciras accord and gave France the right to turn Morocco into a fully fledged protectorate; in return, Germany was given a slice of central Africa. In 1912, a treaty signed by Sultan Abd al-Hafiz confirmed Morocco as a French protectorate.

By this time, the balance of power in Europe had begun to lose some of the flexibility and delicacy that had preserved the peace in the past. Britain was ever fearful of Russian expansion towards India and of naval threats to the Suez route to India; in 1907 it took advantage of a weakened Russia to forge an agreement with the tsarist government that allayed these fears. Facing the Triple Alliance of Germany, Austria-Hungary and Italy, there was now a 'triple entente' of Britain, France and Russia. Germany was conscious of a feeling of encirclement.

The diplomacy of kings

Kaiser Wilhelm, Tsar Nicholas II of Russia and King Edward VII of England were all related, but this counted for little in the game of nationalist and imperialist ambition. It did, however, keep open a high-level corridor of informal exchange.

In October 1908, an indiscreet interview with the kaiser, published in *The Daily Telegraph,* revealed

that Morocco remain independent in order to allow it free access to trade and commerce; but the French claimed that they needed to secure the Moroccan frontier with French Algeria. Meanwhile, the French and Spanish secretly carved up Morocco, effectively cutting out Germany. Although this issue seemed settled by an international agreement reached in Algeciras in 1906, the Agadir Incident

provoked by Germany in 1911 threatened for a while to pitch all the European powers into a major conflagration.

Subsequent events in Morocco followed a familiar pattern. In the face of increasing unrest there, France dispatched more and more troops. In November 1911, the French government concluded a treaty with Germany

WITH UNCLE BERTIE IN BERLIN Wilhelm II is driven through the streets of Berlin beside his uncle Edward VII, during the British monarch's state visit in February 1909. Edward also exchanged less formal visits with Wilhelm, exerting an avuncular influence where state diplomacy proved inadequate.

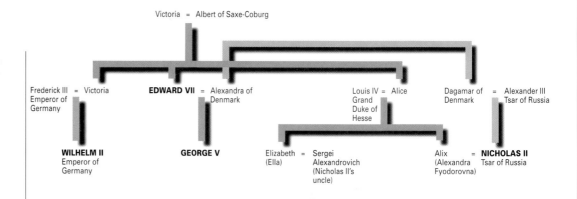

Victoria = Albert of Saxe-Coburg

Frederick III = Victoria
Emperor of
Germany

EDWARD VII = Alexandra of
Denmark

Louis IV = Alice
Grand
Duke of
Hesse

Dagamar of = Alexander III
Denmark   Tsar of Russia

WILHELM II
Emperor of
Germany

GEORGE V

Elizabeth = Sergei
(Ella)   Alexandrovich
            (Nicholas II's
            uncle)

Alix   = **NICHOLAS II**
(Alexandra   Tsar of Russia
Fyodorovna)

THE TERROR OF EUROPE A German cartoon of 1909 shows peasants scattering in fear before a grotesquely armed German warrior backed by a Zeppelin airship.

that, during the Boer War, there had been secret talks between Germany, France and Russia, in which they had discussed ways to 'humiliate England to the dust'. These disclosures brought howls of rage from the British press, and deep embarrassment to the Germans – and especially to the chancellor, Prince von Bülow, who had casually sanctioned publication. In February 1909 Edward VII, the kaiser's uncle, was in Berlin, claiming that good relations had been restored. The British popular press, however, was not so easily quelled and maintained a

FAMILY TIES Nicholas II and George V were first cousins through their mothers; George V and Wilhelm II were both grandsons of Queen Victoria. A complex web of relationships bound Europe's royal houses to one another.

background rumble of anti-German sentiment from now on.

A year later, Edward VII was dead. The funeral for this genuinely respected man brought heads of state from all over the world. Wilhelm was accorded the role of the leading foreign mourner. In the years that followed, however, the atmosphere of international distrust intensified. Germany felt increasingly

CONCENTRATION OF POWER The funeral of Edward VII brought together an array of crowned heads. In a photo taken at Windsor Castle, Wilhelm II stands behind the new British monarch, George V.

threatened, and the kaiser constantly reaffirmed his ties with Austria-Hungary. As Count Berchtold, the Austrian Foreign Minister, related of one meeting with Wilhelm: 'As often as opportunity offered . . . to touch upon our relations as allies, His Majesty ostentatiously used the occasion to assure me that we could count absolutely and completely on him.' This was a reckless attitude, given that Austria-Hungary was simultaneously toying with the Balkan powder keg.

In September 1913, the Triple Alliance of Germany, Austria-Hungary and Italy was reaffirmed, but by now – due to a clash of interests over the Balkans – the commitment of Italy was in doubt. Indeed, on the eve of the First World War, Italy declared itself neutral. It was against this backdrop of growing rivalry that the ruinous arms race took place, fuelling patriotic chauvinism, military posturing and a sense of impending doom.

THE ARMS RACE

THE IDEA WAS TO MAINTAIN THE BALANCE OF POWER WITH AN ARMS RACE – PEACE WAS TO BE PRESERVED THROUGH THE THREAT OF WAR

Between 1897 and 1900, the German parliament passed a series of Naval Laws, a programme of legislation aimed at massively increasing the navy – building some 45 new battleships over the next 20 years. Germany's rulers reasoned that their country needed a stronger navy to protect its colonies and its overseas trade routes. It was also a question of imperial prestige. The kaiser had a great admiration for the British Royal Navy, and felt that Germany should have its equivalent. There was nothing exceptional in this: France, the USA, Japan, even Italy had all hugely extended their navies in recent decades.

At this stage there was no question of Germany competing directly with the British navy, which was by far the most powerful in the world. Indeed, at the turn of the century, Britain's navy was almost twice as strong as all the European navies put together. As the years passed, however, it became increasingly clear that the German navy, in alliance with a foreign power, might begin to threaten British naval supremacy. The kaiser also calculated that, by building up his navy, the British might yet be enticed to form an alliance with Germany rather than confront it.

That was not the outcome. Britain watched Germany's expanding naval power with alarm. When in 1903 a new Naval Law threatened to double the German contingent of battleships, Britain appeared to be losing its edge.

That same year, Britain responded by initiating its own wave of naval shipbuilding. The answer, the British thought, lay in speed and power and in 1906 they unveiled the first of a new class of massive ships: HMS *Dreadnought*. The fastest and biggest warship in the world, it attained a record speed of 21.5 knots (25 mph/40 km/h), and was built so that it could fire eight of its ten huge 12 in (300 mm) guns simultaneously. The *Dreadnought* was said to render all previous naval vessels obsolete: no other navy in the world had anything that could match it. More dreadnoughts were planned as part of a programme to build 50 new warships.

Not to be outdone, Admiral Alfred von Tirpitz, Chief of the German Naval Staff, announced the following year that Germany

DIRE WARNINGS A German cartoon entitled 'Dreadnought Fever' shows the dreadnoughts of rival nations racing along the path to oblivion, supported on the back of Death. Dated 1909, it presaged the outcome that many in Europe foresaw and feared.

would build a set of its own dreadnought-class ships. The first of these, the *Nassau*, was launched in March 1908. By this time Britain had seven dreadnoughts, but the public wanted more and egged on the government, rallying around the slogan: 'We want eight and we won't wait.'

The threat of torpedoes

Naval warfare was changing rapidly. In technology, naval architects and engineers were racing ahead of their counterparts in the army. They were producing ever bigger and more powerful guns with ever longer ranges. Also increasing combat range was the self-propelled torpedo; this had a mini-engine and propeller that drove the torpedo through the water once launched. It was fired from torpedo boats and larger ships, as well as from a new kind of vessel altogether: the 'submarine torpedo boat'.

The first practical submarine had been developed in the USA by the Irish-born American John Philip

TERRORS OF THE DEEP By 1909 several dozen British submarines lined the jetty at Haslar Creek, Gosport, on the other side of the harbour from Portsmouth. The Royal Navy had taken delivery of its first submarines only seven years earlier.

Holland – paradoxically, he had received funding while developing an early prototype of his vessel from the anti-British Irish organisation, the Fenians. The US navy took a Holland submarine into service in 1900, and the following year the British navy followed suit. Before long, the USA, Britain, Germany and many other nations had built up significant submarine fleets.

The long range of torpedoes meant that ships had to engage each other at greater and greater distances, until virtually out of sight of one another. This called for new armaments and new tactics. Winston Churchill, as First Lord of the Admiralty, put it succinctly in a speech to the House of Commons in March 1914: 'If you want to make a true picture in your mind of a battle between great ironclad ships you must not think of it as if it were between two men in armour, striking at each other with heavy swords. It is more like a battle between two egg shells striking at each other with hammers . . . The importance of hitting first, of hitting hardest, and of keeping on hitting really needs no further proof.'

The cost

All the major European countries were caught in an upward spiral of military spending. The armies were expanding as fast as the navies, and consumed at least 50 per cent of the defence budgets – although with less conspicuous symbols of investment than ships. By 1914, the European powers could call upon armed forces numbering nearly 20 million men, of which Russia had 5.5 million, and Germany – with the second-largest armed forces – 4.5 million.

The spending on armaments rose and rose. In Britain it stood at about £50 million per annum in 1900; by 1910 it was £70 million, and by 1914 it was £75 million. Germany in 1900 was spending £40 million, £60 million in 1910 and £110 million in 1914, when 14 new battleships entered service.

As early as 1908, naval spending was beginning to play a major and disruptive role in national budgets. Efforts to raise taxes in Germany in order to fund both social reforms and naval spending were rejected, contributing to the downfall of the chancellor, Prince von Bülow, in 1909. Likewise, David Lloyd George, in his 'people's budget' of 1909, proposed a range of tax increases to raise funds for a new national pension scheme, but also for naval spending. This, too, was rejected. Funds simply had to be squeezed from elsewhere.

Meanwhile, arms and armaments became an immensely profitable industry. The burgeoning domestic market, as well as exports, made huge fortunes for arms manufacturers such as the Essen-based family firm of Krupp in Germany.

Many people, particularly on the left wing, criticised the frenzy of military spending as sheer wasteful folly, and claimed that the money would be far better spent addressing the burning social needs of the day. Rearmament coincided with increasingly bitter and

RULING THE WAVES 'War in Peace' reads the cover of a 1903 German publication. Many Germans argued that a powerful navy led to stability, and were reassured by pictures of battleships such as the *Deutschland* (below).

1908 The first of Germany's dreadnought-class ships, *Nassau*, is launched

1909 Lloyd George's budget brings in tax increases to fund naval expansion

1912 Talks between Britain and Germany fail to limit naval spending

1914 Review of the Fleet at Spithead

SIZING EACH OTHER UP A passenger-carrying Zeppelin glides through the sky over British warships on a visit to the German naval base, Kiel. Dreadnought-class warships (below) were capable of engaging the enemy over a huge distance, beyond the range of torpedoes.

increasingly warlike clamour. The British popular press suggested, for example, that the country was riddled with foreign spies. The *Daily Mail* advised: 'Refuse to be served by a German waiter. If your waiter says he is Swiss, ask to see his passport!' In the foreword to his novel, *Spies of the Kaiser: Plotting the Downfall of England* (1909), William Le Queux was keen to point out that he had not invented the threat, but he felt 'compelled, even at the risk of being again denounced as a scare monger, to present the facts in the form of fiction'. This mood also helped to engender the British Secret Service Bureau, the precursor of MI5 and MI6.

International rivalry extended to all fields of endeavour: in shipping the battle was not just between navies, but between passenger ships as well. There was great rejoicing in Britain in October 1907 when the new Cunard liner *Lusitania* broke the record for the transatlantic run (4 days, 19 hours and 52 minutes) and took the Blue Riband from the Hamburg-Amerika Line's *Deutschland*.

violent strikes and demonstrations organised by the trade unions, socialists and syndicalists, who had little sympathy for nationalistic and imperialist ambitions.

Spies and infiltrators

But all the while, patriotism and xenophobia were being stirred up by the press, in music halls, by stage plays and novels, creating an

Sliding towards war

It was the Agadir Incident of 1911 that alerted many world leaders to the notion that war between the great powers could occur at any moment. Churchill in particular was haunted by this vision. When the Germans announced a new round of naval spending in 1911, he responded by saying, 'for us a great fleet is a necessity, for Germany a luxury. It is existence for us; it is expansion for them.' It was the kind of statement guaranteed to inflame German sensibilities.

In 1912, talks were arranged between Britain and Germany in an effort to curb the

'KAISER BILL' – THE WASP AT THE PICNIC

To the dangerous world of international rivalries, Kaiser Wilhelm II added the frisson of uncertainty. No one, not even his ministers or his relatives in the royal families of Britain and Russia, had any clear idea what he might do next. He was, in the words of the English writer Rebecca West, 'like a wasp at a picnic'.

Wilhelm was the son of an unhappy union between Prince Frederick William of Prussia, later Emperor Frederick III, and Queen Victoria's eldest daughter. An accident at birth had left him with a withered arm and partial deafness, which affected his balance. To overcome these deficiencies, he was subjected as a child to a merciless regime of physical exercise and horse-riding, which improved his physique, but left him emotionally stunted. One of his rare pleasures was to spend holidays with his grandmother, Queen Victoria, at Osborne House on the Isle of Wight, where he developed a lasting passion for the sea.

On his father's death in 1888 Wilhelm was 29. Within two years he had dismissed the chancellor, Otto von Bismarck, the architect of unified Germany and its pilot for the last 28 years. 'There is only one master of this country, and I am he', he declared. Presiding over a country undergoing rapid economic development, he felt himself to be on the crest of a surge towards German greatness. Believing in the divine right of kings, he had no qualms about dominating the supine and largely conservative coalitions of the elected parliament. The German people were generally supportive, seeing him as the embodiment of national greatness.

Wilhelm was not without talents. He was energetic, quick-witted, eloquent and could be companionable to those in his favour. He married Princess Augusta of Schleswig Holstein, and presented himself as a dignified and pious family man. But he was also restless, irascible, inconsistent, vain and disturbingly vulnerable to flattery. With his upturned moustache and his penchant for spiked military helmets, Wilhelm was an easy target for cartoonists in the foreign presses. In Britain, he became known dismissively as 'Kaiser Bill'.

Often the cause of international dismay, Wilhelm managed consistently to irritate the leaders of the other big powers. His support for the Boers made him detested in Britain. In 1905 his excursion to Tangier infuriated the French. In brief, he was the single greatest contributor to the atmosphere of international tension in the run-up to the First World War. In 1918, and 10 million deaths later, he fled to the Netherlands, along with 20 railway carriages of baggage. Reviled in Germany for the defeat and his desertion, he remained in exile in the Netherlands, living the life of a country gentleman until his death in 1941 at the age of 82.

HONOUR AND PRIDE Personal ambition and the Prussian militaristic tradition combined in Wilhelm II. He liked to pose in the uniform of the Gardes du Corps, a regiment raised by his forebear Frederick the Great.

relentless cycle of naval spending, but they broke down when Germany demanded that either side remain neutral if the other engaged in war with a third party. Now the race began in earnest.

Churchill enticed out of retirement the former First Sea Lord, Admiral John ('Jackie') Fisher, now aged 70, the mastermind of the original dreadnought programme. Having secured a contract with the Anglo-Persian Oil Company, they converted as much of the fleet as possible to oil power, which gave the ships greater range. By the end of 1912, Britain had 30 new warships under construction. Its naval planners adopted two catch phrases: 'speed is armour' and 'ruthless, relentless, remorseless'. In 1912 and 1913, massive 15 in (380 mm) 'hush-and-push' guns – capable of firing a shell weighing nearly a ton a distance of 12 miles (19 km) – were installed on five of the new dreadnoughts, creating a class of 'super-dreadnoughts'.

British military planners feared that Germany might take a sideswipe at Britain as it launched an attack on France – especially if Germany felt that Britain was preoccupied by problems in Ireland. So in July 1912, Britain withdrew its fleet from the Mediterranean and posted it in the North Sea, ready to confront the German navy head on.

On July 18, 1914, just before the Austrian ultimatum to Serbia, the British fleet was assembled at Spithead for a grand review. Journalists were instructed to report only general impressions, not the details. One of these journalists, Hugh Martin, later described the scene: 'It was an amazing affair, this hush-hush review. Steaming at 15 knots (28 km/h), it took six hours for the 200 ships to pass the saluting point. There were 70 000 officers and men on board.'

Lord Kitchener, Secretary of War, later said to Churchill, an old adversary: 'There is one thing they cannot take from you. The Fleet was ready.'

THE BALKAN CRISIS

A CORNER OF SOUTH-EASTERN EUROPE BECAME THE FOCUS OF BIG-POWER TENSIONS, AND WAS THE CATALYST FOR THE FIRST WORLD WAR

For some 200 years the once-great Ottoman Empire had been in decline, earning itself the nickname 'the sick man of Europe'. Backward, corrupt and close to bankruptcy, it had gradually lost ground in North Africa, the Middle East and southern Europe to the covetous imperial nations.

Largely to thwart Russian ambitions in Asia, some European governments had helped their traders and industries to infiltrate Ottoman markets – in the building of railways, by developing mines and installing banking systems. As a result, many larger Ottoman cities, such as Constantinople (Istanbul) and Beirut, were beginning to blossom in the early years of the century. But, generally, the Ottoman world remained closed, idiosyncratic and little understood. On the one hand, the crumbling empire signified opportunities for the European powers; on the other, it was a liability. And the most worrying zone of the empire was right on Europe's doorstep, in the Balkans, where ancient religious, ethnic and political rivalries made up a complex patchwork. Here, three powers converged: the Ottomans, who generally retained the loyalty of the Islamic populations; the Austrians, who exploited anti-Ottoman sentiment to shore up their ragged southern frontier; and the Russians, to whom the Slavs in Romania, Bulgaria, Serbia and elsewhere turned for support. The prospective fate of this region was referred to as the 'Eastern Question'.

Balkan wars

During the 19th century Greece, Romania, Montenegro and Serbia had won their freedom from the Ottoman Empire. In 1908 Bulgaria and neighbouring Eastern Rumelia also declared full independence. Austria-Hungary responded by formally annexing Bosnia-Herzegovina, which had been under its administration since 1878; the motive was to create a buffer zone against the newly enlarged, independent Slavic region, but the move was guaranteed to antagonise the large Serb population in Bosnia. These changes still left a dissatisfied and unresolved band of territory stretching from Macedonia to Albania, containing a volatile mixture of national and religious groupings, which periodically flared up in violent unrest.

In 1908 a group of patriotic reformers calling themselves the Committee for Union and Progress – known in the West as the 'Young Turks' – carried out a successful coup in Constantinople, and took over the government. They restored a constitution that had been suspended in 1878; they promised elections, freedom of the press and freedom of worship. The following year, after an abortive counter-coup, they replaced Sultan Abd al-Hamid with his brother Mohammed V. There was some hope among Western governments and among subject nations within the Ottoman Empire that this would bring about a more enlightened and effective regime, but hopes were soon disappointed. The Young Turks had many of the autocratic failings of their predecessors, and proved also to be vehemently nationalistic and anti-Christian.

In September 1912 Bulgaria, Serbia, Montenegro and Greece –

BRUTAL MEASURES 'Turkey discourages ideas of independence in Macedonia' was the title of a German cartoon (left) of 1903. The public hanging of Turkish prisoners in 1911 in Trieste, then the chief port of Austria-Hungary, shows that Turkey had no monopoly on brutality.

CHANGING HANDS In March 1913 Crown Prince Constantine of Greece enters Yannina after Greek troops seized it from the Turks.

THE CAILLAUX CASE

In the run-up to the First World War, France was distracted by a high-profile murder. On March 16, 1914, the wife of Joseph Caillaux, the finance minister and a former prime minister, went to the offices of Gaston Calmette, editor of the newspaper *Le Figaro*, and shot him dead. Calmette had been waging a bitter campaign against her husband, mainly over the imposition of income tax, and had threatened to publish personal and compromising letters. In the sensational trial that followed in July, Madame Caillaux declared that she did not intend to kill Calmette, just to threaten him to make him hand over the letters; but 'I lost my head when I found myself in the presence of the man who had done so much harm, who had ruined our lives for 13 months.' She was acquitted. Caillaux felt compelled to resign, but later made a successful return to politics.

banded together as the Balkan League – launched an all-out war against the Turks, principally to demand independence for Macedonia. The Turks were taken by surprise and quickly overrun; some 200 000 died in the opening weeks of the war. By November, they had effectively been pushed out of Europe, except for an enclave around Constantinople. On November 30, with the Bulgarians at the gates of Constantinople, the Turks signed an armistice. Meanwhile, Albania had declared its independence.

The big powers attempted to take control of events at a peace conference that opened in London on December 16, 1912. But the war rumbled on. In April 1913 a Turkish garrison at Scutari (Shkodër) in Albania fell after a six-month siege. Fighting flared up between the Bulgarians and the Turks over the ancient city of Adrianople (Edirne) which the Turks refused to cede. This rearguard action turned into another costly setback for the Turks. They were forced once more to the negotiating table, and signed the Treaty of London on May 30, 1913, by which they lost Adrianople.

Almost immediately, fresh conflict erupted as the Balkan League itself collapsed in squabbles over the territorial spoils, particularly in Macedonia. The Bulgarians began fighting the Serbs and the Greeks; the Romanians were also drawn into the conflict. Turkey seized the opportunity to reclaim some of its losses. This brief Second Balkan War was concluded by the Treaty of Bucharest signed on August 10, 1913; Bulgaria had now lost all its earlier

BEWARE THE SNIPER A Romanian cavalry patrol operates with wise circumspection, as it goes about its business during the war against Bulgaria in July 1913.

gains (including Adrianople), and even some of its pre-1913 territory. For the great powers, these events sounded alarm bells. It was difficult to predict or to control the outcome of such instability.

An engagement in Sarajevo

It was a routine visit that took the heir to the Austro-Hungarian throne, Archduke Franz Ferdinand, to the Bosnian capital, Sarajevo, on June 28, 1914. After inspecting troops on military manoeuvres, he arrived by train to begin a widely publicised motorcade procession that would take him to the town hall, a new museum and lunch with the governor.

The Balkans were in a state of high tension, and there had been warnings that

WITHDRAWING TO ASIA After 1913 Turkey was left with just the rump of its former European possessions (below). Refugees head for the 'Stamboul Ferry' to take them across the Bosporus to Asian Turkey (right).

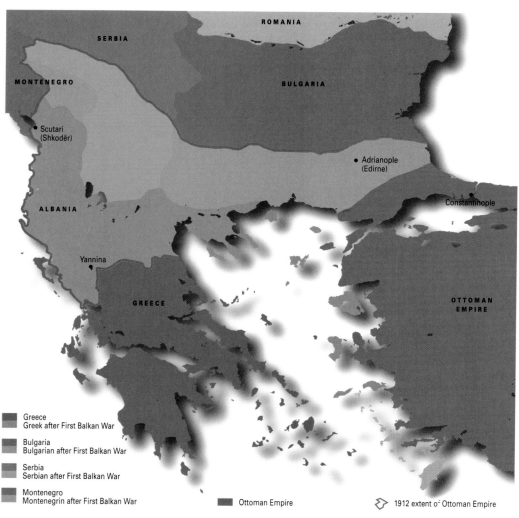

Greece
Greek after First Balkan War

Bulgaria
Bulgarian after First Balkan War

Serbia
Serbian after First Balkan War

Montenegro
Montenegrin after First Balkan War

Ottoman Empire

1912 extent of Ottoman Empire

MEMOIRS OF THE BALKAN WAR

As a young man, fresh out of university, the Irish-born writer Joyce Cary went to the Balkans in the sincere belief that war was about to become a thing of the past and he was curious to witness it. He became a stretcher-bearer for the Red Cross in southern Montenegro near Scutari (Shkodër), where the Turks were besieged for six months in 1913. In his diary he records the strangely unreal feel of the war:

'One had the . . . impression sometimes . . . that it was more easy to fancy the country in deep peace than war. From the outpost here, high up in clear wind, we could watch the sheep browsing in Scutari meadows and a shepherd or two sitting under a tree. The line of wire [defences] in the plain shone like a stream, it could be distinguished from water only by its shewing [sic] more blue and not changing colour with the sky. The gun emplacements were hidden in clumps of trees, the tents half buried in their pits behind the trench – they suggested at most Tunbridge Wells cricket week, or a fair. This is not written or pretended for caprice – it is true that, what with the ordinary course of life being by the nature of man to seven-eighths of its consistency invariable and unchanging whatever you do, whether it is eel-fishing, flying, gambling, or polar-exploring, and what with the large indifference of hills, skies, sun, moon, and stars to small scuffles (the largest battle is small by comparison), it is by an imaginative effort rather than direct realisation that danger and the possibility of bullets can be understood. The sniper waits for the failure of the imagination and shoots you because you have forgotten that you must believe in him.'

SLAVS ON PARADE Russian infantry stride out with bayonets drawn in 1914. As self-appointed protectors of the Slav peoples, the Russians had an important stake in the Balkan tangle.

Serbian nationalists might attempt an assassination; but neither Franz Ferdinand nor the governor, Oskar Potiorek, took much heed. Indeed, their long route through the centre of Sarajevo was protected by only 120 police. Franz Ferdinand travelled in a semi-open car with his wife, Sophie, beside him. Facing them were Potiorek and Count Franz Harrach, the car's owner. There were seven cars in the motorcade altogether, and Franz Ferdinand's was the third.

No fewer than six would-be assassins lurked in the crowd. All were young Bosnian Serbs who had been recruited and trained in Belgrade, the Serbian capital, by a shadowy nationalist society called the Black Hand. Four of the assassins failed to carry out their preplanned attack. But as the motorcade passed down Appel Quay, the city's main riverside thoroughfare, Nedeljko Cabrinovic lobbed a bomb at the archduke's car.

It hit the roof and rolled away; or perhaps, as some witnesses described it, the bomb landed in the car, the archduke picked it up and threw it out of the back. The bomb then exploded beneath the following car, wounding two royal aides and a number of people in the crowd. Franz Ferdinand stopped his car and went back to survey the damage, then he stoically resumed his tour. Cabrinovic was arrested and ushered away.

At the town hall, the mayor launched into a banal speech of welcome, which Franz Ferdinand testily interrupted: 'What is the good of your speeches! I come to Sarajevo on a visit and I get bombs thrown at me. It is outrageous! . . . Very well, now go on with your speech.' This was the archduke's only outward sign of being shaken. He suggested

ARCHDUKE FRANZ FERDINAND: HEIR TO AN EMPIRE

When Archduke Franz Ferdinand (1863-1914) and his wife Sophie were shot in Sarajevo, there was much public grief in Vienna – but in truth he was not greatly missed. Indeed, he was considered perhaps to be playing his most useful role as an assassination victim and an excuse for Austria to attack Serbia.

Franz Ferdinand was the nephew of the ageing Emperor Franz Josef. He had been an obscure duke until he was shoved into the limelight after the mysterious death of Franz Josef's only son Rudolf in an apparent double suicide with his mistress at Mayerling in 1889; and then the death of his own father, the brother of Franz Josef, in 1896. Although Franz Ferdinand was now next in line to the throne, the emperor did not hold him in fond regard, and when Franz Ferdinand was diagnosed with a lung complaint, the court in Vienna widely assumed that his younger brother Otto would become the real heir. This embittered Franz Ferdinand, a sentiment reinforced by the wrangle over his marriage to Sophie, Countess Chotek, in 1900. Franz Josef declared her too common and ruled that the marriage could not go ahead unless Franz Ferdinand agreed it would be morganatic – that their offspring would not be recognised as proper heirs to his titles. This arrangement would eventually favour Otto's son Karl.

Franz Ferdinand attempted various diplomatic moves in preparation for his reign – to improve relations with Russia and to give a greater role to the Slavs within the empire. He was a major protagonist in the annexation of Bosnia-Herzegovina in 1908. Largely ignored by the emperor, however, Franz Ferdinand became ever more temperamental and testy. His main hobby was hunting, and he is said to have killed some 250 000 animals.

As Inspector General of the Armed Forces, his role was to travel around the empire monitoring troops and defences – which is what brought him to Sarajevo in June 1914. No ruler or prince of the day could be unaware of the serious threat of assassination posed by nationalists and anarchists. But Franz Ferdinand dismissed the danger: 'We are all constantly in danger of death,' he declared. 'One must simply trust in God.' As he lay dying in Sarajevo he muttered dismissively: 'It is nothing, it is nothing.'

LOVE MATCH Franz Ferdinand with his wife Sophie, a former lady-in-waiting. He was only allowed to marry Sophie on the condition that their children were not to succeed him.

ON THE WARPATH German field artillery is brought to the front during the invasion of France. One by one, the powers were pulled into the conflict, making it truly a world war.

to Sophie that she return to the governor's palace, but she refused. It was her belief that her presence somehow helped to shield her husband from assassination.

Meanwhile, the commotion surrounding the bomb incident had disrupted the plans of another young would-be assassin, 19-year-old Gavrilo Princip, who stood in the crowd armed with a Browning automatic pistol. Princip decided to defer his attempt until later, when Franz Ferdinand's motorcade was on the way to the museum. So he stationed himself on this route, waiting on the pavement outside a corner food shop.

Franz Ferdinand was determined to go ahead with the scheduled visit, but he made one alteration: he wanted to visit the wounded adjutant in hospital on the way to the museum. This meant a change to the route, but somehow the drivers were not informed. As the cars headed off towards the museum, the governor noticed the mistake and ordered the car to stop and reverse to take the correct route. It stopped directly outside the food shop where Princip stood 5 ft (1.5 m) away. Seizing his opportunity, Princip stepped forward, pointed his pistol at Franz Ferdinand, averted his head and shot him in the neck. Sophie threw herself in front of her husband and received the second bullet in her stomach. Both died within the hour.

Initially, to the world's press, this seemed like just another in a long string of assassinations. The archduke and his wife were buried with due public ceremony. Sarajevo erupted into riots as Croatians and Muslims torched Serbian homes and businesses. Princip and his fellow conspirators were rounded up. But to the Austrian government, the incident was a pretext for crushing independent Serbia, which had been an irritant for decades. Encouraged by Germany, and egged on by anti-Serbian demonstrations in Vienna, the Austro-Hungarian government put pressure on Serbia. It demanded that Austrian officials be allowed to investigate and bring to book the nationalists in Serbia who were behind the assassination. This represented an insulting breach of Serbia's national integrity, and Austria knew that it would be unacceptable. It was a pretext for invasion.

On July 23 Austria issued a 48 hour ultimatum to Serbia to comply, and began to amass troops on the Serbian border. As the ultimatum ticked away, Russia warned Austria's ally Germany that it would not be able to stand by idly if Serbia was invaded.

On July 25 the ultimatum expired; two days later, Austrian troops poured into Serbia. Russia mobilised its troops. On July 30 Germany issued an ultimatum to Russia that it would mobilise if Russia refused to order its troops to stand down. Russia refused. On August 1 Germany declared war on Russia, and France began mobilising in support of its ally. On August 3 Germany declared war on France. On August 4 German troops marched into neutral Belgium to attack France.

Britain could no longer stand aside: it was under obligation both as a guarantor of Belgian neutrality, and by the terms of the Entente Cordiale with France. Britain issued an ultimatum to Germany to withdraw.

Over a warm bank holiday weekend, the railway stations had been busy with family seaside groups mingling with the scores of soldiers and sailors recalled to barracks and bases. There was a feeling of excitement. A welcome spirit of resolve and unity permeated Britain, for so long riven by strikes, unrest and division. When the ultimatum expired at 11 pm (midnight in Germany) on Tuesday, August 4, 1914, the British declared war on Germany. In London joyous crowds hurried from Big Ben to Buckingham Palace, singing patriotic songs. The war so many people had anticipated had at last broken out: the great showdown with Germany had begun. And as Field Marshal Sir John French, commander of the British Expeditionary Force, asserted, it would all be over by Christmas.

HASTENING THE DAY Bank holiday crowds cheer the appearance of George V, Queen Mary and the Prince of Wales on a balcony of Buckingham Palace on the evening of August 3.

TIMECHART

1900

JANUARY

24-25 In the **Boer War**, the British suffer shocking losses as they fall into a trap on the open-top hill called Spion Kop.

FEBRUARY

28 The town of **Ladysmith** is relieved by British troops after a 118 day siege by the Boers.

MARCH

6 One of the key figures in the development of the motor car, the German engineer **Gottlieb Daimler**, dies, aged 73.

HUMAN COST OF WAR **The dead lie scattered on the hilltop where they fell during the Battle of Spion Kop.**

APRIL

4 A 16-year-old anarchist, protesting against British action in the Boer War, makes a **failed assassination attempt** on the Prince of Wales, Britain's future king Edward VII, at a railway station in Brussels.

14 The **Paris Universal Exposition** opens. The centrepiece is the Palace of Electricity; other highlights include the 'moving pavement', a giant Ferris wheel, and an escalator. Art Nouveau is promoted as the latest fashionable style.

24 London's *Daily Express* newspaper is founded.

30 Hawaii becomes a US territory. It was annexed in 1898 at the request of islanders following the overthrow of the monarchy.

30 The express train driver John Luther **'Casey' Jones** creates a legend when he dies clutching the

brake during a collision. His passengers owe their lives to this sacrifice.

MAY

17 The town of **Mafeking** is relieved by British troops after a 215 day siege by the Boers.

31 The **Boxer Rebellion** gathers momentum in northern China. By now foreign communities in Tianjin (Tientsin) are under siege. Meanwhile, Russia takes advantage of the disorder to annex Manchuria.

JUNE

7 Boxer rebels destroy key sections of the railway line connecting Tianjin and Beijing (Peking). The German ambassador in Beijing is murdered by Boxers on June 16.

23 The dome of the **Basilique du Sacré Coeur** in Montmartre, Paris, is opened, providing a new and controversial landmark for the city.

JULY

2 The first **Zeppelin airship**, the brainchild of Count Ferdinand von Zeppelin, is launched near Lake Constance.

3 In Crete the British archaeologist Arthur Evans begins a 30 year excavation of the **Palace of Knossos**, believed to be the setting for the legend of King Minos and the Minotaur.

22 The second modern **Olympic Games** open in Paris, coinciding with the Universal Exposition. Baron Pierre de Coubertin, responsible for the revival of the ancient games in 1896, serves on the organising committee.

29 Umberto I, King of Italy, is assassinated by an anarchist at Monza. He is succeeded by King Victor Emmanuel III (reigns 1900-46).

AUGUST

10 The first of the men's international **Davis Cup** tennis tournaments is won by the competition's founder, the American Dwight F. Davis, and his partner Holcombe Ward.

13 The Hamburg-Amerika liner *Deutschland* takes the **Blue Riband** for the fastest transatlantic crossing: 5 days, 11 hours and 45 minutes.

14 The **Boxer Rebellion** is effectively crushed when an international army of 10 000 troops from Britain, Germany, France, Japan, the USA and Italy enters Beijing to lift a two-month siege.

27 Bubonic plague breaks out in Glasgow.

31 Coca-Cola is promoted in Britain for the first time. It was first produced in the USA in 1886.

SEPTEMBER

7 The Italian Polar explorer **Umberto Cagni** comes the closest yet to the North Pole, about 237 miles (381 km). He is taking part in an expedition led by the Duke of Abruzzi.

OCTOBER

18 In Germany, **Bernhard, Prince von Bülow** takes over as chancellor.

NOVEMBER

6 The Republican **William McKinley** is re-elected as President of the USA. His vice-president is Theodore Roosevelt.

9 The *Mikasa*, a Japanese warship built in Britain, is launched, and enters the record books as the largest and **most powerful warship** in the world.

30 The Irish wit and writer **Oscar Wilde**, imprisoned and disgraced in 1895 after a trial concerning his homosexuality, dies in Paris, aged 46.

DECEMBER

2 Paul Kruger, the Boer leader, receives a warm welcome as he arrives in Germany.

MAIDEN FLIGHT **Zeppelin's airship rose 1000 ft (300 m) above Lake Constance and remained airborne for 18 minutes.**

SCIENCE

The German physicist Max Planck proposes his theory of **'quantum physics'**; the Austrian scientist Karl Landsteiner identifies three **blood groups**; Sigmund Freud, father of **psychoanalysis**, publishes *The Interpretation of Dreams*.

NEW PRODUCTS

The American inventor of the Kodak camera, George Eastman, introduces the **Brownie**, a camera simple enough for children to use. Other new products include the **paper clip** (Norway), the **hamburger** (USA).

THE WRITTEN WORD

Publications include *Lord Jim* by Joseph Conrad and *The Wonderful Wizard of Oz* by the American Lyman Frank Baum.

MUSIC

The opera *Tosca* by Italian **Giacomo Puccini** is first performed in Rome in January; in the USA 'Maple Leaf Rag' by **Scott Joplin** proves a huge hit in sheet music sales.

PRIME MINISTER **As imperial chancellor until 1909, von Bülow sought to restrain the impetuous kaiser.**

1901

JANUARY

1 The **Commonwealth of Australia** is inaugurated, uniting the colonies of Australia under one government. Edmund Barton is the first prime minister.

22 After a reign of 64 years, **Queen Victoria** dies at Osborne House on the Isle of Wight. She is succeeded by her 59-year-old son, Edward VII.

27 The Italian opera composer **Giuseppe Verdi** dies, aged 87.

FEBRUARY

1 The American film actor **Clark Gable** is born.

26 Leaders of the Boxer Rebellion are subjected to **public execution** by beheading in Beijing.

MARCH

17 In widespread student riots in Russia, 500 students, angered by the excommunication of Leo Tolstoy, storm the **Kazan Cathedral** in St Petersburg.

23 News breaks about the dire conditions in the **concentration camps** into which the British have herded thousands of Boer families in South Africa.

27 The Filipino rebel **Emilio Aguinaldo** is captured by American

PATRIOT Aguinaldo acknowledges the defeat of his anti-US insurrection – as depicted by a French newspaper.

troops, after leading a two-year revolt against the USA in the Philippines.

APRIL

27 A crowd of 100 000 attends the **Football Association Cup Final** at Crystal Palace. Tottenham Hotspur beat Sheffield United, 3-1.

MAY

15 The British government authorises the construction of three huge **new battleships**.

JUNE

9 The rebel leader and holy man Mohammed bin Abdullah receives a temporary setback at the hands of British troops in Somaliland. Resisting the British from 1899 to 1920, he is dubbed the **'Mad Mullah'** by the press.

14 The first **Gordon Bennett motor race** is held in France, organised by the son of the editor-in-chief of the *New York Herald*.

JULY

2 A **heat wave in New York** claims the lives of almost 400 people, when temperatures rise to 44°C (110°F) in the shade.

AUGUST

5 **Empress Victoria**, Queen Victoria's eldest child, mother of Kaiser Wilhelm II and sister of King Edward VII, dies, aged 60.

21 The **Cadillac** motor company is founded. It is named after the 18th-century French founder of Detroit, Antoine de la Mothe, sieur de Cadillac.

SEPTEMBER

4 The **Taff Vale judgment** by the House of Lords means that British trade unions may be liable to colossal damages in the event of strikes.

6 US President **William McKinley** is shot and fatally wounded by a Polish anarchist at an exhibition in Buffalo, New York. Theodore Roosevelt takes over as president.

8 The sporadic civil war in Colombia, known as the **'War of a Thousand**

Days' (1899-1901) escalates as neighbouring Venezuela, Ecuador and Nicaragua threaten to invade.

9 The French painter **Henri de Toulouse Lautrec** dies, aged 36. His celebrated posters have come to symbolise the louche and tantalising world of contemporary Parisian night life.

STRIKE COST The union representing striking Taff Vale railwaymen was obliged to pay out some £50 000 in all.

OCTOBER

2 *Holland I*, the British Royal Navy's **first submarine**, is launched at Barrow-in-Furness.

4 The **America's Cup** sailing race series is completed, bringing a 3-0 victory to the US yacht *Columbia* over the British entry *Shamrock II*, owned by the millionaire grocer Sir Thomas Lipton.

16 Booker T. Washington becomes the first black American to dine at the White House, at the invitation of President Theodore Roosevelt. This inspires race riots in which 34 people die.

19 Brazilian aviator Alberto Santos Dumont circumnavigates the Eiffel Tower in Paris in a **dirigible balloon** in order to win a $50 000 prize.

NOVEMBER

30 The Akouphone **hearing aid** is introduced to the public. Developed by electrical engineer M.R. Hutchinson, it consists of a transmitter placed on the lap or a handy table and a telephone that the deaf person holds to his or her ear.

DECEMBER

5 The American film animator **Walt Disney** is born.

10 The first **Nobel prizes** are awarded, a legacy of the Swedish industrialist Alfred Nobel, who was concerned about the implications of his invention, dynamite. The German Wilhelm Roentgen wins the prize for physics for his discovery of X-rays.

11 The Italian **Guglielmo Marconi** sends the first wireless signal across the Atlantic. Listening in Newfoundland, he picks up the letter S in Morse code transmitted from Cornwall.

18 The Liberal MP **David Lloyd George** attempts to make a pro-Boer

REFORMER Booker T. Washington was the most influential spokesman for black Americans at the start of the century.

speech at Birmingham. In the ensuing riot one man is killed.

NEW PRODUCTS

The British engineer Hubert Cecil Booth invents the prototype of the modern **vacuum cleaner**, but this only catches on after it is developed by the US entrepreneur William Hoover in 1908. King Camp Gillette of the USA patents the **safety razor**, along with disposable razor blades; the business really takes off in 1906. **Table tennis** or 'Ping Pong', invented by the British engineer James Gibb, goes on the market. Daimler produces the first **Mercedes**, named after the daughter of the Austro-Hungarian consul-general in Nice.

THE WRITTEN WORD

The year's new books include *Kim*, a novel about the 'Great Game' by **Rudyard Kipling**, the futuristic *The First Men in the Moon* by **H.G. Wells**, and *Buddenbrooks* by the German author **Thomas Mann**.

1902

JANUARY

30 Britain and Japan sign a treaty; it provides for mutual neutrality in a case where either nation is at war with a third party.

31 Lord Kitchener completes his **blockhouse system** in South Africa, although Jan Smuts and Christian de Wet continue to lead a successful Boer guerrilla campaign against the British.

FEBRUARY

20 A **strike in Barcelona**, Spain, results in violent clashes with the authorities, and leaves some 500 dead.

MARCH

13 Polish schools are closed as pupils refuse to sing the Russian national anthem.

26 Cecil Rhodes, a leading figure in the forging of British policy in southern Africa, dies, aged 48. He gave his name to Rhodesia, and his will left provision to fund Rhodes Scholarships to Oxford for students from the USA, Germany and the British Empire.

APRIL

4 By the terms of the **Russo-Chinese Manchurian Convention** the Russians agree to withdraw from Manchuria.

13 The **record speed** for a motor car of 74.5 mph (120 km/h) is achieved in France by Léon Serpollet.

COMMANDO Guerrilla warfare waged by the Boers delayed, though it did not prevent, eventual British victory.

MAY

8 On the French Caribbean island of Martinique, **Mont Pelée** erupts and destroys the island's commercial capital Saint-Pierre, killing 36 000 people.

31 The Boer War is concluded when the Boer leaders sign the **Treaty of Vereeniging**.

31 Worker unrest in Spain compels the king, 16-year-old Alfonso XIII, to declare martial law.

JUNE

24 An operation for appendicitis is performed successfully on Edward VII at Buckingham Palace; but his illness makes it necessary to **postpone the coronation**, due to take place on June 26.

27 The French government led by Emile Combes orders the permanent closure of 2500 religious schools as part of its campaign of **anticlericalism** to limit the power of the Church in French public life.

28 Approval by the US Congress for the purchase of the French canal concession signals the start of the **Panama Canal** project.

29 Marcel Renault wins the Paris-Vienna motor race, at the wheel of one of the cars constructed by the company founded by himself and his brother Louis.

JULY

5 A **coronation banquet for the poor** is held at Olympia and 700 other venues in London in honour of Edward VII's forthcoming coronation. Some 456 000 guests feast at the expense of the king and a host of donor organisations.

5 The British lawn-tennis player Hugh Doherty wins the men's singles at Wimbledon to begin a five-year reign as **Wimbledon champion**.

14 The 1000-year-old **campanile of Venice** suddenly collapses. Rebuilding is completed in 1912.

AUGUST

9 The delayed **coronation of King Edward VII** and Queen Alexandra takes place at Westminster Abbey.

SEPTEMBER

29 The French realist novelist **Emile Zola** dies, aged 62 – as a result of inhaling the fumes of a blocked bedroom chimney. His last years were dominated by his fight against the injustice meted out to Alfred Dreyfus.

OCTOBER

16 President Theodore Roosevelt negotiates an end to a five-month-old **Pennsylvania miners' strike**.

NOVEMBER

16 An anarchist makes a **failed assassination attempt** on Leopold II, King of the Belgians.

22 Friedrich Krupp, head of the powerful German arms manufacturing company, dies, aged 48. The husband of Friedrich's daughter, Bertha, takes over the company.

DECEMBER

10 The **Nobel prize for medicine** is awarded to Ronald Ross. He discovered that malaria is transmitted by the bite of the female Anopheles mosquito.

10 The first **Aswan Dam** is completed, controlling the annual flood of the Nile for the first time.

10 In a dispute over unpaid debts and compensation, mainly for railways seized by Venezuela in 1899, ships of the British and German navies blockade the **Venezuelan fleet** –

DEVIL'S ISLAND A German postcard shows the island prison where Dreyfus was held before campaigning by men like Zola secured his release. Background: Smoke billows from the erupting Mont Pelée.

consisting of four battleships – in La Guaira. The dispute is resolved in February 1903.

30 The **farthest south** to date is reached by Commander Robert Scott, Ernest Shackleton and Dr Edward ('Bill') Wilson on the British National Antarctic Expedition. They come to within 532 miles (856 km) of the South Pole.

SCIENCE

In France the scientists **Marie and Pierre Curie** identify the new element radium. In Britain the physiologists William Bayliss and Ernest Starling discover the first **hormone**, secretin.

NEW PRODUCTS

Morris Michtom, a Russian immigrant to the USA, creates the first **teddy bear**, inspired by a cartoon showing President 'Teddy' Roosevelt, an avid hunter, sparing a bear cub. Three major new companies are founded in the USA: the Texas Oil Company (**Texaco**); Minnesota Mining and Manufacture (**3M**); and Pepsi Cola.

THE WRITTEN WORD

This year sees the publication of two children's classics: The Tale of Peter Rabbit by **Beatrix Potter** and Just So Stories by **Rudyard Kipling**. Novels include The Hound of the Baskervilles by **Sir Arthur Conan Doyle**, Youth and Heart of Darkness by **Joseph Conrad**.

MUSIC

The Italian tenor **Enrico Caruso** makes his first record, 'Vesti la Giubba', from the opera I Pagliacci. Edward Elgar writes **'Land of Hope and Glory'**, adapted from his Pomp and Circumstance march, written the previous year. **Scott Joplin** publishes his popular 'rag' 'The Entertainer'.

1903

JANUARY

1 Just outside Delhi in India, the British Raj reaches a high point of pageantry with the **Grand Coronation Durbar**, orchestrated by the viceroy, Lord Curzon.

20 King Edward VII and President Theodore Roosevelt communicate by **wireless telegraph**.

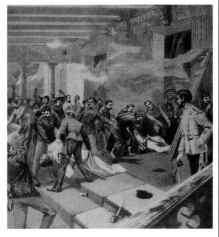

ROYAL MURDER Alexander of Serbia had made himself unpopular with his reactionary policies and his marriage to a widow of dubious reputation.

FEBRUARY

25 Richard Gatling, inventor of the **Gatling machine gun**, dies in New York, aged 84.

MARCH

29 A regular **news service** is established between New York and London using the Marconi wireless.

APRIL

14 Hundreds of Jews are killed in a **pogrom in Kishinev** in Russian-ruled Bessarabia (now Moldova).

14 Over 150 Muslims are killed by Bulgarians in a village near Monastir, in Turkish-ruled **Macedonia**, as the crisis in the Balkans grows.

23 British troops waging a campaign against the **'Mad Mullah'** in Somaliland suffer a disastrous defeat, and lose 190 men.

MAY

1 Britain's Edward VII begins an **official visit to Paris**. Relations between Britain and France have soured because of the Boer War, but improve following the visit.

8 The French painter **Paul Gauguin** dies in the Marquesas Islands, French Polynesia, at the age of 54.

28 An **earthquake in Constantinople** (Istanbul) claims 2000 lives.

JUNE

10 **King Alexander I and Queen Draga of Serbia** are assassinated in their bedroom in Belgrade by rebel army officers. The army appoints its own choice as king, Prince Peter Karageorgevitch (reigns 1903-21).

16 Henry Ford, the pioneer car manufacturer, founds the **Ford Motor Company**. Its first car is a Model A.

JULY

17 **James McNeill Whistler**, the American painter living in Europe, dies, aged 70.

19 The first of the annual **Tour de France** cycle races is won by Maurice Garin, a chimney sweep from Italy. The race was contested by 60 entrants and lasted 19 days.

26 The American motorist H. Nelson Jackson triumphantly enters New York, having become **the first person to cross the USA by car**. The journey took 63 days.

AUGUST

4 A new pope, **Pius X** (pope 1903-14), is elected, following the death of Pope Leo XIII (pope 1878-1903). Widely venerated for his concern for the poor, Pius is canonised as a saint in 1954.

11 A fire on the three-year-old **Paris Métro** kills 84.

SEPTEMBER

8 The **first Western movie**, *Kit Carson*, is filmed, not in the West, but in the Adirondack Mountains of New York State.

8 A Turkish **massacre in Macedonia** claims the lives of up to 50 000 Bulgarians in villages around Monastir.

OCTOBER

10 Emmeline Pankhurst founds the Women's Social and Political Union. A radical pressure group lobbying for votes for women, its members become known as **'suffragettes'**.

NOVEMBER

3 Colombian rebels proclaim independence for Panama, to facilitate US plans to build the **Panama Canal**.

3 The ***Daily Mirror*** is founded by Alfred Harmsworth in London, initially as a women's paper.

12 The French Impressionist painter **Camille Pissarro** dies, aged 73.

17 At the 'Second International' in London, Lenin engineers a split in the Russian Social Democrats, creating the **Bolsheviks** ('majority') led by Lenin, and the Mensheviks ('minority') led by Yuly Martov.

DECEMBER

9 Norway's parliament turns down a proposal to **give women the vote**.

10 **Marie Curie** becomes the first woman to win a Nobel prize. She shares the Nobel prize for physics with her husband Pierre and Henri Becquerel for their work on radioactivity.

14 Japan sends troops into **Korea** to quell rioting labourers, but this causes increased tension with Russia, Japan's main rival in the region.

17 **Orville and Wilbur Wright** achieve the first successful powered flight, when their aeroplane flies 120 ft (37 m) at Kitty Hawk, North Carolina.

18 The USA-Panama Treaty places sovereignty over the **Panama Canal Zone** in the hands of the USA in return for an annual rent.

30 Some 600 lives are lost as the audience panics during the disastrous **Iroquois Theatre fire**, Chicago.

SCIENCE
Dutch physiologist Willem Einthoven invents a galvanometer to measure the voltage changes in the beating heart, the basis of **electrocardiography**.

NEW PRODUCTS
In the USA, the first **Harley-Davidson** motorcycle is produced by William Harley and the three Davidson brothers. The first **oxyacetylene welder** is developed in France.

THE WRITTEN WORD
Novels include *The Ambassadors* by **Henry James**, and ***Call of the Wild*** by Jack London. This year also saw the completion of *Life and Labour of the People of London* by **Charles Booth**, a survey published over four years, providing irrefutable evidence that almost a third of Londoners were living in extreme poverty.

PARTY CONFERENCE Trotsky (top right) and Lenin (top, second left) were among delegates at the second conference of the Russian Social Democratic Workers' Party, held in Brussels and London in 1903.

1904

JANUARY

11 The massacre of 123 German settlers in German Southwest Africa is the start of a **Herero rebellion**.

12 The car manufacturer Henry Ford achieves a new **land speed record** of 91 mph (146 km/h) on the frozen Lake St Clair, near Detroit.

FEBRUARY

8 The **Russo-Japanese War** begins when the Japanese attack and blockade Port Arthur (Lüshun) in north-east China.

10 The scale of atrocities committed by the authorities and traders in the **Belgian Congo** is revealed by the British Consul, Roger Casement.

MARCH

18 Eleven lives are lost as a **British submarine sinks** following an accident with a liner near the Nab Lighthouse, off Portsmouth.

APRIL

1 Race riots at St Charles, Arkansas, result in the deaths of 14 blacks, the victims of **lynching**.

8 Britain and France negotiate closer ties under the terms of an **'Entente Cordiale'**.

18 *L'Humanité*, the French newspaper founded by socialist politicians Jean Jaurès and Aristide Briand, makes its first appearance.

MAY

1 The Czech composer **Antonín Dvořák** dies, aged 62.

4 The **Rolls Royce** company is founded by Charles Stewart Rolls and Henry Royce.

13 The Anglo-Chinese Labour Convention is signed, opening the door to large-scale use of Chinese **'coolie' labour** in the colonies.

JUNE

15 Fire on board a pleasure steamer, the *General Slocum*, causes

FIREBRAND A cartoon illustration of Jean Jaurès, politician and co-founder of *L'Humanité*, dedicated to the cause of democratic socialism.

the death of nearly 1000 people in New York harbour.

JULY

1 The third in the modern series of **Olympic Games** opens in St Louis, Missouri, organised to coincide with the World Fair mounted by the city.

2 The Russian dramatist and short-story writer **Anton Chekhov** dies of tuberculosis, aged 44.

3 The Hungarian-born founder of the Zionist movement, **Theodor Herzl**, dies, aged 44.

14 Paul Kruger, former President of Transvaal, dies, aged 78.

21 The **Trans-Siberian Railway** is completed. The world's longest railway took 13 years to construct.

AUGUST

3 Francis Younghusband, leading a diplomatic mission backed by soldiers from India, reaches **Lhasa**, capital of Tibet, after a series of overwhelmingly one-sided

military encounters with local Tibetan forces.

12 To the great relief of the tsar and tsarina, a **male heir to the Russian throne**, Alexis, is born.

SEPTEMBER

1 The American **Helen Keller**, blind and deaf since birth, graduates from Radcliffe College with honours. She was assisted by the pioneer teacher of the handicapped, Anne Sullivan Macy.

OCTOBER

22 Russian warships of the Baltic Fleet, en route to the Far East, mistakenly fire on British trawlers in the North Sea, killing two of the crew on the trawler *Crane*. This sparks off a major international dispute.

27 The **New York subway** (underground railway) is inaugurated.

NOVEMBER

7 Russian reservists, called up to fight in the war against Japan, **riot in Moscow**.

8 A large majority in the US election reconfirms **Theodore Roosevelt** as president.

28 A **revolt by the Khoikhoi** (Hottentots) in German Southwest Africa is crushed by German troops.

WRITERS TOGETHER The American-born novelist Henry James puts a companionable arm around the Scottish-born James Barrie.

DECEMBER

5 After encircling **Port Arthur**, the Japanese destroy the remnants of the Russian fleet.

10 The Russian physiologist **Ivan Pavlov** wins the Nobel prize for medicine, for his work on digestive glands.

NEW PRODUCTS
Inventions include the **Thermos flask** (Germany), the **teabag** (USA) and the **caterpillar tractor** (USA). British electrical engineer Ambrose Fleming devises the **diode valve**, paving the way towards radio. The French jewellery firm Cartier produces the first **wristwatch**, but this is considered generally too effeminate for men until the First World War.

RISING TO THE CHALLENGE Although deaf and blind, Helen Keller achieved academic distinction and went on to help others to do the same.

ART AND ARCHITECTURE
Scottish architect and designer Charles Rennie Mackintosh creates the **Willow Tea Rooms** in Glasgow, a classic late Art Nouveau work.

THE WRITTEN WORD
Novels include *Nostromo* by **Joseph Conrad**, and *The Golden Bowl* by **Henry James**.

THEATRE AND OPERA
Madama Butterfly, by Giacomo Puccini, receives its first performance, as does the classic children's play *Peter Pan* by J.M. Barrie. *The Cherry Orchard*, performed at the Moscow Arts Theatre in January, proves to be Anton Chekhov's last play.

1905

JANUARY

22 On **'Bloody Sunday'** scores of demonstrators are killed in front of the Winter Palace in St Petersburg, initiating a year of unrest in Russia called the 1905 Revolution.

FEBRUARY

17 Grand Duke Sergei, an uncle of the Tsar of Russia, is assassinated by

OVERKILL Tsarist cavalrymen charged peaceful demonstrators outside the Winter Palace on 'Bloody Sunday'.

a bomb thrown into his carriage in Moscow.

MARCH

18 Eleanor Roosevelt, niece of President Theodore Roosevelt, marries her distant cousin Franklin Delano Roosevelt (president 1933-45).

31 Kaiser Wilhelm II makes a surprise visit to Tangier in **Morocco**, testing British resolve to support France under the 1904 Entente Cordiale.

APRIL

4 An **earthquake in northern India** kills 10 000.

MAY

27-28 The Russian fleet is virtually wiped out by the Japanese at the **Battle of Tsushima**. This is the first major sea battle since 1827, and the first of the modern era.

JUNE

7 The German art movement **Die Brücke** is founded in Dresden by Ernst Kirchner, Karl Schmidt-Rotluff and others. Its predominant style is later described as Expressionism.

29 The British **Automobile Association** is founded to promote the interests of motorists.

JULY

8 The mutinying crew of the Russian battleship **Potemkin** find asylum in Romania. Meanwhile, 6000 people die as Russian troops are brought into Odessa to crush the strikes and mutiny.

8 May Sutton, a 17-year-old American lawn tennis player, becomes the first non-British contestant to win a title at the Wimbledon championships.

30 The Zionist Congress, meeting in Basle, Switzerland, rejects the British proposal to establish a **Jewish state in Uganda**, and restates its preference for Palestine.

AUGUST

19 Tsar Nicholas II issues an Imperial Manifesto, which proposes the creation of an elected consultative assembly, the **Duma**.

SEPTEMBER

5 The **Russo-Japanese War concludes** with a treaty brokered by President Roosevelt and signed at Portsmouth, New Hampshire. It is a humiliating defeat for Russia.

5 The **Baku oilfields** are set alight as Christian Armenians and Muslim Tartars, supported by Turkey, clash in the Russian Caucasus.

19 Dr Thomas John Barnardo, Irish-born founder of over 100 homes for destitute children, dies, aged 60. More than 250 000 children are said to have benefited from his work.

OCTOBER

1 The Salon d'Automne exhibition opens in Paris. It includes colourful work by Henri Matisse, Maurice de Vlaminck, André Derain and others, who are dismissed by a critic as *fauves* ('wild beasts'). **Fauvism** is born.

14 Christabel Pankhurst and Annie Kenney become the first **suffragettes** to go to prison as punishment for civil disturbances.

20 Workers begin a **general strike in Russia**. In St Petersburg they are directed by a newly formed 'soviet' (council) led by Leon Trotsky.

26 Under a Treaty of Separation, Sweden grants **independence to Norway**.

THE ORPHAN'S FRIEND Despite a heart condition, Dr Barnardo worked indefatigably right up to his death.

AN AMERICAN AT WIMBLEDON May Sutton was noted for a powerful forehand drive, rare then among female champions.

NOVEMBER

8 Around 1000 people die in a **massacre of Jews** at the Russian port of Odessa in early November.

9 A **mutiny** breaks out among Russian troops and sailors in Kronstadt, a naval base near St Petersburg.

DECEMBER

10 The German bacteriologist **Robert Koch** wins the Nobel prize for physiology and medicine for identifying the bacteria responsible for the era's greatest cause of death, tuberculosis.

22 Students and workers begin a week-long series of **riots in Moscow**. Several thousand die as government forces are brought in to restore order.

SCIENCE

Albert Einstein publishes four papers, which include his first attempt to describe the **Theory of Relativity**. The British biologist William Bateson coins the term **'genetics'**. French psychologist Alfred Binet devises **intelligence tests**.

NEW PRODUCTS

The first **nickelodeon** opens in McKeesport, near Pittsburgh, Pennsylvania, and is so called because the entrance fee is just one nickel (5¢). Also in the USA, the first **jukebox** is invented by John C. Danton; and the first **American pizzeria** opens in New York.

THE WRITTEN WORD

By popular demand, Sir Arthur **Conan Doyle** revives his detective hero in *The Return of Sherlock Holmes*. *Kipps* by **H.G. Wells** and *The Scarlet Pimpernel* by Baroness Orczy are other popular successes.

ARCHITECTURE AND MUSIC

Vienna Secession architect Josef Hoffman begins the **Palais Stoclet** in Brussels. New musical works include *La Mer* by **Claude Debussy**, and Symphony No. 7 by **Gustav Mahler**.

1906

JANUARY

4 The American dancer **Isadora Duncan** is forbidden to perform in Berlin on the grounds that her act is obscene.

FEBRUARY

7-8 A **typhoon in the South Pacific** kills 10 000 people in French Polynesia and the Cook Islands.

10 HMS *Dreadnought*, the largest and fastest battleship in the world, is launched by Edward VII at Portsmouth. It signals a new era in naval warfare and a major step forward for Britain in the arms race against Germany.

MARCH

7 The Finnish government grants **votes for women** – provided they are over the age of 24 and taxpayers. Men have comparable voting rights.

10 A **colliery disaster at Courrières** in northern France claims the lives of 1290 miners.

APRIL

7 Hundreds of lives are lost as **Vesuvius**, near Naples, erupts.

8 The **Algeciras Conference** on the future of Morocco concludes in Spain. The European powers agree to preserve Morocco's independence, while allowing France and Spain to maintain their spheres of influence.

11 Father Gapon, who led the demonstration in St Petersburg on 'Bloody Sunday' in January 1905, is murdered by social democrats.

18 An **earthquake in San Francisco** triggers a fire which destroys much of the city and causes 2500 deaths.

19 French scientist **Pierre Curie**, aged 46, is knocked down and killed by a horse-drawn wagon on a Paris street.

22 Interim Olympic Games open in Athens to commemorate the tenth anniversary of the first of the modern series.

MAY

10 The elected representatives of the Russian **Duma** meet for the first time, but are immediately plunged into crisis as they clash with the Tsar over amnesty for political prisoners.

23 The Norwegian playwright **Henrik Ibsen** dies, aged 78.

31 The 20-year-old King Alfonso XIII of Spain and his bride, Princess Victoria Eugenie ('Ena') of Battenberg survive an **assassination attempt** at their marriage celebrations.

JUNE

1 The **Simplon Rail Tunnel**, through the Alps separating Switzerland and Italy, opens to rail

FORCE FOR DEMOCRACY? The tsar inaugurates the first Duma. Background: Father Gapon who championed Russia's poor.

traffic. At 12½ miles (20 km) long, this twin-bore tunnel is the longest in the world to date.

7 The fastest and largest liner in the world, Cunard's turbine-driven *Lusitania*, is launched in Glasgow.

14-16 Many die in a **massacre of Jews** in Bialystok, Poland, with the apparent connivance of the Russian authorities.

27 The first **Grand Prix motor race** is held at Le Mans, France, and is won by a Renault.

JULY

12 The French government formally annuls the conviction for treason of **Alfred Dreyfus**; he is awarded the Légion d'honneur on July 22.

AUGUST

25 The Russian premier Piotr Stolypin survives an **assassination attempt**, when a bomb wrecks his home and kills 30 people.

SEPTEMBER

2 The Norwegian explorer Roald Amundsen becomes the first person to sail through the **North-West Passage** to the north of Canada, completing a journey begun in 1903.

14 Some 600 members of the royal court of Denpasar, Bali, commit **mass suicide** when confronted by invading Dutch and Dutch colonial troops.

20 Under an edict issued by the imperial court, the use of **opium** will be outlawed in China within ten years.

OCTOBER

3 The Morse code signal **SOS** is adopted as the international distress signal, at a conference held in Berlin.

22 The French painter **Paul Cézanne** dies, aged 67.

25 Georges Clemenceau begins his first term as French prime minister.

NOVEMBER

15 Japan launches the *Satsuma*, the biggest battleship in the world.

26 President Roosevelt visits **Panama** to inspect work on the

PRESIDENT ON SITE A white-suited Roosevelt watches progress on the Panama Canal from a steam shovel.

canal. This is the first time a serving president of the USA has left the country.

27 The American escapologist **Harry Houdini** narrowly escapes death as he finds himself trapped under ice when performing a feat in the Detroit River.

DECEMBER

10 President Roosevelt is awarded the **Nobel peace prize** for his work in bringing about an end to the Russo-Japanese War.

24 Canadian-born Reginald Fessenden broadcasts the **first radio programme**, consisting of music and spoken words, from Massachusetts.

NEW PRODUCTS

Alva J. Fisher of the USA invents the **electric washing machine**, while fellow countryman Lee De Forest develops the **triode valve**, making wireless transmission considerably more powerful. **William Kellogg** founds a company to market corn flakes, a health food devised by Battle Creek Sanitarium, Michigan. By way of contrast, **'hot dogs'** go on sale for the first time at a New York baseball ground. Karl Nessler, a German-born hairdresser in London, introduces **permanent waving**, achieved with heavy brass curlers.

THE WRITTEN WORD

The children's classic *The Railway Children*, by Edith Nesbit, is first published.

1907

JANUARY

2 The French government bans crucifixes in schools – a measure in its **anticlerical campaign**.

14 Over 700 people are killed in an **earthquake in Jamaica**. The capital, Kingston, is severely damaged.

FEBRUARY

2 The Russian chemist **Dmitri Ivanovich Mendeleev**, creator of the periodic table, dies, aged 72.

MARCH

15 Finland elects the **first women MPs** to its parliament, or Diet.

22 The Indian lawyer Mohandas **Gandhi** begins his campaign of civil disobedience in South Africa.

APRIL

3 Reports from **Russia reveal that famine** has brought 20 million people close to starvation.

26 The British government rejects a bill in favour of building a **Channel Tunnel**; ministers are concerned about the implications for Britain's defence.

MAY

9 Riots in northern India mark the 50th anniversary of the Indian Mutiny.

26 The Hollywood actor **John Wayne** is born.

RECORD BREAKER The *Lusitania* – which would be sunk by a German U-boat in 1915 – docks in New York after its record-breaking transatlantic voyage.

JUNE

14 Votes for women, with certain qualifications, are granted in Norway.

20 French wine-growers riot in Narbonne and several are killed as troops open fire. Overproduction, falling prices and government inaction are the main causes of an increasingly bitter **'wine war'**.

JULY

8 *Follies of 1907* opens at the Jardin de Paris in New York. This is the first of the long-running **Ziegfeld Follies** – show spectaculars produced by Florenz Ziegfeld.

19 The **Emperor of Korea**, Kojong, is forced to abdicate in favour of his feeble-minded son Sunjong, in the face of the growing Japanese dominance in Korea.

29 Sir Robert Baden-Powell, the British hero of Mafeking, founds the **Boy Scout** movement.

AUGUST

10 After a 62 day journey, Prince Scipione Borghese reaches Paris to take first prize in the **Peking to Paris motor race**.

SEPTEMBER

4 The Norwegian composer **Edvard Grieg** dies, aged 64.

8 Sun Yat-sen forms the **Guomindang**, a nationalist party aiming to turn China into a republic.

26 New Zealand ceases to be a British colony, and becomes the **Dominion of New Zealand**.

OCTOBER

4 Widespread **anti-British rioting** breaks out in Calcutta. It is blamed on criticisms of British rule made by the visiting Labour MP Keir Hardie.

11 Cunard's *Lusitania* takes the **Blue Riband** from Hamburg-Amerika's *Deutschland* by crossing the Atlantic in 4 days, 19 hours and 52 minutes.

NOVEMBER

16 Oklahoma becomes the 46th state of the USA.

22 The world's biggest liner, Cunard's new ship the ***Mauretania***, completes her maiden voyage across the Atlantic.

DECEMBER

10 The British author **Rudyard Kipling** wins the Nobel prize for literature.

12 A bloody two-year **Zulu rebellion** against the the poll tax imposed by the Natal government comes to a close when King Dinizulu surrenders.

17 William Thomson, Lord Kelvin, the British scientist who devised the Kelvin scale of temperature, dies, aged 83.

BAEKELAND OF BAKELITE Baekeland had already invented the first commercially successful photographic paper.

NEW PRODUCTS

By means of a photoelectric cell, photographs are transmitted by wire for the first time; this prototype of the **fax machine** is used primarily in the newspaper business. Both Paul Cornu and Louis Breguet of France succeed in lifting their versions of prototype **helicopters** a few feet off the ground. **Persil** detergent is first produced in Germany. The Belgian Leo-Hendrik Baekeland invents the first form of totally synthetic plastic, patented as **Bakelite**.

ART AND ARCHITECTURE

Picasso creates his controversial *Les Demoiselles d'Avignon* signifying a shift that will lead to Cubism. The photographer Alfred Stieglitz shows work by Matisse, Brancusi and Picasso at his influential **291 gallery** in New York. Frank Lloyd Wright begins his greatest 'prairie house', the **Robie House**, in Chicago.

1908

JANUARY

6 Rebels proclaim Mulai Hafid **Sultan of Morocco**, in place of his brother Sultan Abd al-Aziz.

11 Two accidents mar the public enthusiasm for **film**. On January 11, 16 children are killed in the crush at a cinematograph exhibition in Barnsley, Yorkshire; two days later, 160 people are killed in an explosion at a cinema at Boyestown, Pennsylvania.

13 The aviator Henry Farman makes the **first complete circuit in an aeroplane**, near Paris. He stays aloft for one minute 28 seconds to achieve the feat, and wins a £5000 prize.

FEBRUARY

1 King Carlos I of Portugal and Crown Prince Luís Felipe are shot dead by a group of military revolutionaries while driving through Lisbon.

MARCH

7 The German battleship *Nassau*, the equivalent of the British *Dreadnought*, is launched.

21 Henry Farman, the aviator, makes history again by achieving the first aeroplane flight with a passenger.

APRIL

2 In an **accident at sea**, HMS *Tiger* is sliced in two by the cruiser HMS *Berwick* off the Isle of Wight, resulting in the deaths of 34 crew.

MAY

14 The Franco-British Exhibition opens at the **'White City'** in London.

JUNE

4 During a public ceremony to commemorate Emile Zola, **Alfred Dreyfus** escapes assassination by an enraged military journalist.

12 Emperor Franz Josef of Austria-Hungary celebrates his diamond jubilee (60 years as emperor).

21 Some 200 000 women attend a **Women's Sunday** rally held by the suffragettes in Hyde Park, London.

JULY

6 The **Young Turks** stage a revolt in Macedonia, beginning their takeover in Turkey. Their first task is to restore the Turkish constitution and reintroduce representational government.

26 The Bureau of Investigation (later the **FBI**) is founded in the USA.

30 The Italian marathon runner Dorando Pietri provides the dramatic highlight to the fourth modern **Olympic Games** in London. Collapsing at the finish in the White City Stadium, he is assisted over the line to finish first, but is disqualified.

AUGUST

14 An **airship explodes** at the Franco-British Exhibition in London, killing one man.

20 King Leopold II of the Belgians gives up his personal control of the **Belgian Congo**, as he hands this vast African land over to the Belgian government. His rule, and conditions in the country, have attracted widespread international criticism.

23 Sultan Abd al-Aziz of Morocco flees, following defeat by his brother, Mulai Hafid. France and Spain express their support for Mulai Hafid's claim to be the new sultan.

25 The French physicist **Henri Becquerel**, pioneer researcher into radioactivity, dies, aged 55.

SEPTEMBER

1 The **Hejaz Railway**, linking Damascus to Medina, opens. The project was initiated by the Sultan of Turkey in 1900 to facilitate travel to the holy cities of Islam.

14 The Detroit car manufacturers Buick and Oldsmobile are merged to form **General Motors**.

17 The **first aeroplane fatality** occurs at Fort Myer, Virginia. A US Army officer flying with Orville Wright dies after a propeller breaks and their plane crashes. Orville Wright is injured.

25 In the **'Casablanca Incident'**, German deserters from the French Foreign Legion who have sought refuge with a German official are forcibly retaken by the French.

OCTOBER

5 Ferdinand I of **Bulgaria** declares his country's full independence from the Ottoman Empire – hitherto Bulgaria had been an autonomous principality within the empire.

6 Austria-Hungary announces the **annexation of Bosnia-Herzegovina**.

7 The island of **Crete** formally disengages itself from the Ottoman Empire to join Greece.

27 *The Daily Telegraph* publishes an **interview with Kaiser Wilhelm II** in which he discloses his country's efforts to humiliate Britain during the Boer War.

NOVEMBER

3 The Republican **William Taft** is elected president of the USA.

14 The **Guangxu Emperor** of China dies. He is succeeded by a two-year-old infant, Puyi, 'the last emperor'.

FIRST BUT DISQUALIFIED This last-minute helping hand had marathon runner Dorando Pietri disqualified.

KING OF DARKNESS Conrad's novel *Heart of Darkness* was inspired by conditions in the Belgian Congo under the rule of Leopold II (above).

DECEMBER

10 The New Zealand-born physicist **Ernest Rutherford** wins the Nobel prize for chemistry, for his work on radioactive elements.

26 The American **Jack Johnson** becomes the first black boxer to win the world heavyweight champion's title. He holds the title until 1915.

28 An **earthquake in Sicily and Calabria** in southern Italy kills 156 500 people.

NEW PRODUCTS

The Ford Motor Company begins production of the **Model T** using assembly-line techniques. Swiss chemist Jacques Brandenberger patents **Cellophane**. German physicist **Hans Geiger**, working with Ernest Rutherford, invents a machine for measuring radioactive emissions. **Mother's Day** is celebrated for the first time in Philadelphia, Pennsylvania.

THE WRITTEN WORD

New books include **A Room with a View** by E.M. Forster; *The War in the Air*, a futuristic novel by **H.G. Wells**, and the children's classic **The Wind in the Willows** by Kenneth Grahame.

ART AND ARCHITECTURE

The term **Cubism** is coined after an exhibition of work by Pablo Picasso and Georges Braque at the Salon d'Automne in Paris. The German **Peter Behrens** designs the influential AEG Turbine factory in Berlin.

1909

JANUARY

1 The national **old age pension** scheme comes into force in Britain, providing five shillings a week for men and women over 70.

LOOKING AFTER THE ELDERLY
In Britain, pension books brought new financial security to those over 70.

5 The Colombian government recognises the **independence of Panama**, its former province.

INTREPID EXPLORER Ernest Shackleton during his unsuccessful attempt to reach the South Pole. Right: Gordon Selfridge and his Oxford Street store.

9 The explorer **Ernest Shackleton** comes within 97 miles (156 km) of the South Pole – the closest yet.

23 Two **armed Russian anarchists** rob a payroll from a clerk in Tottenham, London, then kill a policeman and a 10-year-old boy and wound 17 others as they try to escape.

FEBRUARY

8 The British government announces the construction of **six new dreadnought-class warships**.

20 The Italian poet Filippo Tommaso Marinetti publishes the **'First Futurist Manifesto'** in the French newspaper *Le Figaro*.

24 An **American shoots his wife** in the National Portrait Gallery in London, then commits suicide.

MARCH

2 The great powers intervene to avert war between **Serbia and Austria-Hungary** over the annexation of Bosnia-Herzegovina. The crisis is eventually resolved on March 30.

15 American retail tycoon Gordon **Selfridge** opens his department store in Oxford Street, London.

24 The Irish playwright **J.M. Synge**, author of *Playboy of the Western World*, dies, aged 37.

APRIL

6 On his fifth attempt, the American Commander **Robert Peary** reaches the North Pole, accompanied by his black assistant Matthew Henson and four Eskimos. However, his records leave room for doubts about his claim.

10 The English poet **Algernon Swinburne** dies, aged 72.

18 The 15th-century French heroine **Joan of Arc** is beatified by Pope Pius X, the first stage towards being formally declared a saint in 1920.

27 The Young Turks depose the tyrannical **Sultan Abd al-Hamid**,

replacing him with his brother Mohammed V (reigns 1909-18).

29 David Lloyd George, the British Chancellor of the Exchequer, introduces the **'People's Budget'**. Designed to raise funds for the old age pension scheme as well as naval spending through increased taxes, it takes six months to pass through the House of Commons and is rejected by the House of Lords on November 30.

MAY

1 In an atmosphere of spiralling racism and incidents of lynching in the USA, the foundations for the **National Association for the Advancement of Colored People** (NAACP) are laid.

18 The **Ballets Russes**, directed by Russian impresario Sergei Diaghilev, perform for the first time, in Paris, in a season of Russian opera and ballet.

28 During a strike by white firemen protesting against the employment of blacks on the **Georgia Railroad** in the USA, a mob attacks black staff on a mail train.

JUNE

7 The French contribute to the **arms race** by announcing that they will spend £120 million in a new naval shipbuilding programme.

26 The **Victoria and Albert Museum** in London is officially opened by King Edward VII.

JULY

14 Bernhard, **Prince von Bülow** resigns as German chancellor. He is replaced by Theobald von Bethmann Hollweg (in office 1909-17).

25 The French pioneer aviator **Louis Blériot** becomes the first person to fly across the English Channel in an aeroplane, and wins a £1000 prize.

AUGUST

1 In Spain, some 1000 people are killed in widespread **anti-government riots in Barcelona** and elsewhere in Catalonia.

2 On his arrival in England, **Tsar Nicholas II** reviews the British fleet at Spithead. The visit is marked by socialist-led demonstrations by workers.

SEPTEMBER

28 In Britain **force-feeding of suffragette prisoners** on hunger strike begins; this is acknowledged in the House of Commons.

OCTOBER

13 The militant anarchist leader of the **Spanish anticlerical movement**, Francisco Ferrer Guardia, is executed in Barcelona, accused of inspiring anti-government unrest. This causes widespread demonstrations at Spanish embassies in Europe.

26 Prince Ito Hirobumi, the noted Japanese statesman, former prime minister and first resident-general of Korea, is assassinated by a Korean patriot in Harbin, Manchuria.

NOVEMBER

13 A **coal mine disaster** at Cherry, Illinois, claims the lives of 250 miners.

14 Pearl Harbor in Hawaii is chosen by President Taft as the site for a new US naval base in the Pacific.

DECEMBER

16 The Liberal government of **Nicaragua** led by José Santos Zelaya falls with the intervention of US marines. US interests begin to dominate Nicaraguan politics.

17 King Leopold II of the Belgians dies, aged 74. He is succeeded by his nephew Albert (reigns 1909-34).

NEW PRODUCTS
The first **electric toaster** is marketed by the General Electric Company in the USA. *A Visit to the Seaside*, filmed in Kinemacolor in Brighton, Sussex, becomes the world's **first commercial colour movie**.

THE WRITTEN WORD
Books include a children's classic, Lucy Maud Montgomery's **Anne of Green Gables**.

MUSIC
While **Gustav Mahler** works on his Symphony No 9, his final completed symphony, fellow-Austrian **Arnold Schoenberg**, the new *enfant terrible* of classical music, produces Three Pieces for piano, marking his complete break with tonality.

1910

JANUARY

26 Heavy rains cause **floods in Paris**. Thousands are forced to abandon their homes.

FEBRUARY

1 The first 60 state-run **labour exchanges** in Britain open, signalling the government's willingness to intervene directly in the job market.

20 Boutros Ghali, Prime Minister of Egypt and a Christian Copt, is fatally wounded by a young nationalist and dies the following day.

23 The **Dalai Lama** flees from Tibet into India, in the face of Chinese incursions.

MARCH

10 Slavery is abolished in China by edict from the imperial government.

21 The French photographer **'Nadar'** (Félix Tournachon) dies, aged 89.

28 Henri Fabre of France makes the first successful flight in a **seaplane**.

APRIL

10 Over 250 000 socialists attend an **anti-government demonstration in Berlin** as tempers flare over suffrage reform.

12 A revolt in **Albania** is put down by Turkish troops.

21 The American writer **Mark Twain** (Samuel Langhorne Clemens) dies, aged 74.

MAY

6 The popular **King Edward VII dies**, aged 68, at Buckingham Palace, after falling ill at Biarritz in France. He is succeeded on the British throne by his 44-year-old son George V.

10 The British House of Commons resolves to restrict the power of the **House of Lords** and to reduce the maximum duration of a government to five years.

20 Halley's Comet, which passes the Earth every 76 years or so, comes

EXILED RULER The Dalai Lama, high priest of Tibet. Background: Herbert Asquith, British prime minister 1908-16.

closest today, when it is some 13 million miles (21 million km) away.

31 The South Africa Act is passed, uniting the four colonies of Transvaal, Orange River, the Cape and Natal in the **Union of South Africa**, a dominion under the British Crown.

31 The **Girl Guides** movement is created by Sir Robert Baden-Powell and his sister Agnes.

JUNE

22 The *Deutschland*, the newest airship designed by Count von **Zeppelin**, makes the first commercial flight carrying passengers, but is wrecked in a storm on June 28.

HANG OUT THE FLAGS Cape Town's Adderley Street railway station is decked with flags to celebrate the new Union of South Africa.

JULY

12 Charles Stewart Rolls, co-founder of Rolls Royce, is killed in an air accident at Bournemouth. He was 32. Six weeks earlier he made aviation history with a non-stop flight across the Channel, from Dover to Calais and back.

31 A British detective boards the SS *Montrose* in Quebec, Canada, to arrest Dr H.H. **Crippen** for the murder of his wife. Crippen, with his mistress Ethel Le Neve, were recognised in mid-ocean by the captain, who alerted Scotland Yard by wireless telegraph.

AUGUST

13 Florence Nightingale, pioneer of modern nursing, dies, aged 90.

27 Mother Teresa of Calcutta, the Albanian-born leader of the Missionaries of Charity, is born.

28 Montenegro proclaims its independence from Turkey.

30 Japan formally annexes **Korea**.

SEPTEMBER

2 The French primitive painter **Henri 'Le Douanier' Rousseau** dies, aged 66. He had been championed by Picasso and others since about 1906.

7 The British Pre-Raphaelite painter **William Holman Hunt** dies, aged 83.

15 The first election in the new Union of South Africa is won by the South Africa Party led by **Louis Botha**.

OCTOBER

1 Cotton workers in Britain are locked out as they go on strike in sympathy with striking dockers, shipbuilders and Welsh miners.

5 Portugal is declared a republic as revolutionaries force the last king, Manuel II, to flee to Britain.

NOVEMBER

18 On **'Black Friday'**, a riot outside the British House of Commons results in the arrest of 120 suffragettes, many of whom complain of maltreatment by the police and male onlookers.

20 The Russian writer **Count Leo Tolstoy** dies at a railway station, after fleeing his home following a dispute with his wife. He was 82.

DECEMBER

21 A **colliery disaster** at Pretoria Pit near Bolton, Lancashire, claims the lives of 344 miners.

NEW PRODUCTS

Black & Decker, the tool manufacturer, is founded in Baltimore, Maryland, by Duncan Black and Alonzo Decker. The **largest cinema in the world**, the luxurious 5000 seat Gaumont Palace, opens in Paris. French chemist Georges Claude invents

THE BIGGEST The first-ever Gaumont Palace was just that: a palace for the new entertainment of moving pictures.

neon lighting and demonstrates it at the Paris Motor Show. The **Ford Motor Company** sets up a factory to build cars in Britain.

MUSIC AND DANCE

The Ballets Russes' *L'Oiseau du Feu* (**Firebird**) – with music by Igor Stravinsky, costumes by Leon Bakst, and starring Tamara Karsavina in the lead role – causes a great stir in Paris.

1911

JANUARY

3 A fire demolishes the house in east London where a small band of armed anarchist criminals held hundreds of police and troops at bay in the so-called **Sidney Street Siege**.

FEBRUARY

27 Aristide Briand resigns as French prime minister. After Ernest Monis's brief spell in power, his place is taken by Joseph Caillaux in June.

MARCH

31 A Shops Bill introduced by the Liberal government seeks to limit the working week for British **shop assistants** to 60 hours.

APRIL

23 French troops are sent into **Morocco** to quell unrest in Fez and Casablanca.

PRESIDENTIAL POSE   Until his fall in 1911, Porfirio Diaz had ruled Mexico more or less continuously since 1877.

31 The White Star liner **Titanic,** proclaimed the largest and fastest liner in the world, is launched at Belfast.

JUNE

16 In Morocco, French troops occupy **Fez**.

JULY

1 The Germans unexpectedly send the gunboat *Panther* into the Moroccan port of Agadir in protest

THE NEW MASTERS   Italian soldiers march a group of Libyan prisoners through the streets of Tripoli.

MAY

1 In continuing **trust-busting** action in the USA, John D. Rockefeller's Standard Oil Company is found to contravene monopoly laws, and is subsequently split up into 34 separate companies.

25 The dictator Porfirio Diaz is ousted as president of **Mexico** as the country slips into civil war. The liberal Francisco Madero becomes provisional president, with the support of rebel leaders such as Pancho Villa and Emiliano Zapata.

against the increasing French presence in the country. This **'Agadir Incident'** provokes a crisis which brings the European powers to the brink of war, but it is resolved in November.

20 With **widespread strikes across Britain**, nine people are killed during a confrontation with troops at Llanelli, South Wales. Three are shot, and the others die in an explosion on a train which strikers have attempted to stop.

24 In the Peruvian Andes, the American historian Hiram Bingham discovers the ruins of a lost Inca city, **Machu Picchu**.

AUGUST

22 Leonardo da Vinci's **Mona Lisa** is stolen from the Louvre by an Italian house painter. It is eventually recovered in Florence in 1913.

SEPTEMBER

29 Italy declares war against Ottoman Turkey and launches an attack on Tripoli in **Libya**.

OCTOBER

9 HMS *King George V* is launched, destined to be the first of the **'super-dreadnoughts'**.

26 After a series of provincial mutinies, the **Republic of China** is proclaimed. Sun Yat-sen is appointed provisional president. The old imperial government is confined to Beijing and the north.

NOVEMBER

1 The Italians use aeroplanes to bomb Turkish troops in Libya, marking the **first military use of aviation**.

DECEMBER

10 The French scientist **Marie Curie** becomes the first person to win a second Nobel prize. Her Nobel prize for chemistry is awarded for the discovery of radium and polonium.

12 King George V is crowned **Emperor of India** at the Delhi Durbar. He also formally founds New Delhi as the capital of India, in place of Calcutta.

15 Roald Amundsen and four fellow Norwegians reach the **South Pole**, a month ahead of the British expedition led by Captain Robert Scott.

SCIENCE

The physicist Ernest Rutherford discovers the nucleus and puts forward the idea of the **nuclear atom**. Dutch physicist Heike Kamerlingh-Onnes discovers **superconductivity**, the reduction of electrical resistance in some substances at very low temperatures.

NEW PRODUCTS

The Delco **self-starter** for an automobile is fitted to a model built by Cadillac. it was the first self-contained system that performed ignition, starting and lighting the car. Painted

white lines, down the centre of the road, are introduced as a safety feature in the USA.

THE WRITTEN WORD

Books include the children's classic **The Secret Garden** by Frances Hodgson Burnett, and *Ethan Frome* by the American writer Edith Wharton.

MUSIC AND ART

The opera **Der Rosenkavalier** by Richard Strauss is performed for the first time in Dresden, Germany; and the Ballets Russes' production of Igor Stravinsky's **Petrushka** starring Vaslav Nijinsky, is given its premiere in Paris. Meanwhile, Irving Berlin's song **'Alexander's Ragtime Band'** becomes a popular success. **Der Blaue Reiter** group of painters, led by Franz Marc, Auguste Macke and Vassily Kandinsky, is founded in Munich, and the term **expressionism** is coined.

RAGTIME AND A BLUE RIDER
Aged 23, Irving Berlin (above) was near the start of a career as one of the most successful songwriters of the 20th century. The Russian-born lawyer-turned-artist Vassily Kandinsky designed this cover (below) for a Blue Rider exhibition.

1912

JANUARY

6 New Mexico becomes the 47th state of the USA.

22 An election in Germany leaves the **Social Democratic Party** (SPD) as the strongest political party, but it still does not form part of the government.

FEBRUARY

8 The German government announces the construction of **six new dreadnought-class warships**.

10 Joseph Lister, the British surgeon who introduced the use of antiseptics, dies, aged 84.

12 The reign of Puyi, the **last emperor of China**, comes to a close as his mother signs abdication papers on his behalf. China is formally declared a republic.

14 Arizona becomes the 48th state of the USA.

26 A **British miners' strike**, begins. It soon gathers momentum and wins the support of a million workers.

MARCH

1 At St Louis, Missouri, Albert Berry becomes the first person to jump from an aircraft with a **parachute**.

1 A sudden and concerted outbreak of **window-smashing** by suffragettes causes widespread damage in the West End of London. It results in the arrest of over 120 women.

7 Guglielmo Marconi wins a contract with the British government to set up wireless telegraph stations in London, Egypt, Aden, Bangalore, Pretoria and Singapore. Government ministers are later implicated in a shares scandal relating to this deal.

29 Captain Robert Scott makes his last diary entry in the Antarctic before perishing with his companions Dr Edmund 'Bill' Wilson and Henry 'Birdie' Bowers.

30 Sultan Abd al-Hafiz of Morocco signs a treaty with France formally

making **Morocco** a French protectorate. A treaty between France and Germany, signed on November 3, 1910, had paved the way for this.

APRIL

13 The **Royal Flying Corps** is established in Britain, acknowledging the military potential of aircraft.

14 The *Titanic* hits an iceberg and sinks in the Atlantic on its maiden voyage, with the loss of some 1500 passengers and crew.

MAY

14 The Swedish playwright **August Strindberg** dies, aged 63.

23 The Hamburg-Amerika line's *Imperator*, the **world's biggest ship**, is launched by Kaiser Wilhelm II in Hamburg.

29 Strikes in the Port of London, in pursuit of a union closed shop, are supported by other transport workers and bring London to a standstill.

WHITE STAR DISASTER After the *Titanic* disaster ships had to have lifeboat spaces for everybody on board.

30 Wilbur Wright, pioneer aviator, dies of typhoid at the height of the Wright brothers' success. He was 45.

JUNE

26 The first **Alexandra Day** is held in Britain, raising £12 000 for the

AIR WARRIORS An airman prepares for takeoff at the new Royal Flying Corps' Central Flying School in Wiltshire.

charities sponsored by Alexandra, the Queen Mother.

29 The fifth modern **Olympic Games** open in Stockholm.

JULY

30 Emperor Meiji of Japan dies, aged 60. He had reigned since 1867. He is succeeded by Yoshihito.

AUGUST

1 The first **airmail service** between London and Paris begins.

21 William Booth, founder of the Salvation Army, dies, aged 83.

SEPTEMBER

28 Some 250 000 Protestant Ulstermen sign the **'Solemn League and Covenant'** in Northern Ireland, pledging their opposition to Catholic-dominated Irish Home Rule based in Dublin.

OCTOBER

8-17 Bulgaria, Serbia, Greece and Montenegro form the Balkan League and declare war on the Turks, thereby triggering the **First Balkan War**.

12 The British **super-dreadnought** HMS *Iron Duke* is launched; this takes the lead as the largest and most powerful warship in the world.

14 A gunman tries to **assassinate** Theodore Roosevelt, campaigning to be re-elected as US president. Roosevelt escapes with slight wounds.

18 A peace treaty signed by Turkey cedes Tripolitania and Cyrenaica in **Libya** to Italy.

NOVEMBER

5 The Democrat **Woodrow Wilson** is elected president of the

USA after Theodore Roosevelt's Progressive Republican ('Bull Moose') Party splits the Republican vote and ousts Taft.

19 Suffragettes in Britain begin their campaign of setting fire to **letterboxes**.

28 Albania declares its independence from Ottoman Turkey.

DECEMBER

10 A **peace conference**, aimed at putting an end to the Balkan War, opens in London.

23 Lord Hardinge, **Viceroy of India**, is wounded when a bomb is thrown into his howdah on the back of an elephant, at a durbar to inaugurate New Delhi as capital.

SCIENCE
German geologist Alfred Wegener first proposes the concept of **continental drift**, but only in the 1950s does this idea become widely accepted.

NEW PRODUCTS
Car windscreen wipers, still operated by hand, are first manufactured on a commercial basis. The **Wurlitzer** Company of North Tonawanda, New York, produces its first cinema organ; the designer, British-born Robert Hope-Jones, is such a perfectionist that he has to be locked out of the workshop to prevent further delays.

THE WRITTEN WORD
Publications include *The Psychology of the Unconscious* by the Swiss psychoanalyst **Carl Jung**, and *The Montessori Method* by the Italian educationalist **Maria Montessori**. Novels include *The Lost World* by Sir Arthur **Conan Doyle**.

MUSIC AND DANCE
The Ballet Russes' production of *L'Après-midi d'un faune (The Afternoon of a Faun)* to music by Claude **Debussy** and starring **Nijinsky** is first performed in Paris. Arnold Schoenberg's expressionistic song cycle *Pierrot Lunaire* also receives its first performance. W.C. Handy writes **'Memphis Blues'**; and the British music hall song **'It's a Long, Long Way to Tipperary'**, by Jack Judge and Harry J. Balsall, makes its first appearance. The revue *Hello Ragtime!* causes a sensation when it opens in London in December.

1913

JANUARY

9 The future US president **Richard Nixon** is born.

11 The last **horse-drawn omnibus** is withdrawn from service in Paris.

18 The **Irish Home Rule Bill** is passed by the House of Commons, but rejected by the House of Lords on January 30.

23 A revolt by the Young Turks breaks out. The Turkish commander-in-chief **Nazim Pasha** is assassinated, and on January 31, Grand Vizier Kiamil Pasha is replaced by General Shefkat Pasha.

FEBRUARY

1 Grand Central Station in New York, the largest railway station in the world, opens.

8 The Australian polar explorer **Douglas Mawson**, leader of the Australasian Antarctic Expedition, struggles into his base camp at Cape Denison after a three-month nightmare journey in which both his two companions died.

10 News reaches the outside world of the tragic deaths in March the previous year of **Captain Robert Scott** and his fellow explorers.

18 Following a coup led by General Victoriano Huerta in Mexico, **President Francisco Madero** is arrested. He is shot four days later when allegedly trying to escape.

AT THE SIEGE'S END A Montenegrin general questions a Turkish prisoner after the fall of Scutari.

19 A **suffragette bomb** wrecks the unoccupied country house belonging to the British chancellor of the exchequer, David Lloyd George, in Walton-on-the-Hill. The next day suffragettes burn down the Kew Gardens Tea House.

MARCH

3 Some 5000 women demonstrate in support of **votes for women** in Washington, on the eve of the inauguration of Woodrow Wilson as the new US president.

18 King **George I of Greece** is assassinated by a Greek in Salonika, a city newly captured from the Turks.

31 Immigration into the USA hits a new record as 6571 arrive at **Ellis Island** in a single day.

APRIL

20 The American dancer **Isadora Duncan** loses her two children, aged seven and five, in a drowning accident in France.

22 The Turkish-held city of **Scutari** (Shkodër) in northern Albania surrenders, after a six-month siege by Montenegrin forces.

MAY

29 The Ballet Russes' *Le Sacre du Printemps* (**The Rite of Spring**), with music by Igor Stravinsky, causes a riot when first performed in Paris.

30 The **Peace of London** is signed, bringing the First Balkan War to a close.

JUNE

4 The suffragette **Emily Wilding Davison** attempts to stop the king's horse during the Derby, and is fatally injured.

30 The **Second Balkan War** begins as Bulgaria attacks its former allies Serbia and Greece.

JULY

12 Turkey re-enters the Balkan conflict and recaptures **Adrianople** (Edirne) from the Bulgarians.

AUGUST

10 A **peace treaty** signed by the Balkan states in Bucharest brings the Second Balkan War to a close.

SEPTEMBER

23 The French aviator **Roland Garros** becomes the first to cross the Mediterranean, flying 558 miles (898 km) from France to Tunisia in just under eight hours.

OCTOBER

1 The German engineer **Rudolf Diesel**, the inventor of the diesel engine, dies, aged 56.

6 Yüan Shih-kai is elected president of the Chinese Republic as Sun Yat-sen stands down.

10 The **Panama Canal** is officially opened, after seven years under construction.

17 The world's largest airship, the **Zeppelin L2**, explodes, killing all 28 people on board.

NOVEMBER

3 Rebel forces in **Mexico**, led by General Venustiano Carranza, Pancho Villa and Emiliano Zapata, issue an ultimatum to President Huerta as they close in on Mexico City.

5 President Yüan Shih-kai of China dismisses the republican assembly and assumes dictatorial powers.

25 Protests over the imprisonment of the civil rights activist Mohandas **Gandhi** in South Africa result in the death of two Indian demonstrators.

DECEMBER

31 Leonardo da Vinci's **Mona Lisa**, stolen in 1911, is returned to the Louvre.

SCIENCE

Following finds of fragments of a human skull at Piltdown Common in Sussex, England, the fossil hunter Charles Dawson claims to have discovered the 'missing link' between humankind and its ape-like ancestors. The find is immediately surrounded by controversy, and definitive tests in 1953 prove **'Piltdown Man'** to be a hoax.

CAR AFTER CAR Ford's new assembly-line method would transform all branches of manufacturing.

NEW PRODUCTS

The **zip fastener** is patented by Gideon Sundback, a Swedish-born engineer in Hoboken, New Jersey. The *New York World* introduces the first modern **crossword puzzle**. An early form of **stainless steel** is created by the English metallurgist Harry Brearley of Sheffield – but was not widely used until the 1930s. The first **moving assembly line** is introduced at the Ford Motor Company in Highland Park, Michigan. **Camel cigarettes** are launched as a new brand in the USA.

THE WRITTEN WORD

New European fiction includes *Sons and Lovers* by **D.H. Lawrence**, *Le Grand Meaulnes* by Henri Alain-Fournier, the first part of *A la recherche du temps perdu* by **Marcel Proust**, and *Tod in Venedig (Death in Venice)* by **Thomas Mann**. In the USA *The Inside of a Cup* becomes the fifth novel by the American author Winston Churchill to top the bestseller lists.

MUSIC AND DANCE

While the **Ballets Russes** makes the news with its highly controversial *Le Sacre du Printemps (The Rite of Spring)*, the **tango** has become all the rage in the dance halls of Europe, but this is being overtaken by the **foxtrot** in the USA.

ART

Nude Descending a Staircase No 2, a Futurist-style painting by French artist **Marcel Duchamp**, causes a sensation and outrage at the Armory Show (the 'International Exhibition of Modern Art') in New York, but Duchamp has already moved on to produce his first 'ready-made' assemblage, *Bicycle Wheel*. The neo-Gothic **Woolworth Building** in New York, designed by Cass Gilbert, is destined to remain the tallest skyscraper in the world until the 1930s.

1914

JANUARY

27 US Marines land in **Haiti** to restore order, after the president resigns in the face of a revolt.

FEBRUARY

26 Suffragettes torch a Scottish church in a campaign.

MARCH

10 The *Rokeby Venus* by Velázquez in London's National Gallery is slashed by the **suffragette** Mary Richardson. Greater security is introduced in public places, causing widespread irritation.

20 In the **'Curragh Mutiny'**, British officers serving in Ireland declare that they would prefer to be dismissed rather than obey orders to take arms against Ulster Unionists fighting against Irish Home Rule.

APRIL

21 King George V and Queen Mary receive an enthusiastic welcome as they arrive in Paris.

22 US forces seize the port of Veracruz in **Mexico** to prevent German arms reaching the forces of President Huerta.

MAY

22 More than 60 women, including Emmeline Pankhurst, are arrested at a **suffragette demonstration** at Buckingham Palace, at which a deputation tries to deliver a petition to King George V.

JUNE

4 Some 2 million British workers are on **strike** as miners and transport workers take industrial action in sympathy with striking builders.

13 The socialist **René Viviani** becomes prime minister of France. He remains in power until October 1915.

20 In Hamburg, Kaiser Wilhelm II launches the *Bismarck*, the **world's biggest passenger ship**.

28 The heir to the Austro-Hungarian throne, **Archduke Franz**

SLASHER Mary Richardson leaves court during the trial following her attack on the *Rokeby Venus*.

Ferdinand, and his wife Sophie are assassinated by the Bosnian Serb nationalist, Gavrilo Princip, in the Bosnian capital of Sarajevo.

JULY

3 The **telephone link between New York and San Francisco** comes into operation for the first time.

23 Austria-Hungary issues an **ultimatum to Serbia**. Vienna is demanding that its own representatives should be allowed to pursue the Serbian nationalist conspirators behind the assassination of Archduke Franz Ferdinand.

26 In Dublin members of the **Irish Citizen Army** and British troops clash over weapons smuggled into Ireland by Roger Casement and Erskine Childers. Three civilians are killed and 38 wounded.

28 Austria-Hungary declares war on Serbia.

31 The French socialist leader and anti-war campaigner **Jean Jaurès** is shot dead by an overwrought patriot in a Parisian café. He was 55.

AUGUST

1 Germany declares war on Russia. It signs a treaty with Turkey, to bring Turkey into the war as an ally.

1 Ernest Shackleton leaves London on the *Endurance*, leading an expedition that aims to cross the Antarctic continent. Despite Shackleton's misgivings about the onset of war, he is instructed by Winston Churchill to proceed.

2 Russia invades east Germany. Italy declares its neutrality.

3 Germany **declares war** on France.

4 German troops enter neutral Belgium. At 11 pm, following the expiry of its ultimatum, **Britain declares war on Germany**. The USA formally declares its neutrality in the European conflict.

6 Austria-Hungary **declares war** on Russia.

8 The **British Expeditionary Force** lands in France.

10 France **declares war** on Austria-Hungary.

12 Britain **declares war** on Austria-Hungary.

20 After the flight into exile of President Huerta and his successor, the rebel army led by General Venustiano Carranza takes **Mexico City**.

23 Japan **declares war** on Germany.

SEPTEMBER

1 The **last passenger pigeon** dies in the Cincinnati Zoo. Once numbering billions, in less than a century this bird has become victim – mainly through human predation – of one of the most dramatic extinctions on record.

15 In London, the **Irish Home Rule Act** receives royal assent, but a Suspending Bill passed by the British government delays its enactment until the end of the war.

OCTOBER

4 The first bomb is dropped on London. Bombing from the air and **aerial combat** signal a new era in both warfare and aviation.

28 Gavrilo Princip is found guilty of the assassination of Archduke Franz Ferdinand, but escapes execution because he is under 21.

NOVEMBER

2 Russia **declares war** on Turkey.

5 Britain and France **declare war** on Turkey.

23 US forces withdraw from **Veracruz**, Mexico.

DECEMBER

10 No **Nobel peace prize** is awarded this year.

SCIENCE

Following the discovery of effective ways to preserve blood, the Belgian

READY FOR WAR The French coast looms for British soldiers. Background: German sailors march into Brussels.

surgeon Albert Hustin is able to create a **blood bank** and conduct blood transfusions without the presence of the donor.

NEW PRODUCTS

The first modern **brassiere** is designed and popularised by the US socialite Mary Phelps Jacob. The first **traffic lights** are put into operation in Cleveland, Ohio. George Eastman develops Eastman Kodak's **colour photographic process**.

THE WRITTEN WORD

The Irish writer **James Joyce** publishes his short-story collection *Dubliners*. *Pygmalion* by **George Bernard Shaw** receives its first stage performance. The American writer Edgar Rice Burroughs produces the first of his Tarzan novels, *Tarzan of the Apes*.

MUSIC

W.C. Handy publishes the blues classic, **'St Louis Blues'**. The British composer Ivor Novello writes the famous wartime song, **'Keep the Home Fires Burning'**.

ART

The Romanian sculptor **Constantin Brancusi** has a one-man show of his abstract sculptures at 291 gallery in New York. The **Vorticist** movement of British artists and writers, led by the painter and novelist Wyndham Lewis, publish their manifesto in the magazine *Blast*.

INDEX

ACKNOWLEDGMENTS

Abbreviations:
T = Top; M = Middle; B = Bottom; R = Right; L = Left

AKG = AKG London
BB = Brown Brothers
BAL = Bridgeman Art Library
CB = Corbis-Bettmann
CPI = Culver Pictures Inc
GI = Getty Images
MEPL = Mary Evans Picture Library
POP = Popperfoto
RMN = Agence Photographique de la Réunion des Musées Nationaux, Paris
TP = Topham Picturepoint
UB = Ullstein Bilderdienst

3 Vintage Magazine Co, L; Jean-Loup Charmet, LM; UB, RM; Richard Lancelyn Green Collection, R. 6 Vintage Magazine Co, MM, BL. 7 AKG, TL; GI, BR. 8 CB, TL. 8-9 ÖTV Hauptverwaltung. Haus der Geschichte Baden- Württemburg, Sammlung Metz 9 BB, TL. 10 CPI, TR; AKG, MM; BB, BL. 11 UB, TL; Roger-Viollet, BR. 12 BB, TL; Jean-Loup Charmet, MM; Library of Congress, BL. 13 GI, TL, B; Museum of London, TM. 14 Velocity of Cars and Light, 1913, Giacomo Bally, Moderna Muselt, Stokholm, Sweden/BAL /© DACS, London/ADAGP, TR; Jean-Loup Charmet, ML; GI, BR. 15 Science & Society Picture Library; MEPL, L; Jean-Loup Charmet, LM; Colin Woodman, RM; Science & Society Picture Library, R. 16-17 Roger-Viollet, B. 17 Roger-Viollet, T; Jean-Loup Charmet, MR. 18 AKG, TL; Jean-Loup Charmet, BL. 18-19 AKG, BM. 19 Roger-Viollet, ML; GI, TR. 20 Toucan Books Archive, MM; Jean-Loup Charmet, BL; BAL, Private Collection, BR. 21 UB, TL, ML, TR. 22 AKG, ML, BM; Science & Society Picture Library, BL, MR. 23 Science Photo Library, TL; UB, BR. 24 Science & Society Picture Library, TL; Colin Woodman, TR; Science Photo Library, B. 25 Colin Woodman, TL; Science & Society Picture Library, TR. 26 AKG, ML; UB, TR. 27 AKG, BR; Photomontage, Bradbury & Williams, BR. 28 Jean-Loup Charmet, MM; UB, BM, BR. 29 Christine Vincent, BL; John Frost Archive, BM; Vintage Magazine Co, BR. 30 CB, TL; MEPL, MM; Science & Society Picture Library, BR. 31 Sygma, MR; Marconi Co Ltd, BL, BR; Martin Woodward, BM. 32 TP, ML; CB, B. 33 Kobal Collection, TL, MM, BM. 34 MEPL. 35 GI,

ML; Library of Congress, BM; Ellis Island Immigration Museum, MR. 36 CB, TR; CPI, BL; Ellis Island immigration Museum, ML. Bradbury & Williams, BR. 37 Ellis Island Immigration Museum. 38 Library of Congress, TM. 38-39 AKG. 39 Library of Congress, BR. 40 CB, BL, BM, MR. 41 MEPL, TL; TP, BR. 42 AKG, BL; CB, MM; MEPL, BM. 42-43 CB, T. 43 MEPL, BR. 44 GI, MR; Canon de Chelly, Edward S. Curtis/The Amon Carter Museum Collection, B. 45 Image Library NSW, B; Andromeda/ National Film Archive, Australia, MR. 46 CPI, ML; BB, BL; Image Library NSW, TR. 47 Library of Congress, TR; CPI, B. 48 GI, BL; Museum Africa/Reader's Digest, South Africa, MM. 49 Museum Africa/Reader's Digest, South Africa, TL; Bradbury & Williams, BR. 50 Arcaid/Richard Bryant, ML; Hunterian Art Gallery, University of Glasgow/Arcaid/Ken Kirkwood, TR; Death and Life, c.1911, Gustav Klimt, Private Collection, BAL, BR. 51 Madame Matisse; The Green Line, 1905, Henri Matisse, Statens Museum for Kunst, Copenhagen, © DACS, London/ADAGP. 52 Les Demoiselles d'Avignon, 1907, oil, Pablo Picasso, The Lillie P. Bliss Bequest/The Museum of Modern Art, New York, © DACS, London/ADAGP. 53 Still Life with Chair Caning, 1912, collage, Pablo Picasso, Musée Picasso, Paris/RMN, © DACS, London/ADAGP, TL; Braque in his studio at 5, impasse de Guelma, c.1912, Laurens Collection, TR; Bicycle Wheel, assemblage, Marcel Duchamp, New York, 1951 (Third version, after lost original of 1913), The Sidney and Harriet Javis Collection/Museum of Modern Art, New York, © DACS, London/ ADAGP, BR. 54 Self Portrait with Model, Ernest Ludwig Kirchner, Kunsthalle, Hamburg/ Copyright by Dr.Wolfgang & Ingeborg Henze-Ketterer, Wichtrach/Bern BAL, TR; Dynamism of a Dog on a Leash, 1912, Giacomo Balla, Albright-Knox Art Gallery, © DACS, London/ ADAGP, BL. 55 Improvisation 28, second version, 1912, Wassily Kandisky, Solomon R. Guggenheim Museum, New York, © DACS, London/ADAGP/BAL. 56 Jean-Loup Charmet, MM; UB, BR. 57 Toucan Books Archive, TL; Mander & Mitchenson, MR; BB, BR. 58 GI, TL; Richard Lancelyn Green Collection, TR; MEPL, MR, BR; The Kipling Archive, University of Sussex, BL. 59 BB;

National Museum of Labour History, L; IG Metall, LM; Roger-Viollet, RM; Jean-Loup Charmet, R. 60 Popperfoto, BL; AKG, BR. 60-61 CPI. 61 MEPL, MR; Arcaid, BR. 62 Diana Philips, TL. 62-63 AKG. 63 British Museum, London, TR. 64 AKG, TL, BR; TP, BM; Photomontage, Bradbury & Williams, BR. 65 Bradbury & Williams, TL; CB, BR. 66 David King Collection, BL. 67 BAL, TR; David King Collection, ML, MR. 68-69 David King Collection, TL, TM, B, TR. 70 David King Collection, TL, TM, BR. 71 David King Collection, BR; Photomontage, Bradbury & Williams, BR. 72 David King Collection, TL; David King Collection, B. 73 David King Collection, TR. 74 TP, MR; British Library, B. 75 AKG. 76-77 British Library. 78 AKG, TR. 79 Bradbury & Williams, TL; Royal Tropical Institute, Netherlands, TR, BR. 80 MEPL, TR; Christine Vincent/Royal Commonwealth Society, BL. 81 Bradbury & Williams, TL; Christine Vincent/ Royal Commonwealth Society, BR. 82 Popperfoto, ML; Jean-Loup Charmet, MM. 83 AKG, TL; Popperfoto, MR; TP, BR. 84 Jean-Loup Charmet, TR; AKG, BR. 85 Roger-Viollet, TL; CPI, MR; BB, BM. 86 AKG, B. 87 UB, TL, TM; Jean-Loup Charmet, MR; UB, BL. 88 CB, TL; Roger-Viollet, MR; MEPL, BM. 89 GI, BL, BR. 90 CB, TL, TR; National Museum of Ireland, Dublin, BL. 90-91 GI, B. 91 GI, T. 92 CB, BL; BB, TR. 93 Ulster Museum, Welch Collection. 94 Roger-Viollet, TL, B; Joseph Rowntree Foundation, TR. 95 AKG, ML; Roger-Viollet, BR. 96 GI, TR; CPI, ML. 96-97 Roger-Viollet. 97 CPI, TR. 98 National Museum of Labour History, TM, ML; IG Metall, TR; GI, B. 99 CPI, TR, BL. 100 National Museum of Labour History, MR; GI, BL 101 MEPL, TR; Roger-Viollet, BM. 102 MEPL, TR, BL. 103 AKG, ML; UB, B. 104 Roger-Viollet, TL, MR; Jean-Loup Charmet, TR. 105 London Metropolitan Archive. 106 AKG, TR; MEPL, MR; TP, BL. 107 UB, MR; AKG, B. 108 David King Collection, T; UB, BM. 109 Roger-Viollet, B. 110 CPI, BM; AKG, MR. 111 GI, TR; National Museum of Labour History, MR. 112 MEPL, TL; UB, BL. 113 CPI, TM; GI, MR; MEPL, BM. 114 BB, ML; CPI, BL. 115 Jean-Loup Charmet, TM, TR; Museum of London, B. 116 MEPL, TL, TR, BL. 117 MEPL, TL.

Camera Press, B. 118 GI, MR, B. 119 ET Archive, MR; UB, B. 120 Jean-Loup Charmet, TR; GI, BL. 121 Roger-Viollet, TR; Süddeutscher Verlag, BL. 122 Royal Geographic Society, T, BL. 123 Süddeutscher Verlag, T; UB. BR. 124 UB, TM; Jean-Loup Charmet, ML; UB, BM. 125 AKG, MEPL, L; Süddeutscher Verlag, LM; CB, RM; AKG, R. 126 Süddeutscher Verlag, TR, MM; Roger-Viollet, BL. 127 MEPL, TL; Süddeutscher Verlag, BR. 128 GI, MM; Roger-Viollet, BL. 129 MEPL, TL; Roger-Viollet, MR; Popperfoto, B. 130 Jean-Loup Charmet. 130-1 AKG, B. 131 AKG, TL; Bradbury & Williams, TR; UB, BR. 132 AKG, TR; UB, BL. 133 Jean-Loup Charmet, MM; CPI, BR. 134 GI, TL. 134-5 Roger-Viollet, B. 135 Imperial War Museum, MM; Süddeutscher Verlag, BL; UB, BM. 136 MEPL, ML; GI, BL. 137 Popperfoto, TL; Imperial War Museum, BR. 138 Imperial War Museum, TR; Bradbury & Williams, BL. 139 GI, TM; CB, BR. 140 Imperial War Museum, TL, BR. 141 MEPL, TR; TP, ML; Popperfoto, BR. 142 National Museum of Labour History, TM; TP, MR; Jean-Loup Charmet, BL. 143 Jean-Loup Charmet, MM, TR; Museum Africa/Reader's Digest, South Africa, BL. 144 MEPL, ML; David King Collection, BR. 145 Jean-Loup Charmet, TL; BB, MR, BR. 146 BB, TR; David King Collection, ML; Barnardos Photographic & Film Archive, BM. 147 TP, TR; David King Collection, BL, MM. 148 BB, TR; CPI, BM. 149 UB, TR; GI, BM. 150 MEPL, TL; GI, ML; MEPL, BL. 151 GI, M, TL; Roger-Viollet, MR; Museum Africa/Reader's Digest, South Africa. 152 UB, TL, ML; BB, MR; Catalogue cover for Der Blaue Reiter, Wassily Kandinsky, Stadtische Galerie Im Lenbachaus, Munich, © DACS, London/ ADAGP/BAL, BR. 153 Imperial War Museum, TM; MEPL, MM. 154 CB, TR; Imperial War Museum, BL. 155 CB, M; Imperial War Museum, TM, TR.

Front cover: GI, T, B; AKG, L; Museum of London, LM; Jean-Loup Charmet, RM; MEPL, R.

Back cover: GI, T, B; MEPL, TL; Hunterian Art Gallery, University of Glasgow/Arcaid/Ken Kirkwood, TR; CB, BL; David King Collection, BR.

Endpapers (front and back): All from John Frost Historical Newspaper Service except, AKG, TL, TR; Vintage Magazine Co, BL, BR; Museum of London, MR.

The editors are grateful to the following individuals and publishers for their kind permission to quote passages from the books below:

Aitken, Stone & Wylie Ltd, from Paris Cavalcade by Eric Welpton, 1959.
Aurum Press, from The People's Almanac Presents the 20th Century, edited by David Wallechinsky. Manchester Guardian, January 28, 1905, reprinted 'Past Notes' © The Guardian, January 28, 1997.
Macmillan Magazines Ltd, from Nature, 118 (Supplement) 51, 1926.
John Murray (Publishers) Ltd, from Dangerous Trade, edited by Thomas Oliver, 1902.
Reader's Union/Michael Joseph, from Memoir of the Bobotes, 1965, © University of Texas Press, 1960.
Rogers, Coleridge & White Ltd, from Lives of the Great 20th Century Artists, Weidenfeld & Nicolson, 1986.
The Strand Magazine, 1905.
Sutton Publishing, from The Suffragettes In Pictures by Diane Atkinson, 1996.
The Times, from 'Launching Of The Dreadnought', © Times Newspapers Ltd, 1910.
Weidenfeld & Nicolson, from 1900, by Rebecca West, 1982.

MERTHYR BOROUGH

VOTE FOR
KEIR HARDIE

FIRST WIRELESS PRESS

Signalizing the Opening of the Ma...
a Message of Congrat...

In order not to miss The
New York Times of to-mor...
...k will be printed

...Y, SEPTEMBER 7, 1909.

3:45 P. M.---EXTRA---3:45 P. M

AN FRANCISCO WRECKED AND HELPLESS
FROM EARTHQUAKE AND UNCHECKED F

WHOLE BUSINESS
DISTRICT GOES
INTO THE RUINS

VIVID PANORAMIC VIEW OF ST...
(FROM A RECENT PHOTOGRAPH).

TITAN...
866 R...
ISMA...

Col. Astor and Bride,
Isidor Straus and Wife,
and Maj. Butt Aboard.

"RULE OF SEA" FOLLOWED

KYRLE
PICTURE-
PALA
ROSS.

THE PEKIN MASSACRE.

ALL WHITE MEN, WOMEN, AND CHILDREN PUT
TO THE SWORD.

SPECIAL ARTIST
EACH WEEK.

MOVING PICTURES
SHEWN EACH DAY,
7,000 FEET IN LENGTH.

...ANGE OF PROGRAMME,
MONDAYS & THURSDAYS

...ist, Miss MAY WYATT, of Matlock.

...rs Open 7-30 Commence at 8
...nees Thursdays & Saturdays, at 3.

...ices—1s., 6d. & 3d.
...hildren, on Saturdays—1d. 2d. & 3d.

...ORY OF THE 6TH & 7TH JULY.

AWFUL

HOW 0...

WHEN SHALL THEIR

HISTORY'S MOST HEROIC DEFENCE

THE BOERS' LAST GR...

MAFEKING AND BADEN-POWELL'S GAL...

"LET ME
TELL MOTHER."

FULL D...

HOW THE "EXPRESS" FIRST
GAVE THE...